THE ULTIMATE WORLD WAR TWO TRIVIA BOOK

THE ULTIMATE WORLD WAR TWO TRIVIA BOOK

UNBELIEVABLE FACTS, EXTRAORDINARY ACCOUNTS AND TALL TALES FROM THE SECOND WORLD WAR

A 'WEIRD WAR TWO' OMNIBUS

RICHARD DENHAM & M. J. TROW

INTRODUCTION
The Second World War 1939-45

The Causes
The older generation still call it 'Hitler's War' but monumental events that lead to the deaths of millions cannot be placed at any one man's door. To understand how war came about in September 1939 we have to go back to the Treaty of Versailles that ended the First World War.

The victors at Versailles – Britain, France, Italy and the United States – decided that Germany had caused the First World War (which they hadn't) and that Germany must pay. To that end, territory which once belonged to Germany was taken away, German armed forces were cut to almost non-existence and the country was saddled with a massive reparations bill of £3.5 billion (at least $46 billion today) and it couldn't possibly pay.

The weak democratic Weimar government struggled on for ten years, but the financial disaster of October 1929 – the Wall Street crash – plunged Germany particularly deeply into recession and that gave a new impetus to Adolf Hitler's National Socialist party, which, until then, had been regarded as something of a lunatic fringe. In a series of underhand political manoeuvres, Hitler became Chancellor of Germany in 1933 and set up a state he promised would last a thousand years – the Third Reich. In fact, it lasted just twelve and a half years and the steps that led to the Second World War also led to Germany's second defeat in thirty years.

The Steps to War 1933-39
1933   Hitler becomes Chancellor of a bitter and angry Germany.

1934   On the death of President Hindenberg, Hitler becomes President, giving himself the title *Fuhrer* (leader).

All members of the German army (Wehrmacht), air force (Luftwaffe) and navy (Kriegsmarine) swear a personal oath of allegiance to Hitler.

1935   In an Anglo-German naval agreement, Germany is allowed to build warships again.

Saarland (Germany's smallest federal state) is returned to Germany after a referendum, having been removed from its control as part of the Treaty of Versailles.

1936   Hitler invades the demilitarized Rhineland, devoid of troops since Versailles, claiming that he has that right. Britain and France complain but do nothing.

Civil war breaks out in Spain and Hitler supplies General Francisco Franco's Fascists with aircraft, experts and cash. The Luftwaffe's Condor Legion bombs Guernica, giving the world the first taste of Blitzkrieg (Lightning War).

The Rome-Berlin Axis (the Pact of Steel) is signed between Hitler and Benito Mussolini, the Fascist duce (leader) of Italy, but not ratified until three years later.

Germany and Japan sign the Anti-Comintern Pact against the left wing countries of the Communist International, spearheaded by Russia (the Union of Socialist Soviet Republics).

1938   The *Anschluss* with Austria. On the face of it, a peaceful union, it is actually a Nazi coup.

Hitler claims the Sudetenland, part of the new state of Czechoslovakia, as German because of the large number of Germans living there. He needs *lebensraum* (living space) for his rapidly growing country.

At the Munich Conference in September, Hitler promises Neville Chamberlain, the British Prime Minister and Edouard Daladier, his French counterpart, that he has no further ambitions in Europe.

1939   Ignoring Munich, Hitler invades Prague and Memel in March.

Anxious to expand to the east and to regain East Prussia, Hitler signs a non-aggression pact with Josef Stalin, the Russian leader.

Two days later, Britain signs an agreement with Poland that is clearly Hitler's short-term target. On a pretext, on 1 September, Hitler launches *Fall Weiss* (Case White) and invades Poland.

On 3 September, with Hitler ignoring Chamberlain's ultimatum to withdraw his troops, Britain declares war on Nazi Germany. So does France.

The Second World War has begun.

The Phoney War 1939-40

The French called it the Funny War (Drôle de Guerre); to the Germans it was Sitzkrieg (the Armchair War). The British coined the word 'phoney' from an article by an American journalist based in London. In the west, nothing happened. The east was a different story, however. Poland fell in the September War, crushed between Hitler's Germany and Stalin's Russia and the execution squads of the einsatzgruppen went to work rounding up and shooting Jews – another step towards the Holocaust.

There was action at sea too. Two British aircraft carriers, the newest and most expensive ships afloat, had been sunk by October, and there were air raids on British naval bases in Scotland. The Kriegsmarine's pocket battleship, the *Admiral Graf Spee* was scuttled by her crew in the River Plate on 17 December. In terms of military capability, the Royal Navy had the edge, but the Luftwaffe, whose aircraft had been built secretly for years, were far ahead of the Royal Air Force, thanks to years of appeasement under Prime Ministers Baldwin and Chamberlain. In November, the USSR invaded Finland. This was the Winter War, in which the Finns, with their local knowledge, proved more than a match for the Red Army.

With spectacular mistiming, Neville Chamberlain told that House of Commons that, in delaying an all-out attack in the west, Hitler had 'missed the bus'. Five days later, the Germans invaded Norway.

Collapse of the West 1940

It was the British who had misread the bus timetable! Norway was crucial to both sides, because of its strategic position overlooking the North Atlantic and its production of heavy water. The Germans moved first and despite a half-hearted British involvement, overran the country and set up a puppet government under Vidkun Quisling, whose name became synonymous with traitor (in fact, he had never made any secret of his Nazi sympathies). Denmark, hopelessly feeble against the power of the Reich, surrendered after only one day and the threat to flatten Copenhagen. Of the 16,000 troops in the Danish army, only thirteen were killed.

Failure in Norway led to a no-confidence vote in the Commons and Chamberlain was forced to resign. His replacement, on 10 May, was the First Lord of the Admiralty, Winston Churchill. He had been warning of the Nazi threat for years and this was to be his finest hour.

Churchill's first day at Number Ten was the start of *Fall Gelb* (Case Yellow), the simultaneous invasion of Holland, Belgium and France. On paper, the Allied and Axis armies were exactly matched but no one was prepared for the speed of the German advance under blitzkrieg. Aerial attacks, using a mixture of bombers (*Heinkels* and *Dorniers*) and fighters (*Messerschmitts* and *Stukas*) were followed by pincer movements on the ground spearheaded by the *panzers*, the tanks that had replaced horsed cavalry. The Allies had no leaders of the calibre of Heinz Guderian, Erwin Rommel and Gerd von Rundstedt and despite valiant defence, Holland surrendered in five days.

A British expeditionary force was rushed to France (exactly as in 1914) but was driven back to the coast at Dunkirk. The 'miracle' that happened there was the result of private boats – 'the little ships of England' – that crossed the Channel and carried back as many men as they could. It was all part of Churchill's genius that he turned what was actually an embarrassing defeat into a victory and the 'Dunkirk spirit' is still occasionally heard of today. Belgium surrendered at the end of May and France soon after. The armistice was signed in the same railway carriage at Compiegne where the Germans had surrendered in 1918 and an ecstatic Hitler went sightseeing in Paris. Versailles was avenged.

The People's War 1940-41

The summer of 1940 has become the 'Spitfire Summer'. Hitler's invasion of Britain – Operation Sealion – was heralded by the blitzkrieg tactic of knocking out the RAF first. All over the south east of the country, dogfights were fought daily in what became known as the Battle of Britain, but the RAF – 'the few' as Churchill called them – held out and Herman Goering, head of the Luftwaffe, was forced to change tack and bomb civilian cities instead.

'The Blitz', beginning in earnest on 30 August, is a prime example of Britain's 'finest hour'. Guernica came to London, Coventry, Plymouth and Hull. Industrial, war production areas were the target but the bombing technology of 1940 was not that precise and homes, schools, hospitals and *people* were all caught up in it. A paranoid government, convinced that there was a Fifth Column of spies operating in the country, gave draconian powers to the police, the armed forces and an army of 'little Hitlers' in and out of uniform, to curb civil liberties. Much of this has never gone away. Bombing raids, the blackout, spivs selling rationed goods illegally on the black market, all this became part of a legend. By May 1941, 40,000 British civilians had been killed, another 46,000 badly injured. Over a million homes were shattered. But the world learned a lesson that still has to be driven home – mass bombing does not lead to collapse; it just increases resistance.

The Wider War 1941-42

Countries overrun by the Germans coped as best they could. Most people kept their heads down and did as they were told. Some collaborated openly – Quisling in Norway, Marshal Petain in Vichy France. Others resisted, either passively or actively, like the Maquis in France, sabotaging German occupation and staying in touch by radio with Britain, now 'fortress Britain', standing alone.

With dreams of recreating another Roman Empire, Mussolini sent his troops into North Africa in June 1940. Egypt had been in British hands since the nineteenth century and General Archibald Wavell stopped the Italians at Sidi Birrani in December. It was depressing proof to Hitler that his Italian allies weren't worth the candle and he sent in Erwin Rommel and his Afrika Korps to bail them out. Wavell was beaten back.

The extraordinarily tortuous politics of the Balkans re-emerged, resulting in a German attack on the new state of Yugoslavia (today's Croatia) and the invasion of Greece. The British attempt to police the Mediterranean (they had Gibraltar at the western end, Malta in the centre and Cyprus in the east) met with disaster and Crete fell to the Germans by June 1941.

On the 22nd of that month, Hitler made the biggest mistake of the war by launching Operation Barbarossa, the invasion of the USSR. This had been his plan all along, taking *lebensraum* to a logical conclusion and Josef Stalin seemed blissfully unaware. The long drawn out Eastern Front saw the deaths of millions. To the Russians, it was the Patriotic War, defending their own territory against a treacherous enemy. Stalin was quite prepared to sacrifice as many millions as it took. For their part, the Germans had underestimated both the tenacity of the enemy and the severity of the Russian winter. Petrol froze in the tanks of mechanised transport and blitzkrieg ground to a halt in sieges like Stalingrad.

On 7 December – 'a day that will live in infamy' as President Franklin D Roosevelt said – the Japanese bombed the US naval base at Pearl Harbor in the Hawaiian Islands. America had sat on an isolationist fence throughout the Twenties and Thirties, its population made up of the descendants of both sides who faced each other in 1939. Roosevelt's natural inclination was to join the Allies but there was a powerful German lobby at home and he had promised America's mothers that their boys would not be involved. Instead, the Lend-Lease programme was set up – vital money and equipment lent to Britain (the debt was finally repaid in 1994).

Japanese ambitions in the Pacific (they had been at war with China since 1937) were unrealistic. America's actual military strength in 1941 was feeble, but the wealth of the country and its military capability were awesome. The 'double whammy' of Barbarossa and Pearl Harbor in the same year made it inevitable that Hitler would lose the war.

Initially, the Japanese did well, driving the British out of Singapore in one of the most embarrassing defeats in modern history. The creation of the Burma railway, where thousands of British prisoners of war were worked to death, ranks alongside the Holocaust in terms of inhumanity, although of course the numbers going routinely to the gas chambers of Europe by 1943 have no comparison.

Now that Soviet Russia had joined the Allied camp, there was need to relieve them as far as possible. Convoys of British merchant ships ploughed the icy waters of the North Atlantic to achieve this, at the mercy of the dreaded Kriegsmarine U Boats. A huge propaganda coup was struck when the iconic new battleship the *Bismarck* was sunk by the British in May 1941.

Turning Points 1942-43

We have already seen how important Hitler's decision to invade Russia was. The attack on Pearl Harbor was another gamble too far. In the Pacific, the Americans fought back at the battle of Midway, in which the Japanese lost four aircraft carriers, 332 aircraft and 3,500 men.

In July, Bernard Montgomery's British Eighth Army stopped Rommel's Afrika Korps at El Alamein, near Alexandria and Operation Torch saw the invasion of Italian-held Morocco, Algeria and Tunisia by the British and Americans.

In the east, the Wehrmacht was losing men daily at an horrific rate and by 31 January 1943, General Friedrich von Paulus was forced to surrender the Sixth Army.

The Invasion of Europe 1942-44

With Rommel's Afrika Korps destroyed and the Italians on the run, an Anglo-American force invaded Sicily and Italy, making for Rome. It was the first assault of Hitler's Europe-wide Reich and one of its first casualties was Mussolini, kicked out by his own government and put under house arrest. Stiffened by the Germans, Italy held on for months, fighting battles at Anzio and Monte Cassino, but in the end, they surrendered and were effectively out of the war by the end of 1943.

In the summer of that year, the Red Army under General Georgy Zhukov began to push the exhausted Wehrmacht back to the German border they had crossed with such high hopes during Barbarossa two years earlier. Zhukov's ultimate destination was Berlin.

For the RAF it was payback time. With the USAAF flying out from British bases, Air Chief Marshal Arthur 'Bomber' Harris unleashed raids on German cities. Dresden was hit by a firestorm unparalleled in history and today Harris is regarded by many as a war criminal. In fact, he was just doing his job and no one at the time had a problem with that.

All of this was crowned on 6 June 1944 by Operation Overlord, the biggest amphibious assault in history. 27,000 airborne troops had landed in Normandy the previous night to take vital bridgeheads and road crossings before the 'ducks' ran up the beaches codenamed Omaha, Utah, Sword, Gold and Juno. The Germans were caught napping. Only at 'bloody Omaha' was there serious resistance; Rommel was on leave in Germany at the time and Hitler dithered. The next weeks after D Day (D for Deliverance) saw the Allies driving the Wehrmacht across France, liberating towns and villages as they went.

The Race for Berlin 1944-45

By the end of September 1944, twenty-five of thirty-seven German divisions of Army Group Centre had been destroyed by the Red Army. Berlin was panicking – the

Cossacks were on the German border and the Communist threat had never loomed so starkly. By the end of the year, the Germans had pulled out of the Balkans, consolidating and regrouping to defend their homeland.

1944 saw a sting in the tail with the return of the Blitz over Britain. Hitler's rocket scientists, working on jet and unmanned aircraft technology, came out with the V1 and V2 missiles – 'doodlebugs' – that rained down on British cities as conventional bombs had three years earlier.

Advancing steadily from the west, the Allies, under the command of General Dwight Eisenhower, drove all before them. There were disagreements as to how exactly this should be done and hotheads like Montgomery and George Patton constantly clashed. Operation Market Garden, an airborne attempt to capture the bridges at Arnhem, was a disaster however with a loss of life that was all the harder to take because the end of the war was now surely in sight. In a last ditch gamble, the Germans attacked in the Ardennes forest – the battle of the Bulge. Probably only a lack of equipment meant that it failed.

At the beginning of 1945, Hitler became increasingly delusional. The Allies crossed the Rhine in February and March as the Russians swept through eastern Germany to take territory they would refuse to give up for forty years. In the event, it was the Red Army that got to Berlin first, fighting street by street for the enemy capital. The names of some of them are still there, scratched into the plaster of the Reichstag, Berlin's parliament building. In an appalling act which the Russians still deny, thousands of German women and girls were raped by Soviet troops.

Gotterdammerung 1945

Hitler was hiding in his bunker under Berlin while the fighting raged overhead. On 29 April he married his mistress Eva Braun and they committed suicide, either by poison or gunshot (exact details are unclear) and their bodies were doused in petrol and burned. Admiral Karl Doenitz was Hitler's successor, all other leading Nazis now on the run and he negotiated the Reich's surrender over the next few days. 8 May was officially designated VE (Victory in Europe) Day and there were street parties all over Britain and the newly-liberated countries of the west.

In the far east, General William Slim's 14th Army drove the Japanese out of Burma and the Americans captured island after island in the South Pacific ('island hopping', it was called). Iwo Jima and Okinawa became enshrined in American folklore as a result but it was felt that everyone was too exhausted to go on; and to the Japanese, surrender was unthinkable. With that in mind, the new president, Harry S Truman, authorised the first use of the newly-created atomic bomb. 'Little Boy' and 'Fat Man' flattened the cities of Hiroshima and Nagasaki, bringing nuclear terror to the world with which we all still live. In seventeen seconds at Hiroshima, 80,000 people were dead with a further 70,000 badly injured. VJ Day (Victory in Japan) was officially 15 August.

What next?

As the Allies liberated German-held Europe, the reality of the Holocaust came to light. Six million people, Jews, homosexuals, gypsies and political dissidents had been exterminated in death camps like Auschwitz, Dachau and Treblinka. The Nazi high command scattered but most of them were captured and faced trial for war crimes at Nuremberg, the scene of the pre-war Nazi rallies, in 1946. Sixteen of the twenty-one were hanged by the British executioner Albert Pierrepoint.

Various high level Allied conferences over the last two years of the war set out the post-war world. Soviet Russia refused to hand back captured German territories and used the war as an opportunity to extend the limits of the Soviet bloc to include large sections of eastern Europe that had never been either Communist or Russian. Germany itself was divided between the Allies, east and west Berlin suffering the same fate. Winston Churchill, ousted in a post-war election, prophesied that an 'iron curtain' would come down across Europe and so it proved, leading to the Cold War and espionage fictions without number.

A devastated world struggled to come to terms with what had happened, rebuilding, reshaping and trying to forget the past. But some things – the Holocaust, the blanket bombing, the Burma railway, the A bomb – are unforgettable. We will always have them with us.

Richard Denham & M. J. Trow

AHNENPASS

Central to the ideology of the Third Reich was the concept of race. Only those who could claim pure Aryan blood going back four generations were allowed to hold professional posts in government, the armed forces, teaching and the law.

Parenting in the Nazi mindset was everything; to be a pure German was essential to have much chance of having a successful life. As well as 'pure' Aryans and 'full' Jews, there were also those with three, two or just one Jewish grandparent and various government officials spent years defining various categories. Even a German who was just one quarter Jewish was considered to be a '*Mischling* (mixed-blood) of the second degree'. The *Ahnenpass* (ancestor passport) was another of the countless forms and papers to come out of the Reich, a state obsessed with paperwork. It wasn't an official government document, but a way for Germans to prove their Aryan parentage by tracing and documenting their family tree. Eventually it would be needed to go to school or get married. The work of tracing family trees was difficult and arduous (long before the internet!), relying on people tracking down their own family trees via church and civil records. Unsurprisingly, the services of genealogists rocketed during the Reich.

Such an arbitrary system could be turned on its head, although many women were successful in court in convincing the judge that any offspring with Jewish fathers were the results of adultery with Aryans. Bribery and corruption was also rife in the justice system with back-handers ensuring people weren't classified as mixed-blood. Sometimes on the whim of the leadership, Jewish ancestry would be 'forgiven' and people would be given Aryan blood certificates. A classic example was Erhard Milch, a *Wehrmacht* field marshal with a Jewish father. It is possible that up to 160,000 *mischlinge* fought for Hitler during the war. The *Ahnenpass* was available in all good book stores and cost 0.60 Reichsmarks.

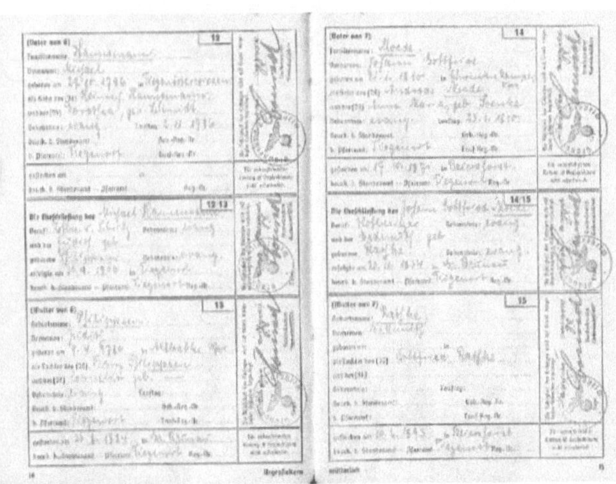

'AND ALL THAT JAZZ!'

Nazi ideology frowned on much that was acceptable elsewhere and Jazz, which was spreading in popularity around the world as the party grew, came in for special criticism. It was popular in Germany at the time but was classified by the Nazis as 'degenerate negro music seen through the eyes of Jews'. Performances by black musicians were banned in Germany in 1932 and by 1935 they were not allowed to be heard on the radio.

Interestingly, similar doubts were being expressed in America, but there it was more of a generational issue, rather as rock 'n' roll would horrify the Moms and Dads who fought the Second World War. A rebellious group in Germany, 'The Swing Kids', continued to listen to Jazz music in private and opposed the Hitler Youth and League of German Maidens. Over three hundred Swing Kids were arrested in 1941, their punishments ranging from having their hair cropped to being sent to concentration camps.

Despite all this, Josef Goebbels still found a place for Jazz music in his propaganda repertoire. Lead by front man Karl 'Charlie' Schwedler, Charlie and His Orchestra became a surreal part of the propaganda machine in 1940. The band would play Swing and Jazz classics to their listeners in Britain every Wednesday and Saturday at 9pm but with altered lyrics, supposedly with the help of 'Lord Haw-Haw' (William Joyce), boasting of the strength of the Reich and mocking Churchill and the Allied war effort. Their cover of Walter Donaldson's 'You're Driving Me Crazy' contains a bizarre section of Schwedler impersonating Churchill, being driven crazy by the military might of the Nazis and the Jews. The ominously upbeat 'Let's Go Bombing' gives us the cheery point of view of a raid on neutral areas, civilians and churches far from the areas of conflict.

The band was broken up after the war, but treated leniently and most of them continued to have successful musical careers.

ANTI-TANK DOGS

Animals and warfare have been linked for centuries. Horses charged into battle and pulled war chariots; pigeons carried messages in the First World War; dogs pulled equipment sledges over frozen battlefields.

For dog lovers, their deployment in the Second World War was perhaps going too far. The idea was particularly popular with the Russians, who carried on using anti-tank dogs until the nineties! As the name suggests, the dogs were strapped with explosives and trained to run under German tanks and use their teeth to release the bomb before running back to safety. The second part of this proved too difficult however, and it was thought more effective for the dogs to be blown up once they reached their target. The training of this involved leaving the dogs' food under tanks, so they instinctively learned to run under any tank to find their supper. Quite how the food was to be put there in the first place is not clear!

Anti-tank dogs did not always (unlike most Nazis) follow orders. In the confusion and noise of battle, having had their explosives primed, the animals would often run back to their handlers, leading to a grisly end for both of them. Of the first thirty dogs deployed on the Eastern Front against the Reich, four blew up under German tanks and six blew up returning to their handlers.

THE ARMISTICE CARRIAGE

Nothing typifies the contempt that Hitler felt for the French more than his use of the Armistice carriage in 1940. The original train belonged to Marechal Ferdinand Foch and was chosen for the signing of the 1918 armistice because the siding in the quiet forest of Compiegne, thirty-seven miles north of Paris, was remote and discreet. The train was briefly still in use after the First World Warbut then was handed over to the Army Museum in Paris.

Hitler, bitter and humiliated, as were many Germans, by losing the first World War, clearly remembered this. The blitzkrieg against France in 1940 was overwhelming, the Wehrmacht simply bypassing the Maginot Line with its impenetrable line of fortifications by going through Belgium. When France sued for peace against the Reich, Hitler insisted the surrender be offered inside the very train carriage of 1918. He had it removed from the Army Museum and returned to the exact same spot it had been in in November during the first armistice. In fact, he deliberately sat in Foch's seat of 1918 when France officially surrendered to him on 21 June. This was not, said Colonel General von Keitel on the day itself, an act of revenge, but merely to right a wrong.

The carriage was then taken to Germany where it was on display in Berlin until 1943. It remained there until it was destroyed by the SS in Thuringia in 1945.

ATLANTIS

Heinrich Himmler, as Reichsfuhrer of the SS, was a man fascinated by mysticism and the foundations of 'Aryan' history. Many of the stories of his obsession for the occult that have survived seem rather far-fetched and the archaeology of the Nazis has been fertile ground for conspiracy theorists ever since, even finding its way into the Indiana Jones film franchise starring Harrison Ford.

It is known that many expeditions were conducted by the Nazis under the *Ahnenerbe*, a department set up to find evidence of the Aryan racial theory and history and personally run by Himmler.

Atlantis, mentioned by Plato, Aristotle and various writers of the ancient world, was a highly advanced and sophisticated civilization destroyed, according to legend, in a single day by some unknown catastrophe. Whether Himmler actually believed this or simply wanted to create a mythology for propaganda purposes is a matter of opinion but either way he put great efforts into the pursuit of it. The *Ahnenerbe* thought that Atlantis could have been a sunken island somewhere between Britain and Portugal – Plato refers to the Pillars of Hercules, i.e. the Straits of Gibraltar – and that those who survived made it to Tibet over 5,000 miles away. A team of scientists and archaeologists travelled there where they used their pseudo-science to study the faces and head-shapes of the locals and decided they were in fact descended from the Atlanteans. However, in the Nazi view of racial purity, the bloodline had been poisoned by interbreeding with the Tibetans.

One theory that interested Himmler in the legend of the lost civilization of Atlantis was the idea the survivors were Aryans, thereby explaining why there was no archaeological evidence of an ancient Aryan culture.

THE AVENGERS

Abba Kovner was born in Belarus in 1918. By the time of the Second World War, Abba was in Vilna, Lithuania when the Reich conquered it. Abba and his friends, being Jewish and at risk of persecution, went into hiding in a Dominican convent. He was disgusted and outraged with what was happening to people in the Jewish ghetto with thousands of victims having been murdered. Abba had seen first-hand what the Nazis were capable of. But many in the ghettos could not believe the wickedness of it all. Even as the ghettos began to be cleared out, there was much disbelief about the destination and the so-called resettlement.

Abba gave a passionate speech in the ghetto to the surviving remnant:

> 'Jewish youth! Do not trust those who are trying to deceive you. Out of the eighty thousand Jews in the "Jerusalem of Lithuania" only twenty thousand are left. Ponary is not a concentration camp. They have all been shot there. Hitler plans to destroy all the Jews of Europe, and the Jews of Lithuania have been chosen as the first in line. We will not be led like sheep to the slaughter! True, we are weak and defenceless, but the only reply to the murderer is revolt! Brothers! Better to fall as free fighters than to live by the mercy of the murderers. Arise! Arise with your last breath!'

A group named FPO (United Partisan Organisation) began in January 1942, but many Jewish people feared their resistance was simply antagonising the Nazis and would not openly support it. The FPO soon came to the attention of the Gestapo. It was announced that if their leader, Yitzhak Wittenberg, did not hand himself in, they would kill the 20,000 remaining Jews in the city. Wittenberg did the honourable thing and did in fact hand himself in to save the lives of those he had sworn to protect. Before submitting to certain death he appointed Kovner as the FPO's new leader. Wittenberg would be found dead in his cell the next day on 16 July, 1943. Kovner continued the struggle, carrying out acts of sabotage, forging links with the Red Army and sending word to other ghettos not to volunteer themselves onto the trains, as they too would be going to their deaths. By September 1943 the ghettos of Vilna were desolate.

The FPO escaped Vilna and met up with Soviet partisans and continued the fight. As the war was nearing its end, the FPO assisted in helping Jews flee to Palestine via the *Beriha* (Escape) movement. Over 250,000 people would make it.

When the war was finally over, the full scale of the atrocities committed by the Nazis became evident, and many wanted revenge. The FPO joined forces with sympathetic soldiers from within the Jewish Brigade, a unit made up of war veterans serving in the British Army, and formed *Nakam* (Revenge).

Although many high-ranking Nazis were convicted at the Nuremburg War Trials, countless others escaped punishment in the chaos and confusion of post-war Europe. To those who had suffered, this 'justice' was woefully inadequate. Of an original list of 13 million suspects, by 1949 only 300 would face prison or worse. The prosecution was exhausted and the task in front of them was never ending. The world wanted to forgive and move on – Nakam couldn't. Every member of Nakam had his own story, returning to their homes to find it being lived in by strangers and awkward glances from neighbours who only years before had informed on them to the enemy. This new atmosphere of forgiveness and reconciliation did not sit well with them.

Nakam planned to poison the water supplies of German cities, in the hope of killing six million people. The plan never came to fruition. It is believed this operation, which was appalling in its scale of brutality and arbitrary punishment, was sabotaged or stopped by those overseeing the Nakam operation itself. They feared the world could not support an organisation capable of such a murderous act. Not to mention the hindrance this may pose in the creation of a Jewish nation.

Plan B was the planned poisoning of 15,000 Axis POWs who were being held in an American camp near Nuremburg. A Nakam cell discovered all of the food was prepared on site except for the bread, which came from a nearby bakery where two Nakam agents were able to find work. They pasted 3,000 loaves of bread with arsenic. When it was delivered to the POW camp, the agents fled. After the event, the *New York Times* reported over 2,000 POWs became ill and 400 died as a result, though later evidence suggests the poisoned bread didn't actually kill anyone. Experts claim the poison could have killed 60,000, so it is a mystery as to why this failed.

Nakam gradually faded away as its members found peace and gave up their desire for revenge. Abba Kovner moved to Israel, becoming a renowned poet and eventually retired on a kibbutz where he lived with his wife until his death in 1987.

The morality and justification for the actions and motives of Abba Kovner and Nakam remain a subject of discourse. Some suggest Nakam was a terrorist organisation, though German prosecutors dismissed a case against them due to the 'unusual circumstances' they found themselves in.

Elsewhere, SS officers and high-ranking Nazi officials who had successfully faded back into normal life, were being found dead in suspicious circumstances across the world.

BALLOON BOMBS

One of the more bizarre facts of history is that war gives a stimulus to technology and more money has been spent on arms manufacture than anything to do with peace. Leonardo da Vinci is today remembered as a genius, a 'universal man' renowned as a painter, sculptor and theoretical physicist; but he made his money designing weapons for various Italian noblemen.

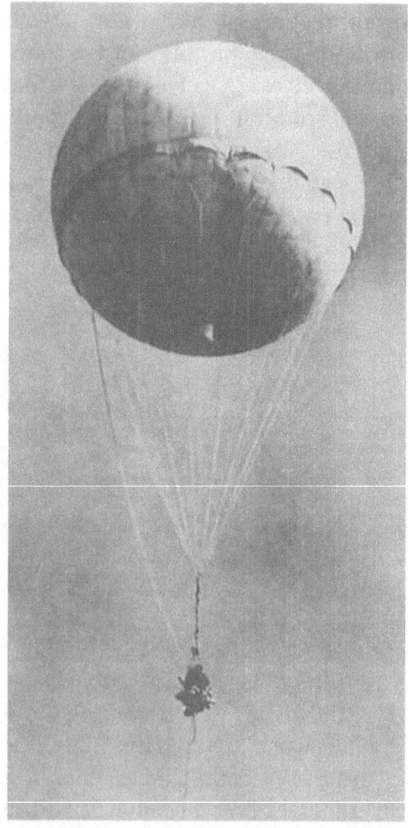

No less ingenious were the Japanese in the Second World War. Harnessing the power of jet streams that blew east across the Pacific Ocean, they came up with the idea of balloon bombs. The idea was relatively simple; explosives attached to paper balloons. These bombs would then float silently to the USA and cause untold damage, the brilliance of the weapon lying in the fact that there was no way to stop it until it detonated.

First created in 1944, the balloons were launched from Japan, taking approximately 30 to 60 hours to reach their destination. The first was launched on 3 November. Figures vary wildly but it is estimated that between 1,000 and 9,000 balloon bombs were created and sent to the west coast of America. Only 284 were discovered according to American reports.

The US government were quick to hide these balloon bombs from the general public, and they appeared to be ineffective, but there was one tragedy. On 5 May 1945, a group of five children and a pregnant woman having a picnic in Bly, Oregon, came across one of the balloons. With no reason to suspect it was a bomb, they accidentally detonated it, becoming part of a very small list of mainland American casualties during the war from enemy activity.

BAMSE THE DOG

Bamse (teddy bear) was a St. Bernard from Norway who refused to let the Nazi occupation of his homeland dampen his spirits. With the coming of war, Bamse and his owner Erling Hafto saw their whale-catcher vessel *Thorodd* drafted into the Norwegian navy. Bamse was officially enrolled on 9 February 1940.

The Nazi war machine devastated Norway and by 10th June the Scandinavian nation was conquered. The British and French mismanagement in failing to aid their ally would lead to the replacement of then Prime Minister, Neville Chamberlain, with the untested Winston Churchill on 10 May. Winston Churchill was a controversial figure and distrusted by many politicians, he had left the Conservative party to join the Liberals in 1904, only to rejoin the Conservatives in 1924. Even worse, he was half-American to boot!

Only thirteen Norwegian naval vessels were able to escape to Britain, *Thorodd* was among them. With French forces crumbling and their government weeks from surrender, the 'lifeboat of democracy' was the last free country in open opposition to Hitler. The vessel was converted into a minesweeper and spent the remainder of the war stationed in Montrose and Dundee in Scotland.

Bamse lead from the front, earning fame and prestige among his crew and the locals thanks to his heroism. In battle, he stood defiantly at the front of the *Thorodd*, wearing his custom-made helmet. He saved the life of Olav August Johan Nilsen, who was walking the docks, by pushing a knife-wielding attacker into the sea. He saved another who had fallen overboard by jumping into the sea and dragging him to shore. He would calm down his crew when tensions got high and scuffles developed by placing a paw on their shoulders. He even rounded up his crew who were due to return from shore leave by travelling on local buses, unaccompanied, with a bus pass attached to his collar. He then turned up at the favourite pub of his men, the Bodega Bar, and escorted his worse-for-wear friends back to their ship. If he didn't find them, that was fine. He'd come back another time.

Bamse passed away in July 1944 and was buried with full military honours in Montrose. He became a mascot for both the Free Norwegian Forces and the charity PDSA (People's Dispensary for Sick Animals). In 2006 a bronze statue of the heroic dog was unveiled on Montrose's Wharf Street, facing Norway. In 2009, the Norwegians erected their own statue of Bamse in Honningsvag, facing Scotland. In 2016, a 17-acre forest, 'Bamse's Wood', in Cumbria was planted in his honour.

BAT BOMBS

Natural scientists may be fascinated by them, but in folklore and even today's occult world, bats are associated with death, vampirism and Count Dracula himself. A dentist from Pennsylvania, Lytle S. Adams, saw a new role for them in January 1942 when he sent a written proposal to Franklin D. Roosevelt's White House. The concept was to drop bats fitted with tiny incendiary devices onto Japanese cities, giving the animals enough time to find a building to roost in. It was estimated by experts that a bat bomb could cause ten times as many fires as an ordinary bomb, with no loss of life unlike conventional bomber units.

Adams knew Eleanor Roosevelt, the formidable wife of the President and she persuaded her husband to take the dentist's nonsense seriously. The National Research Defense Committee, headed for this project by Donald Griffin, a famous psychologist, carried out experiments. 'This man is not a nut,' F.D. Roosevelt wrote and Project X-Ray, using Mexican free-tailed bats, took wind in March 1943. Initial tests had mixed results. In one case bats were accidentally released, setting fire to an airbase and a general's car. Two million dollars were spent and then the notion of bat bombs was discarded as the development of the atomic bomb was considered a more effective way to bring the war to an early end.

BATMEN

Batman, aka millionaire Bruce Wayne, first appeared in #27 of Detective Comics in May 1939, four months before the war began. Developing over the years since, the caped crusader has adapted via the intensely serious world of comics and Hollywood, but could some of his extraordinary powers have been harnessed for real?

The element of surprise is one of a soldier's greatest weapons, and what could be more surprising than a regiment of winged soldiers gliding down silently from the sky? This was the idea of Major Malcolm Wheeler-Nicholson of the California State Guard. Nicholson was the brains behind DC Comics, for which Batman was created and had served as an officer with the 9th cavalry, the Buffalo Soldiers, before serving as an envoy in Russia and Japan. When his military career nose-dived, he began writing lurid pulp fiction to make ends meet. But Wheeler-Nicholson never fully abandoned a serious interest in things military and made sure, via his many useful contacts, that prototypes and testing began, with the hope that eventually all paratroopers could be equipped with jump suits fitted with diving wings, in addition to their parachutes which would be deployed later, that could then be controlled to dodge and weave enemy fire as they descended. Practicalities and lack of cash got in the way and the plans were abandoned but the concepts put forward are still used by skydivers to this day.

THE BATTLE OF LOS ANGELES

After Pearl Harbor the Americans didn't know what Japan would throw at them next. The only direct air raid on the American mainland to cause any death or injury took place at Ellwood, near Santa Barbara, California on the night of 23 February, 1942. The next night one of Los Angeles' strangest incidents happened. The air raid sirens began to sound out and a black out was enforced. Air Raid Wardens dashed into action. Ed Murrow and other reporters based in London had been broadcasting regularly to American cities and everyone was on high alert, expecting aerial bombardment by the Japanese, mirroring the Luftwaffe's Blitz over England. The anti-aircraft guns fired off over 1,500 rounds into the night sky and sporadic firing continued for nearly an hour. The 'All Clear' finally sounded at 7.21am. Five civilians died – three in car crashes in the chaos of the alarm and two others from heart attacks

This 'battle' remains controversial to this day. The Secretary of the Navy, Frank Knox, said the following day 'it was a false alarm' and no enemy aircraft was shot down or spotted. Despite this, newspapers cried out that it was a cover up and there are a large number of people today who believe it was in fact a UFO, a theme that would capture the imaginations of Americans in the following decades.

Experts believe it was a combination of a stray air balloon, shaky nerves and that the barrage simply followed the first shot. The public's reaction to the government's official response may be the first time that Americans began to doubt the integrity of their leaders.

THE BATTLE OF SCHOENFELD

The Battle of Schoenfeld was the last successful horseback cavalry charge of the Second World War, or since, happening on 1 March 1945.

Attached to Soviet forces, the Polish First Army was assisting in the push to the Baltic Sea. The Germans were dug in at the village of Schoenfeld and it fell to the Polish forces to take it. Infantry forces and tanks were initially unsuccessful in their attack, due to the Germans having anti-tank guns and the advantage of elevation. It was now the turn of the 1st Warsaw Independent Cavalry Brigade. They led a new assault, using a ravine and the smoke of burning tanks to hide their approach.

The charge took the defending Germans completely by surprise, cutting swathes through their ranks. The horsemen then overran anti-tank positions and lead the assault on the village itself. Joined by their infantry and tanks, they forced the defenders to flee.

The Polish lost 147 men, including just seven cavalry, to the Germans loss of 500. A plaque in the village, now called Żeńsko, commemorates the attack.

The fact cavalry were still being used may seem odd enough, but there was also poetic justice in their success. Six years earlier, the Nazis and Soviets had openly mocked the Polish and their supposed reliance on horses. They invented an incident, for the mockery of the world press, that the Polish cavalry had foolishly and suicidally charged panzers.

The age of cavalry was over, but the battle of Schoenfeld was an apt last hurrah.

THE BATTLE OF THE TENNIS COURT

Think of Thermopylae and you think of Leonidas and his three hundred Spartans facing impossible odds against the Persians in narrow mountain passes. Think of Stalingrad and you have a ghastly image of death and destruction when the might of the Wehrmacht broke against the immovable wall of the Red Army.

But there is another battle, unknown alongside Thermopylae and Stalingrad, a battle voted by the National Army Museum in London in 2013 as the greatest battle ever fought by the British. It is the battle of Kohima, the battle of the tennis court.

The war in Burma, today's Myanmar, was brutal, if only because the Japanese had a different mindset to the West. The little country had punched above its weight taking on China in the 1930s and the attack on Pearl Harbor brought the opposition of the United States. On 4 April 1944, as part of their push towards British India, the 31st Japanese Division encircled the British position at Kohima. With the town cut off, the Commonwealth forces were running low on water and three days later the 161st Brigade of General Montague Stopford's XXXIII Corps were later surrounded at

Jotsoma near the town.

The District Commissioner's bungalow came under attack on 8 April and drove the British back to the nearest high ground, the tennis court. This was hand-to-hand combat at its most lethal, one British Tommy buried temporarily under the mud and the bodies of his comrades. He played dead until dark, then dug his way out and dashed back across the tarmac to his own lines.

Attacks came every half an hour, including mortar fire directed at the field hospital in full view of the tennis courts themselves. Time was of the essence for two reasons. General William Slim of the 14th Army was bound to send help (it came first in the form of aerial support) and the monsoon season was about to break, after which all military operations would be severely compromised.

From their entrenched positions on either side of the tennis court, the Allies and the Japanese hurled grenades at each other, like a bizarre centre court at Wimbledon. Air drops were not that effective, ammunition and water landing in thick jungle and often ending up in the hands of the Japanese. When Stopford's tanks arrived, the onslaught continued until 10 May when the Japanese were driven back.

The war cemetery in Kohima has 1,420 graves to Allied soldiers. It was built on the site of that tennis court in the Commissioner's bungalow's garden and carved into the central memorial there are the now famous and poignant lines –

'When you go home, tell them of us and say,
For your tomorrow, we gave our today.'

'BAVARIAN' JOE

Scandalous cases of sexual impropriety do not belong exclusively to our own time. One of them may have removed an obstacle to Hitler's path to the war. 'Bavarian' Joe was actually a Berliner, Otto Schmidt, a career criminal and low-life who specialised in blackmailing male celebrities. The Nazi leadership, many of whom were notorious for their heterosexual flings, frowned on homosexuality and it emerged that Schmidt had had an encounter in the toilets of a Potsdam railway station with Colonel General Werner Freiherr von Fritsch, commander of the Wehrmacht, in 1933.

There had been a file on all this submitted by Reinhard Heydrich, in his position as head of the Reich Security service, the SD. At first, Hitler purported not to believe it, but the fact was that von Fritsch was an old-school soldier, appalled by Hitler's headlong rush to a war that he was convinced Germany was not ready for. Von Fritsch was in the way. The Gestapo interrogated him on 27 January 1938 and he was confronted by Schmidt, brought from Börgermoor internment camp for the purpose. He claimed that, in the Potsdam encounter, von Fritsch had smoked a cigarette (he had given up smoking in 1925); wore a fur coat (he never owned one) and told the lad he was commander of the army (a role he was not given until a year later). Despite the arrant nonsense spouted by Schmidt, von Fritsch did the honourable thing and resigned.

He was recalled to the army just before the outbreak of war and was killed near Warsaw, Poland, on 22 September 1939. It was generally believed at the time that he had done this deliberately.

THE BEE BOMBS OF PRESTER JOHN

Prester John (John the Priest) never existed. He was believed throughout the Middle Ages and much later, to be a Christian king who lived in the far east and would one day (he was immortal) save the crusading west against Islam. By the nineteenth century the legend still stood, but he was now an ancestor of the Selassie rulers of Ethiopia in East Africa. The Rastafarian cult of which the emperor Haile Selassie was the leader, believed the man to be a messiah and were as appalled as their emperor when European politics muscled its way into their territory.

Benito Mussolini, Italy's Fascist dictator, wanted to create a new Roman Empire and one obvious place to do it was in a backward society like Ethiopia. War broke out over this in October 1935 and a horrified world's press carried reports of natives armed with spears and shields, trying to hold back a modern, mechanical Italian army bent on destruction.

Haile Selassie himself, dignified and solemn, with complete justification on his side, appeared before the League of Nations to demand justice. The League had been set up after the First World War to arbitrate such international disputes, but it had no teeth and proved itself wholly inadequate. Adolf Hitler, for instance (now teaching Mussolini a lesson by sending guns to the Ethiopians) refused to join the League and simply ignored them.

Having to cope as best they could, the Ethiopians came up with an ancient weapon of which Prester John (had he ever lived!) would have approved. Soldiers would jump on to Italian tanks and throw a bee-hive into the vehicle's sights before getting out, fast. Pandemonium ensued when terrified Italians could be seen baling out of their tanks, much to the delight of Haile Selassie's men.

BEEFSTEAK NAZIS

Within the political ideologies that contended in Europe in the 1920s and '30s, Fascism and Communism dominated. The Bolshevik Revolution in 1917 terrified the west who saw their long-held interest in capitalism under attack. To combat the Red threat, Fascism became the order of the day, accepted in Germany, Italy and Spain by the 1930s, but the way there was strewn with corpses, from street fighting in German cities to all-out civil war in Spain.

Even within Hitler's Nazi party there were shades of opinion. One of these was spearheaded by the Strasser brothers, Gregor and Otto, who advocated a more radical, working class strand of National Socialism. These people were contemptuously called 'beefsteak Nazis' – brown on the outside (the colour of the SA uniform) and red inside (the colour of the Communist flag).

When the Russian army was closing in on Germany by late 1944, there is evidence that some of these men tried to defect to them. The *Daily Press* (California) of 22 September said,

> 'Their change will fool nobody. Like some beefsteaks, they will probably be done to a turn.'

THE BELLAMY SALUTE

The extending of the right arm out with a flat hand will now always belong to the shadow of the Fascists, but it wasn't always theirs. American schoolchildren throughout the country had been doing it every day for decades and no one thought anything of it. Both the Fascist and the American versions probably stem from the ancient Roman salute given to emperors, superior officers and legionary standards, although we are not exactly sure what form this took.

In an act of fervent patriotism in 1892, a magazine owner named Daniel Sharp Ford set out on his mission to get a US flag in every classroom and with the American Civil War still in living memory, this was seen as a unifying gesture. Sharp asked one of his writers, the Christian Socialist minister Francis Bellamy, to come up with a form of words that could be recited by the children. He wrote 'The Pledge of Allegiance' which was extremely popular and was soon being spoken by millions of students - 'I pledge allegiance to my Flag and the Republic for which it stands; one Nation indivisible, with Liberty and Justice for all.'

Sharp and Bellamy thought something was missing, and a salute was necessary to complement the words, so they advised all young patriots to stretch out their right hand, slightly upwards in the direction of the flag. The Bellamy salute began to make people uncomfortable by the 1930s and the identical salute of the Fascists in Europe raised many concerns. As relations between the US and Germany became hostile, leading to outright war in December 1941, a law was passed a year later replacing the Bellamy salute with the right hand instead being placed over the heart. The ultra-traditional Daughters of the American Revolution resisted at first, but eventually fell into line with everybody else.

THE BERLIN OLYMPICS

The Olympic Games have a long tradition, going back to ancient Greece. The games were eventually banned by the Romans when they turned to Christianity as they believed them to be a pagan celebration. In these ancient games, fires were lit in the temples of various gods to honour them.

It would be over 1,400 years until the games were reborn as the modern Olympics in 1896. The Olympic flame made its return in the 1928 summer games in Amsterdam. But it was the Nazis, in the 1936 Berlin Olympics, who conceived of the idea of running the torch from Greece to the host nation. Using over 3,000 people, the runners managed the relay in twelve days, where the final runner lit the torch to mark the start of the games. This tradition survives to this day.

As well as giving the world the Olympic Torch, the Berlin Olympics are known for a much better reason. Although much has been made of the black athlete Jesse Owens' historic victories at the 1936 Berlin Olympics, this is another case that doesn't quite tell the full story. The myth is that Owens winning so many gold medals infuriated Hitler and belittled his claims of Aryan physical supremacy. Adolf was so incensed, he stormed out and a moral victory was gained for black people, democracy and America.

Jesse Owens was in fact warmly received by the German public who cheered his name and congratulated his four gold medals, with admiring fans asking for his autograph. Jesse said the reaction at Berlin was the best he ever received. Hitler *did* refuse to speak to a black athlete, Cornelius Johnson on the first day. But this wasn't personal. Hitler was in attendance and congratulated the German athletes, but the Olympic officials protested the neutrality of the event and insisted he had to receive all the athletes, or none of them. So he chose the latter - and did not congratulate any of the athletes again.

Jesse's victories were on the second day, when Hitler wasn't seeing anyone. Jesse himself was frustrated by the manipulation of the truth and later commented:

'When I passed the Chancellor he arose, waved his hand at me, and I waved back at him. I think the writers showed bad taste in criticizing the man of the hour in Germany.'

The Olympics went better than Hitler could have dreamed, and he was delighted with the results. Not only did Germany win more medals than any other country, Hitler also revelled in such a successful publicity and propaganda campaign.

Some people tried to get the US to boycott the Olympic games, including the American ambassador to Germany, who was well aware of the horrors being committed by the Nazis and the fact it would be an overwhelming victory for Hitler in the propaganda stakes. The opponents to US participation lost the argument.

In fact, it was returning to America where racism was rife, that Jesse Owens faced discrimination. He did receive a ticker tape parade but was soon forgotten by the American people. Three years after Berlin he was declared bankrupt. President Roosevelt received the white athletes from the games but did not invite Jesse to the White House, congratulate him, or acknowledge his victories. According to Jesse's daughter Gloria, when the hero was attending a hotel for his own celebration, he had to use the back door to enter due to the colour of his skin.

What is weird here is that the oppression and persecution stopped in Berlin while the city was hosting the Olympics. It was as if a great, collective, dirty secret was put on hold until the foreigners had left again.

BERNHARD LICHTENBERG

Bernhard Lichtenberg was a German Catholic priest who was brave enough to speak out against the Nazis. A veteran of the First World War, Bernard was 62 years old when the persecution of the Jews was being increased, particularly after *Kristallnacht* on 9-10th November 1938. He was also deeply troubled by the euthanasia program, Aktion T4, aimed at disabled and mentally ill people. The priest found the actions of his countrymen repulsive and would courageously end each mass with a prayer for the Jews and other victims of the concentration camps.

He wrote a letter to Leonardo Conti, the chief physician of the Reich in 1942 saying:

'I, as a human being, a Christian, a priest, and a German, demand of you, Chief Physician of the Reich, that you answer for the crimes that have been perpetrated at your bidding, and with your consent, and which will call forth the vengeance of the Lord on the heads of the German people.'

Typically, such dissent could not be tolerated by the Nazis. Lichtenberg was put before the Berlin District Court and found guilty of 'abuse of the pulpit' and other insidious activity. He was sentenced to two years imprisonment.

During this term, Bishop Prysing visited him in prison. He then brokered a deal with the Gestapo allowing Lichtenberg to go free if he refrained from any further anti-Nazi activity. The priest refused, asking instead to be able to serve as a minister in Lodz, Poland.

This was intolerable to the Reich, who ordered his internment in Dachau concentration camp. He never worked a day, though, having died on 5th November 1943, during the train journey there. For his unyielding courage in the face of adversity he was beatified in 1996 by Pope John Paul II and declared as 'righteous among the nations' by Israel.

Leonardo Conti was arrested after the war and would have been put on trial for his involvement in Aktion T4, but he hanged himself in his cell on 6 October 1945, before this trial began.

THE BIELSKI BROTHERS

The casualty rate in the countries caught between Nazi Germany and Soviet Russia was horrific. In Belorussia, tens of thousands of Jews were murdered and the rest forced into ghettos which were duly 'liquidated' in 1942-3.

Such would have been the fate of the entire Bielski family who were hanged or machine-gunned in the Nowogrodek ghetto in December 1941; except that four of the family's six sons – Tuvia, Asael, Zus and Aharon – escaped and took about thirty others with them. Knowing the local geography like the backs of their hands, the boys disappeared in the impenetrable forests of Zabiedovo and Peralaz. They linked up with Soviet partisans and stole weapons. Tuvia became the leader of a warband that had twentieth century parallels with Robin Hood, striking a blow for freedom against the evil sheriff of Nottingham in Sherwood Forest. He sent agents into the ghettos, recruiting people and escorting them back to the hideout. That way, 100 Jews who would otherwise have died at Iwie were saved. By the summer of 1943, the 'merry men' had grown to an astonishing 700 people! Naturally, this irked the Germans. Twenty thousand Einsatzgruppen and Wehrmacht troops were unleashed, hunting for the Bielskis. There was a price of 100,000 Reichsmarks on Tuvia's head. From their base in the Nalikoki Forest, the group set up their own mill, laundry, school, synagogue and courthouse. They joined partisan Resistance groups, attacked collaborators and targeted the police, using explosives to sabotage bridges and railways.

By the time Stalin's Red Army had driven the Germans out of Belorussia in the summer of 1944, the Bielski group was 1,230 strong, 70 per cent of them women, children and the elderly. They travelled back to Nowogrodek and disbanded.

Like many Belorussians, at the end of the war they realised that in welcoming the Red Army, the Bielskis had simply swapped one vicious dictatorship for another. Asael was killed, fighting as a Soviet conscript in February 1945. The others fled west, fighting for the new state of Israel in 1948 and then to New York. The last survivor, Aharon, still lives in Florida.

The extraordinary life of Belorussia's Robin Hood was told in the 2009 film *Defiance*, starring Daniel Craig as Tuvia.

THE BITCH OF BUCHENWALD

The appalling story of torture, medical experiments and extermination carried out by the Reich between 1933 and 1945 defies description. Many of the anecdotes in this book are intentionally light-hearted. Humour, especially in beleaguered Britain, was a vital psychological release. But the behaviour of some individuals goes far beyond weird and the career of Ilse Koch, the 'bitch of Buchenwald' is a prime example. The original version was 'witch' (hexe) but the alliteration of the other version took hold and is the one used today.

She married SS Standartenfuhrer (Colonel) Karl-Otto Koch at an open air ceremony in 1936 and three years later the couple were posted to the concentration camp at Buchenwald, he as commandant, she as an SS Helferinnen (assistant). The Nazi mindset did not allow women to told important posts in any capacity – something else that is weird by today's standards. While he made a small fortune out of his exalted position (in direct opposition to the ideals of integrity preached by Heinrich Himmler as head of the SS) Ilse became known as a nymphomaniac with marked sadistic tendencies.

For decade the assumption was made that *all* Nazis had these vicious tendencies which explains the Holocaust in the first place, but Ilse went beyond the 'norms' of abnormality. She was obsessed with tattooed skin and had the skin of camp inmates removed from corpses and made into lampshades, gloves and wallets. She continued working even after her husband was hanged by the Reich early in 1945 and came to trial two years later.

Found guilty of murder, she was sentenced to life imprisonment. Extraordinarily, this was reduced by US General Lucius Clay (who believed that the lampshades were made of goatskin) to four years. In October 1949, she was released, only to be re-arrested for incitement to murder. The Senate examined her war record and she was re-tried in 1951. The decision of the court on the advice of psychiatrists was that she was a 'perverted, nymphomaniacal, power-mad demon'. In prison for life, she seduced an American army warder and gave birth. She hanged herself in Ailsach prison in September 1967.

Just as weird as Ilse, perhaps more so, is the series of Nazi exploitation films featuring sadism, blood and lesbianism produced particularly in Italy and France throughout the 1970s and '80s. The best known, *Ilsa, the She Wolf of the SS* and clearly based on Koch, was made in Canada in 1974.

Slightly less well known than Ilse is Irma Grese, the Belle of Auschwitz, also known as the Blonde Angel of Hell. She became a camp guard at the age of twenty-one and spent hours whipping inmates and gloating over medical experiments carried out by doctors such as Josef Mengele, the Angel of Death, with whom she may have had an affair. Another lover was probably the commandant of Bergen-Belsen, Josef Kramer. Found guilty of war crimes, she was hanged by Albert Pierrepoint. Staring him in the face, she simply said, '*Schnell!*' (quick!).

THE BLACK BEAST

Pal was a Newfoundland, one of the huge dogs bred for haulage across the frozen wastes of northern Canada. He belonged to the Hayden family, and although gentle, like all his breed, he had scratched the face of the family's 6-year-old, so he had to go. It was a tough decision. Should he be put down or merely moved on? In the end, sentimentality prevailed, and Pal was taken to the Royal Canadian Air Force station at Gander. Accordingly, that became his new name and he was officially instated as the regimental mascot of the 1st Battalion, Royal Canadian Rifles. A dog as loyal and intelligent as Gander was bound to impress; within weeks, he was promoted to sergeant!

At the end of 1941, the Rifles found themselves fighting in unfamiliar territory, defending the British base of Hong Kong against a determined Japanese attack. This was not the Allies' finest hour. The defenders outnumbered the Japanese and should have been able to hold on, but aerial support was lacking and the British surrendered on Christmas Day.

Rifleman Fred Kelly may well have been a formidable fighter, but he took his helmet off to his dog, Sergeant Gander, who was up to his neck in the hand to paw fighting at street level. Three times he drove the Japanese back, snapping at their heels as they ran. When the attackers interrogated prisoners later, they wanted to know about the 'black beast' that had run amok through their ranks, fearing that the Canadians were training such animals as killers.

Gander's number came up in the fight at Lei Yue Mun, the narrow channel leading to Hong Kong's harbour. A group of Canadians, trying to hold off a renewed assault, were under heavy fire, with a number of casualties. When a hand grenade hurtled through the air, the dog grabbed the pineapple in his powerful jaws and dashed towards the enemy lines. He was fast, but not fast enough and the grenade exploded, killing him instantly. His human handlers, however, lived to fight another day.

One thousand nine hundred and seventy-seven Canadians died at Hong Kong and Gander's name is listed with them. His medal is on display in Ottawa's Canadian War Museum and there is a statue to him and Rifleman Kelly at Gander Heritage Memorial Park, unveiled in July 2015. The fighting man's best friend was awarded the

Dicken Medal for Gallantry by the People's Dispensary for Sick Animals in October 2000. Twenty veterans of the Rifles were there that day.

THE BLACK BOOK

One of the sharpest brains in the German secret service (Sicherheitsdienst or SD) was Walter Schellenberg who became, during the later stages of the war, Hitler's spymaster. In 1940 he was deputy leader of Amt IV of the Reich Central Security Office in Berlin, responsible for counter-intelligence. Not only had he captured two top British agents in the Venlo incident on the Dutch border, he was also the mastermind behind Operation Willi, an attempt to coerce the exiled Duke of Windsor (Edward VIII) into the Nazi cause.

Schellenberg's task in the spring of 1941 was to compile the Sonderfahndingsliste-GB (Special search list, Great Britain), effectively a death-list for known opponents of the Reich in the UK, later known as Hitler's Book or the Black Book. It was typed up, complete with entries by secretaries at SD headquarters, in Wilhemstrasse, Berlin while Spitfires and Messerschmitts were slogging it out over the skies of Southern England.

A similar list, containing 61,000 names, had already been compiled for Poland and most of those on it who had not been able to escape the onslaught of the Wehrmacht and the einsatzgruppen, were dead. For those who today question whether the British version was actually a death list, this fact alone speaks volumes.

The 2,694 people in the Black Book could be divided into a number of categories. Inevitably, Britain's political leaders were there, men like Churchill, the Prime Minister and his deputy, Clement Attlee. Neville Chamberlain is there too, even though he was now seriously ill, semi-retired from politics and had, after all, appeased Hitler for most of the past seven years. Ernest Bevin, the Minister of Labour was B131. Alfred Duff Cooper, the Minister of Information, was D114. And there were the 'B' feature men, like Harold MacMillan, the future prime minister; Edwin Duncan-Sandys, the future Foreign Secretary. Women, who held virtually no place in the Nazi hierarchy, are not forgotten. Sylvia Pankhurst is listed, as a feminist and former suffragette, as is Megan Lloyd-George, the daughter of the prime minister of the First World War who was rather impressed with Hitler in the '30s. There was a galaxy of consuls, vice-consuls, envoys and attaches, 'our men' in various countries who had annoyed Hitler's regime in any number of ways. The leader of the eight exiled governments hiding in London (hardly the safest place in the world by September 1940) are on the list, along with their hangers-on. Charles De Gaulle of the Free French; Edouard Benes of the Czech Republic; Wladyslaw Sikorski of the Polish army.

There is of course, a large group in the Black Book who are emigres, intellectuals and politicians who got out of Europe while they still could. Many of these were Jews and British minorities were singled out for destruction come the German invasion because they had given them jobs. And there were home-grown British dissidents too – the left wing publisher Victor Gollancz; Harold Laski; the Socialist liberal, Bertrand Russell, already the grand old man of philosophy.

Institutions, as well as individuals came under Schellenberg's scrutiny. The public schools, as well as the universities, bred the officer class currently leading the war effort against the Reich. Boy Scouts and Girl Guides help with that war effort too. Most businessmen were in league (shock! Horror!) with Churchill and Beaverbrook's shackling of the economy to win the war. Those were traitors in Britain, good Germans who should know better. Spies, naturally, could not be allowed to survive.

Today we tend to scoff at the Nazis with hugely popular TV sitcoms like *Dad's Army* and *'Allo! 'Allo!* and we focus on the mistakes in the Black Book. Albert Einstein, probably the greatest genius of his generation, had fled Germany, but merely bounced in and out of Britain before going to America; Schellenberg believed he was still there. Churchill is listed twice; so is Attlee. And Freud, the famous psychoanalyst, was already dead.

The other side of the coin, however, is terrifying. Given the limited access to information across the Channel because of the war, the Nazis were extraordinarily well-informed. They had aliases, circles of friends and acquaintances, telephone numbers, addresses, even car registration numbers, all of which would have been used to hunt dissidents down in the event of a German invasion.

Let us leave the last word, however, to one of the several 'luvvies' on the list. After the war, when one of the two copies (of 20,000 published) was discovered and the story hit the British press, the novelist Rebecca West sent a telegram to fellow listee, Noel Coward – 'My dear,' she wrote, 'the people we should have been seen dead with.'

THE BLACK DEVIL

Erich Hartmann was a *Luftwaffe* fighter pilot and holds the record as the world's top flying ace with the highest recorded number of kills, earning himself the nickname 'The Black Devil' among the Soviets and the slightly less intimidating 'Bubi' (the kid) from his comrades. He is here not because he was weird but because his kill-list is so extraordinary. His nickname (Chemiy Chort in Russian) comes from the black tulip design on his engine cowling.

Erich's mother was a glider pilot (one of the first in Germany) and set up her own flying school, within which Erich became an instructor at the age of fourteen! Joining the *Luftwaffe* in 1940 he was extremely confident in his own abilities and a stunt where he performed aerobatics showing off over the Zerbst airfield saw him literally grounded and losing two thirds of his pay. This hubris may have saved his life as a friend was killed the same afternoon flying a Messerschmitt Bf109 that should have been Hartmann's.

Despite a rocky start to his career, 'Bubi' would go on to take part in over 1,400 combat missions, shooting down an unbeatable 352 enemy planes. He dodged death and crash landed fourteen times, always due to mechanical failure not enemy action.

What made Hartmann such a killing machine in the air? His philosophy was 'get close [to within 66 feet or less] – when the enemy fills the entire windscreen you can't miss.' He was deadly at stalk and ambush tactics and believed that 80 per cent of the pilots he shot down had literally no idea what hit them.

Hartmann surrendered his I/JG52 unit to the American 90th Division and was handed over to the Soviets. He was tried on trumped up charges of war crimes and convicted, serving ten of his twenty-five-year sentence before being released in 1955. This conviction has since been quashed as a 'malicious prosecution.' The Black Devil became a civilian flight instructor and lived peacefully to the age of seventy-one.

THE BLACKOUT RIPPER

The Blitz has a deservingly prestigious place in British folklore. Through the bombings and terror, the British public generally pulled together with courage, a sense of humour and community which hasn't been seen since, and which is remembered as 'the Blitz spirit'.

In such times, an element of trust was naturally assumed in a person's neighbours. Homes were vulnerable, shops were defenceless and the streets were abandoned. Those who robbed and looted during the blackouts were treated with particular scorn.

One particularly vicious Briton, Gordon Cummins, an RAF serviceman, would use the blackouts and the chaos of bombing as a cover for a brutal murder spree in 1942. His first victim, Evelyn Hamilton, was found gagged and strangled in a West End air raid shelter. The next day saw Evelyn Oatley strangled and slashed across her abdomen with a tin opener in her apartment. 13 February saw two more victims, Margaret Lowe and Doris Jouannet, both alleged prostitutes who suffered equally gruesome deaths.

The newspapers dubbed the killer 'The Blackout Ripper', for his inclination to attack during the blackouts, while most of the city was taking shelter. This, however, made those who did not take shelter such as prostitutes, or 'ladies of the night' particularly vulnerable.

14 February saw two more attacks on Greta Hayward and Kathleen Mulcahy, though both of these victims were able to fight off their attacker and survive the ordeal.

However, the Blackout Ripper would not disappear uncaught into urban legend like his namesake Jack the Ripper, who had terrorized Victorian London fifty years earlier. It was only a matter of time before Cummins slipped up. During his attack on Hayward, he dropped his gas mask case, complete with his serviceman's serial number 525987. Investigators entered his lodgings on the 16 February and arrested Cummins who protested his innocence, though his proclivity for taking a memento from each of his victims was to be his undoing.

Cummins was tried for murder and received the death penalty. In a final dark twist, the Blackout Ripper was hanged by Albert Pierrepoint, ironically during a German air raid.

THE BLITZ WITCH

Helen Duncan was a Scottish medium and clairvoyant who operated during the war. Born to a working class Presbyterian family in Callander, Perthshire, in 1897, she gravitated from teenage hysteria to full blown 'spirit contact' during the 1920s. The mother of six gave séances to people, claiming to be able to speak to the recently departed. The Victorians had loved this cross between spiritualism and parlour trickery and the number of dead in the First World war made séances popular again as bereaved families tried desperately to contact their dear departed. During her performances Helen would have nosebleeds and produce ectoplasm from her mouth, which was actually a mixture of cheesecloth and paper and cuttings from magazines. Tests conducted by British experts on psychic phenomena were not supportive to Helen, to put it mildly. The Society for Psychical Research were not impressed.

Photographs taken in 1928 reveal the various manifestations as laughable. Faces from magazines have clearly been stuck on to lavatory paper in some of them. The 'ghost hunter' Harry Price concluded, 'Could anything be more infantile than a group of grown-up men wasting time, money and energy on the antics of a fat, female crook?' Despite this public humiliation and a number of prosecutions and fines, Helen carried on her work and during a séance in Portsmouth in November 1941, she revealed that HMS *Barham* had been sunk and that she was talking to one of the dead sailors named Sid. The sinking of the *Barham* was not revealed by the government until January 1942 so Intelligence officers began to watch her more closely. Two Naval officers attended a séance in 1944 and were not impressed by her powers though and reported her to the police. Although the loss of *Barham* had not been revealed to the public, the families of the 861 dead had been informed in private so there is no reason to believe she couldn't have found that information out from them and the wartime rumour machine. Winston Churchill's government, via the Ministry of Information, continued the poster paranoia that 'careless talk costs lives' and 'tittle-tattle lost the battle' but the need for secrecy often ran counter to human nature.

The government nevertheless deemed the 'Blitz Witch' a security risk and decided to charge her for various offences so she appeared in court. Duncan and her defence team offered to conduct a séance in the court but this was declined by the jury. She was found guilty and sentenced to be imprisoned for nine months at Holloway, London's female prison. She was originally to be charged for espionage and treason but astonishingly was convicted under Clause 4 of the Witchcraft Act of 1735! 'I have done nothing,' she shouted from the dock. 'Is there a God?'

According to some reports the prison wardens refused to lock Helen's cell and had readings from her. Her séances in front of paying customers seem harmless enough. For a person to be imprisoned in twentieth century Britain as a witch says much about the paranoia of the leaders of the country at the time, although Churchill himself believed the trial was a farcical waste of time and angrily described her charge in a letter to the Home Secretary, Herbert Morrison, as 'obsolete tomfoolery.' Duncan continued to be harassed by the government until her death in 1956. The Witchcraft Act of 1735 was repealed in 1951. In 2012 the Scottish government rejected a petition to pardon her. 'Hellish Nell' remains Britain's last convicted witch.

THE BLOOD FLAG

Die Blutfahne (the Blood Flag) was a Nazi flag that took on an almost sacred quality and was treated like a martyr's relic. The original *blutbannr* was a scarlet flag associated with Medieval states and carried by the German *landsknechte*, mercenaries of the sixteenth century. Hitler's version was that of the 6th SA (*Sturmabteilung*) and was carried by Heinrich Trambauer in November 1923 during the Beer Hall Putsch in Munich, a failed attempt to wrest power from the Communist government. Sixteen Nazis and four policemen died in the violence that ensued. One of the brown shirts, Andreas Bauriedl, was killed and fell onto the flag, staining it with his blood. As the SA fled, one of them took the flag from its staff and stuffed it in his jacket, hiding it away for safekeeping. After serving nine months in prison for his attempted coup, Hitler was given the flag.

Upon receiving it, Hitler had a new staff made and the names of the sixteen brown shirts who died carved into its silver sleeve. *Die Blutfahne* was given to the SS in 1926, after which it took part in Nazi ceremonies, being used to touch other flags to 'sanctify' them as part of a flag consecration ceremony. The flag was housed in the Brown House, the Nazi headquarters in Munich and had an SS guard of honour. Although the glorifying of the dead of the Beer Hall was out of all proportion to what they achieved, the notion of standards as holy relics had a very ancient pedigree, stretching back to the Romans and beyond.

The flag's last known use was on 18 October 1944 after which it disappears from record. It is likely the flag was simply destroyed when the Headquarters were bombed by the Allies, or, at a push, it may have been taken to a place of safety. Either way, the holy relic of the Reich has never been seen since.

BOARD GAMES FOR THE REICH

The lengths the Nazi leadership went to in order to control the minds of their subjects is overwhelming. As part of their total war for the hearts and minds of Germany, they even made children's board games!

Jagd auf Kohlenklau (Hunting for the Coal Thief) was a game designed in 1944 and was used to encourage energy conservation as part of the German war effort. The war economy was driven by Hitler's architect Albert Speer and the speed of war production was astonishing. The game sees players move across fifty squares trying to avoid landing on tiles such as 'left the radio on, miss a turn.' This continues until one of them is declared the winner, thus 'evicting the coal thief'.

The idea of the game is quite benign, compared with two other games made by private companies during the Nazi regime. *Bomber über England* (Bomber over England) was a pinball style game where players would try to direct the ball to holes on a map of Britain, representing key cities, while trying to avoid having their 'bombs' land harmlessly in the North Sea. Players lose points for 'bombing' areas of the Reich.

The most baffling and wicked game to come out of the age has to be the 1936 creation of *Juden Raus!* (Jews Out!) by Gunther & Co. In this board game, playing pieces were pointed hats, representing Jews. Players are then in a race with their opponents to move all of their Jews out of the city and deport them to Palestine before anyone else. Surprisingly, the SS were not impressed by this game, believing it trivialized the Jewish 'problem'. Ironically, the SS solution to the 'problem' was more absurd then the objective of the children's game. Though it would be unfair to blame any child for enjoying a board game without an understanding of its deeper meaning, it is still uncomfortable to picture German families sitting down together playing it.

THE BOLLOCKS OF THE BLITZ

There is no doubt that *the* defining experience of the Peoples' War was the series of bombing raids on British cities in 1940-41 which were visited on German cities by the RAF and the USAAF in 1944-45. The aim of both was to terrify and demoralize the civilian population, forcing their governments to surrender. And, in both cases, it was an abject failure.

In an attempt to outwit the enemy during night-time attacks (raids in the daytime were quickly discovered to be suicidal) a blackout was imposed and the cry 'Put that light out' became a stock catchphrase. Men let their white shirts hang out of their trousers to aid travel on the darkened streets and kerb stones were painted white. Even so, road accidents rocketed in number, at a time when nobody owned a car and journeys were restricted because of petrol rationing. The London firm of Marshall and Snelgrove sold white coats for the dogs of the upper classes and private detectives had their work cut out in divorce cases. 'Adultery,' noted *Reynolds News* in January 1940, 'cannot be proved because identification is impossible in the pitch dark.'

The Blitz, first in London, then in the provincial centres like Coventry, Hull, Plymouth, Liverpool and Sheffield, killed thousands and destroyed property on an unprecedented scale. The sights and sounds and smells that the overstretched rescue services had to witness were often beyond belief. Even so, a grim battle humour shone through, from East Enders 'who could take it' to the bombed House of Commons itself. On 8 October 1940, Churchill told the House that given the rate of bombing and the hit-rate of the Luftwaffe, it would take ten years for half of London's houses to be demolished. 'After that, of course, progress would be much slower.'

The rumour machine kicked in big time. Someone saw a Zeppelin shot down over Essex. Refugees from bombed cities were causing a massive increase in venereal disease among those generous enough to take them in. In London, two million dogs and cats were put down because of a government order – and this was in the first week of the war, long before the Blitz started. When Merseyside was badly hit in May 1941, stories abounded of martial law in the area, train loads of burned corpses carried to the crematoria, rioting was widespread and thousands had taken to the streets carrying white flags of truce and demanding an end to it all. None of this actually happened. People *did* complain, not unnaturally. One London borough put in an official complaint because the reverberation of the anti-aircraft batteries was cracking lavatory seats in council houses.

As early as August 1940, before provincial raids started at all, more than seventy German parachutes were found in the Midlands, 'proof' of an invasion. Luftwaffe pilots and crew shot down over England wore rouge and lipstick. 'The medical profession,' sneered the *Daily Mirror* of 16 April 1941, 'has a word for men of this type. It classifies them as moral deviants ...' No one was too surprised by this. Anybody who could bring such terror from the skies could hardly be normal.

Various reports, all unsubstantiated, told a shell-shocked public that a pilot who bailed out over the East End was torn to pieces by the mob.

And if it weren't so grim, the Blitz had its comic side. A number of East End families swore they emerged from the Tubes and other shelters to find that the only part of their house still standing was the front door; it usually had the pet dog, completely unharmed of course, still tied to the door knob! One lady in Mayfair was rocketed out into the street in her bath. Others were sitting on the loo. Whole cities became beyond exhausted by night after night of raids and sales of Horlicks for 'deep, healing sleep' rocketed. When Madame Tussaud's was hit, some of its inhabitants were scattered along Marylebone Road like so many corpses.

Humour of course came to the rescue. A cardboard, hand written sign outside a shattered London police station read, 'Be good; we're still open!' Shops with no fronts put up signs reading, 'More open than usual'. Others just wrote, 'Blast!' One pub caught the mood of defiance perfectly – 'Our windows are gone but our spirits are excellent. Come in and try them.'

The shelters themselves became little microcosms of the shattered world above, offering sing-songs, stand-up comedians and, in the case of cinemas, as many as five feature films a night. The Blitz mentality saw a camaraderie unknown before the war and unknown since. The fact that it was engendered by fear did not lessen its importance. It cut across barriers of class, race, education and upbringing. Strange superstitions kicked in. The Germans never bombed the same house twice; in one London borough, everybody wanted a local Nigerian as their Air Raid Precautions warden because his black face was less of a target! When Plymouth was hit, several locals swore they heard the beating of Drake's drum, as though their sixteenth century hero had come to save them.

Cities began to look like deserted battlefields and the scars would last for years. The ubiquitous rosebay willow herb that grew on bomb sites came to be called fireweed. Those whose houses had been hit had the additional embarrassment that passers-by on their way to work could see their bedroom wallpaper and would, at the very least, raise eyebrows of disapproval at their lack of taste.

People died. Homes were smashed. The country was brought to breaking point. But it did not break. And the tide of war swept on in a different direction.

THE BOMBING OF BROOKINGS

In the early stages of the Pacific War, Japan's obvious problem was how to contain America's powerful fleet. The answer was to cause havoc at home and force the US navy to return to its own waters for defence.

Nobuo Fujita was a pilot in the Japanese Imperial Navy who carried out the second – and last – continental aircraft bombing on the United States. He and his crewman, Shoji Okuda, flew from a 1-25 submarine that surfaced off the Oregon coast near the town of Brookings, Oregon in 1942. His mission was to use his seaplane to drop incendiary bombs to start forest fires. The damage was minimal and a second sortie was barely noticed. Fujita's one man bombing campaign of continental America was a failure.

Despite this, twenty years later, the terror of the skies was invited back. He was assured by his own government in 1962 he was not going to be tried as a war criminal so accepted the invitation. In an act of honourable remorse, Fujita gave his family's 400-year-old samurai sword to the Americans as a gift. He intended to use the sword to commit *seppuku* (honourable suicide) if he was unwelcome; happily, the people of Brookings forgave him and he was declared an honorary citizen in 1990.

Fujita became an unofficial ambassador for peace, inviting students to Japan and he even received a letter from the office of President Ronald Reagan in admiration of his kindness and generosity. In the last years of his life he planted a tree at the bombing site as a gesture of peace and some of his ashes are scattered on Mount Emily, which he had pointlessly bombed fifty-five years earlier.

THE BOSTON HERALD RUMOR CLINIC

Imagine the horror as an American mother opened a parcel addressed to her, only to find her captured son's eyes staring up at her. Imagine the terror of the people of Curry County, Oregon when they heard that a bomb had exploded in their area, releasing deadly plague bacteria. It was widely known that 90% of the women who served in the Women's Auxiliary Army Corps were prostitutes. Native American soldiers, at Fort Devon, armed and no doubt under the influence of 'fire water', had gone on the rampage, raping any white woman in sight. A woman who had spent a small fortune to have her hair permed, walked into her day job in a munitions factory and her head exploded. And, of course, not a single American ship escaped the Japanese aerial attack on Pearl Harbor.

Nothing in the paragraph above is true. They are all fine examples of 'fake news' long before the phrase came into being. Misinformation and disinformation have been the bane of governments' existence for centuries. When the stones of St. Paul's Cathedral in London exploded because of the heat of the great fire in 1666, people swore they saw French warships bombarding the building from the river Thames. Attempts to damp down on this sort of nonsense have usually met with failure.

One man who tried was journalist Frances Sweeney who wrote regularly for *Life* magazine and *Readers' Digest*. She created the Boston Herald Rumor Clinic, using around 300 'morale workers' to keep their eyes open and their ears to the ground to hunt down tall tales. But there was an irony here. If, just for a moment, you were tempted to believe anything you read in the opening paragraph, that is because it is human nature to do so. The mere reporting of such stories, even when they are debunked, give them oxygen and the United States Office of War Information criticised Sweeney for that reason.

The criticism which could be levelled at the government is that so little information was being released. It was not until ten weeks after Pearl Harbor that President Roosevelt gave out details in one of his famous 'fireside chats' over the radio.

And sometimes, of course, governments lied to their people for the sake of morale. On 10 May 1941, the heaviest blitz of the war rained down on London. The BBC the next day, told a terrified nation (who rarely missed a broadcast) that 28 enemy aircraft had been shot down. In fact, the real total was a measly seven. But somehow, 28 sounded a better balance against the destruction on the ground.

Nazis dressed in nuns' habits patrolled the English countryside. Collaborators were lighting the way for the Luftwaffe with cigarette lighters. The Germans were digging a tunnel under the Channel to surprise the people of Kent. Women were attacking parachutists with pitchforks, stealing their silk to make nylons and knickers. You'd better believe it!!

THE BRIDE OF BELSEN

Gena Turgel was a Polish survivor of the nightmare that was Bergen-Belsen concentration camp. She lost all of her family was sent to Auschwitz. That camp has become synonymous with the barbarity of the Third Reich and remains today a museum and shrine to its millions of victims. As the Red Army was closing in she then endured a forced march to Bergen-Belsen. These 'death marches' served no purpose, as there was no safe place now for the remnants of Hitler's regime. Thousands died on the roads and in the ghastly cattle trucks, moving from camp to camp. Gena shared a barracks with Anne Frank, the most famous of all concentration camp victims, thanks to the diary she kept while in hiding during the German occupation of the Netherlands. The camp was liberated in April 1945 and the appalling conditions there, reported by Richard Dimbleby for the BBC, shocked the world. For most this was their first experience of how terrible the Holocaust was.

Through the unimaginable horror of it all, there was still some hope. A young British soldier named Norman Turgel was one of the first to come across the camp and took part in the overwhelming task of saving as many people as they could. Norman set eyes upon Gena in the camp. He immediately said, 'This is the girl I am going to marry.' He then helped bundle the vicious camp commandant, Josef Kramer, into a cell, looking into his face and telling him, 'I am a Jew.' Norman fell in love with Gena and proposed to her several days later. She said yes.

Her wedding dress was made from a silk parachute and she went to Britain with Turgel in October, being labelled by the press 'The Bride of Belsen.' Gena and Norman had a happy life, with three children. She spent several years telling British school children about her experiences. Of the inmates of Belsen, she said, 'They were ordinary people like you and they were murdered for no reason.'

BRIDE SCHOOLS

Reichsbräuteschule, 'Reich Bride Schools,' were set up by Nazi Germany to train women to become the perfect wives and mothers. It is always hard not to scoff at nonsense like this, and we should try to allow ourselves a pinch of humour when it is appropriate. If you will forgive the mocking tangent, we can almost imagine the lessons of this 'school' as an old fashioned cooking show.

> 'First off ladies, let's make sure there is none of that yucky Jewish or gypsy blood in you. Good, how about any of that horrid physical or mental illness which costs the state so much? You are going to breed healthy children aren't you? Excellent, now if you could just prove your Aryan ancestry back to 1800. Lovely, you truly are on your way to becoming a queen of the hearth and beginning your special task. Now, just grab yourself a tall and handsome SS fiancé and you're ready to begin.'

This 'special task' was to stop working, forget their previous lives and work on their 'spiritual and physical wellbeing'. But before they got to spiritual wellbeing, best to learn how to iron shirts and uniforms properly first. And there was cooking and gardening to be done, and let's not forget to give your husband's boots a once over. Also, make sure to vigorously polish his dagger when he gets home.

Working women were shunned as cold-hearted *Rabenmutter* (Raven mothers), cruelly abandoning their children, pushing them away from the bosom and the hearth.

The Nazi 'ten commandments' of 1934 for choosing a spouse were as follows:

1. Remember that you are a German.
2. If you are hereditarily healthy, you should not remain unmarried.
3. Keep your body pure!
4. You should keep your mind and spirit pure!
5. As a German choose only a spouse of same or Nordic blood.
6. In choosing your spouse, ask about his ancestors.
7. Health is a requirement also for physical beauty.
8. Marry only for love.
9. Seek a companion in marriage and not a playmate.
10. You should wish for as many children as possible.

And for female readers whose blood hasn't quite reached boiling point, six other points were added, particularly for women;

1. Women should not work for a living
2. Women should not wear trousers
3. Women should not wear makeup
4. Women should not wear high-heeled shoes
5. Women should not dye or perm their hair
6. Women should not go on slimming diets

Who said romance is dead?

THE BRITISH PET MASSACRE

In 1939 war was declared, just twenty-one years after the horrors of the Great War that irretrievably changed the world forever. With new threats and technologies available in the new conflict, Britain was taking no chances.

NARPAC, the National Air Raid Precautions Animal Committee, were deeply concerned by the shortages that war would bring. If the enemy could encircle the British Isles, food and other essentials would be in dire shortage, and the country would begin to tear itself apart from within as desperate citizens fought over whatever scraps they could find. NARPAC issued a pamphlet advising people that, if it was impossible to move their beloved pets to the countryside, it would be best to put them down; an advert for a bolt gun was printed next to the information.

Despite protests from animal rights groups such as the RSPCA and PDSA, a panicked population rushed to veterinary centres to have their animals euthanized. In one week, it is believed that as many as 750,000 animals died. Long before the horrors of the final solution were known, this was referred to as the September holocaust. Battersea Dogs' Home managed to save 145,000 dogs from certain death.

What is odd about this incident is the weight of government advice and the panic people must have felt to offer up their pets so quickly. Tragically, with hindsight, the animal cull was clearly unnecessary and years later many pet owners were bitter and angry with the government. Radio broadcaster Christopher Stone stating, 'To destroy a faithful friend when there is no need to do so is yet another way of letting war creep into your home.'

The 2017 book *The Great Dog and Cat Massacre* by Hilda Kean explains this tragic moment of British history in depth.

THE BROTHERS OF THE FOREST

Operation Barbarossa, the German invasion of the USSR instantly turned Russia from an enemy to an ally. From 1941 to '45, Britain regarded Russia as a friend, sending vital supplies via North Sea convoys. The reality, for the states of Estonia, Latvia and Lithuania, is that the Red menace was every bit as deadly as the Nazi occupation. While the world focussed on the evils of Hitler, most people beyond his grasp ignored the equal evils of 'Uncle Joe' Stalin. So, for many countries, their 'liberation' from Nazi Germany wasn't really a liberation at all. After the war, while France and West Germany were celebrating the return of democracy, countries like Lithuania, Ukraine and Poland simply had one form of foreign dictatorship replaced with another. In fact, their liberators were the same people who had conquered them before retreating from the Nazis in 1939.

Stalin's rule of the Baltic states was cruel and totalitarian; over one hundred thousand people would die in fighting and reprisals in the years to come. Tens of thousands joined the 'Forest Brothers', groups of guerrilla fighters that hid from their enemy in the vast forests of their nations in 1940. The partisans suffered heavy losses and were no match for the Red Army, so their tactics resorted to small cells conducting ambushes. Torture and death awaited any captured Forest Brothers whose mantra was 'save the last bullet for yourself.' For these countries, the war did not end in 1945 and Stalin's men were no different from Hitler's. The Soviet Union would continue to occupy the Baltic states until 1991.

BUSY LIZZIE

Nazi scientists were busy throughout the war (as were their Allied counterparts) trying to perfect more deadly weapons than the enemy. The V1 and V2 rockets – 'doodlebugs' – brought a new Blitz to British cities in 1944 and the V3 (*Vergeltungswaffe* 3) was a development of this technology. It was considered a 'revenge weapon'. Built on the northern coast of France, this huge cannon had barrels that were over 400ft long and was claimed to be capable of firing 600 shots every hour towards London. For this reason it came to be known as the London Gun, although the pattern of rocket boosters along its barrel gave it its German codename *tausendfussler* (millipede).

As with many Nazi superweapons, it was theoretically possible, but it was a huge drain on resources and manpower that many military commanders' thought was better placed elsewhere. Scientists also doubted the capabilities of the gun to achieve what it was supposed to. Hitler's obsession meant the plan was to go ahead, but thanks to the work of the RAF's 617 Squadron (the Dambusters), the cannon was damaged by aerial bombardment and put out of action.

The Nazis still had hopes for this weapon, even after D-Day. One of the four V3 cannons was relocated to Germany and used to bombard Luxembourg. The weapon that was meant to change the war was not impressive; a month long bombardment killed only ten people. In the end, time ran out and the German railway network was so damaged by Allied bombing that it was impossible to provide ammunition for the 'Busy Lizzie' as the gun was ironically called. The Americans captured all superweapons they could find and sent them to the US for testing, before giving up on this one in 1948.

CAMP E715

The unbelievable horrors that emerged from the string of concentration camps across Europe is well documented: millions of Jews, disabled people, political dissidents, prisoners of war, and other 'undesirables', suffered to such an extreme that, despite overwhelming evidence, a minority today still cannot – or refuse to – believe it was real.

One of the lesser-known stories is that of Arthur Dodd, a British soldier in the Royal Army Service Corps. Dodd was captured by the enemy at Badir during the Desert War and ended up in several Italian Prisoner of War camps. In 1943 he was transferred to Auschwitz III (Monowitz), a slave labour site for the pharmaceutical giant IG Farben just five miles away from the infamous Auschwitz-Birkenau site.

The horror of this place became apparent immediately to Dodd. As he and his comrades disembarked from the train they were greeted by the site of an SS officer thrashing a topless teenage Jewish girl with a whip. They tried to intervene but the SS officer pulled out a pistol, a Wehrmacht soldier warned them the SS would have no qualms about killing anyone. Leaving the British with no choice but to let the thrashing continue.

Dodd's home for the next 14 months was camp E715, close enough to the crematoria for the smell of burning flesh to fill the air, bodies hung from gallows and the men witnessed the unbelievable treatment of the inmates, particularly the Jews. Some of the men tried to sneak food to the other inmates, but others refused to help, openly admitting they believed that anyone being treated as cruelly as the Jews of Auschwitz were obviously being punished for a crime they had committed of equal ferocity.

Opportunities for defiance were slim, but the soldiers tried. Being forced to work on pipework at Monowitz, the men began to deliberately sabotage them by filling them with stones and other items. A German engineer became suspicious and ordered a test. The men were horrified – their act of sabotage would soon be discovered and the best they could hope for was to be lined up and shot. As the test began, an air raid siren sounded. The men were rushed to an air raid shelter. When they emerged, they discovered the only place that was actually hit by bombs was where their pipes were. All of them were destroyed and their sabotage effort was never discovered.

With the war coming to an end and the Allies closing in, the guards gave Dodd and his men a choice to walk towards the Soviets in the east or the Americans in the west. They choose the westward journey and they were eventually liberated at Regensburg, Germany.

After the war, Dodd returned to Britain, marrying his sweetheart Olwen and starting a family. His account of his time in the war, *Spectator in Hell*, was published in 1998.

THE CARPET CHEWER

The German word is *teppichfresser* and it was a term of contempt applied to Hitler by non-Nazis. To explain the extraordinary rise of the Fuhrer and the hold he had over millions, we have to factor in his explosive temper. How much of this was the genuine bitterness of a sociopath and how much part of his public persona is difficult to tell. He certainly screamed and ranted if he thought he could get his way – he did it at the Munich Conference in 1938 and most of his cleverly crafted speeches ended on an hysterical note. This led some people to make assumptions. Birgir Dahlerus, a Swedish diplomat, found him 'patently unstable'. Neville Henderson, the British ambassador in Berlin before the war, said he was 'quite mad', having 'crossed the borderline of insanity'. Manfred Schroder, a Nazi underling who was with Hitler at the time of Munich, described him as 'an absolute maniac'.

If he behaved like a spoiled child with tantrums, there is no doubt that it often worked in that he got his way and minions were genuinely afraid of him, especially if they had to be the bearers of bad news.

There is no evidence that he ever rolled on the ground, frothing at the mouth and literally chewing the carpet with rage as the nickname suggests, but the same behaviour is ascribed to King John of England, who gnawed at the floor covering at Windsor Castle having been forced to put his seal to Magna Carta in 1215. The problem with *that* story is that in John's day, carpets were tapestries and hung from the walls; the floor was covered in straw.

CARROTS

It was believed that carrots could help you see in the dark. At a stretch there is a truth to this; if you have a Vitamin A deficiency you will develop nyctalopia and carrots help but only to the point of returning your eyes to a normal level. The myth was useful however to the British Air Ministry. In an effort to keep the Germans in the dark as to their recent development of radar, they claimed that the Royal Air Force pilots were being fed carrots to give them night vision and thereby explain why they were quick to find and intercept the *Luftwaffe* on bombing raids. The story focussed on Group Captain John 'Cats' Eyes' Cunningham of 604 Squadron who shot down an enemy aircraft in December 1940 with radar aid.

The public certainly believed it and the myth gave renewed impetus to the Ministry of Food and the 'grow your own' campaign – 'Dig For Victory'.

Carrots of course were the least of it. As rationing became the norm and food supplies dwindled, the public had to make do with substitutes of all kinds. Powdered egg, whale meat, 'snoek' (tinned fish) and much later, Spam, all joined the carrots and turnips of Woolton Pie. Even Christmas puddings had a high vegetable content. The BBC broadcast *The Kitchen Front*, advocated the use of spaghetti and noodles. Most housewives had never heard of these and some refused to buy them because they were foreign and Britain was at war with the Italians.

CARROT ON A STICK

The Second World War hit ordinary people like no other in history. Because of the range of enemy bombers, everybody's home was the Front Line. And even without the Blitz, privation became the order of the day. The Ministry of Food was set up to control the production and intake of food. Rationing, coupons, queues – they became the 'new normal' from 1940 until, in some cases, long after the war was over.

The 'Dig for Victory' campaign encouraged people to turn their lawns and flower gardens into allotments; even the greens of the Tower of London where umpteen Tudors had lost their heads, were planted with vegetables. Pig clubs were set up, 6,000 animals sharing gardens throughout the land; even the Metropolitan Police had one. The family pet was no longer a cat or a tortoise, but a chicken or a rabbit because they were edible. Vegetables, fruit, fish and above all, bread were never rationed, because of the panic that that might cause. But everything was in chronically short supply; by the end of 1942, Britain had lost 728,000 tonnes of imported food to U-boat attacks.

Enter good old British 'make do and mend'. No lemonade? Never mind, just grate carrots and swede, strain them through muslin and you have Carrotade. And don't forget curried carrot, carrot puddings and carrot jam. If you freeze the carrot juice, you can have carrot on a stick. Given the few domestic fridges in Britain during the war, this was luxury indeed.

And of course, the Ministry of |Information insisted, carrots helped you see at night – Bomber command never took off without them. The *real* all-seeing 'eye' – radar – was top secret, known only to a select few in the RAF and Air Ministry. In the States, Walt Disney was doing his bit for this propaganda – Carroty George, Clara Carrot and Pop Carrot all appeared in the cartoons of 1942 and in Britain, kids could rely on the ubiquitous 'Doctor Carrot', 'the children's best friend', ably assisted by his sidekick Potato Pete.

Carrots even found their way into the codes used by the Maquis and other French Resistance groups. As D-day loomed – and happened – on 6 June 1944, wireless sets all over France crackled 'les carottes sont cuites' (the carrots are cooked).

Long after the war, exasperated parents would still try to get food into their uninterested toddlers' mouths by making aircraft noises and calling out patriotically 'One for the king'.

THE CASE OF THE DEADLY DOUBLE

It sounds like a Perry Mason television episode (in fact it was, in 1958!) but this particular double had more sinister and more serious connotations. Two weeks before the Japanese attack on Pearl Harbor, advertisements appeared in the *New Yorker* magazine for a dice game. To draw readers' attention to it, the words Achtung! Warning! and Alerte! were used – all of them heard all too frequently in war-torn Europe at the time. The dice themselves, tumbling in mid-air, showed a series of numbers on the faces – O, 5, 7, 12, 24 and XX. It purported to be Chicago's favourite game and one that could be played in an air raid shelter (something the Americans would never have to do for real).

The Pearl Harbor attack led to high alerts across America and the FBI became convinced that the Deadly Double game was a code on behalf of the Japanese war machine. 12 and 7 on the dice was the date of the attack; 5 and 0 referred to the time of the raid and XX was 20, the latitude of Pearl. 24 was perhaps the code sign of the agent who had placed the ads. The FBI's investigation revealed that the Deadly Double Game did not exist; neither did the Monarch company that purported to make it. To this day, the case remains unsolved.

CASTLE ITTER

Five days after Hitler killed himself, the war would see one of its most unusual battles; an alliance of German and American soldiers fighting the SS in Austria to save Frenchmen. Castle Itter, part of the Dachau concentration camp organization, was used to intern many of France's most powerful people including former prime ministers Edouard Daladier and Paul Raynard, ex commanders of the Army Maxime Weygand and Maurice Gamelin and even a famous tennis star, Jean Borotra. In May 1945 the guards fled, fearing execution from the SS; two prisoners set off to find help. They came across a Wehrmacht major, Josef Gangl, opposed to the Nazis and working with the Austrian resistance. As he only had twenty men he wasn't able to provide an adequate defence. Under the truce of a white flag, Gangl met up with the 23rd Tank Battalion of the US XXI Corps, led by Captain Jack Lee and explained the situation to him. Lee agreed to help defend the castle.

The men took up defensive positions and waited for the inevitable attack. On 5 May a 150 strong unit of the 17th Panzergrenadier Division, Waffen SS attacked the castle and blew up a tank and laid siege. Captain Lee was able to radio for help and reinforcements were dispatched, but the communication was intercepted before it was completed. So tennis star Borotra vaulted the castle walls, survived the gunfire of the encircling enemy and met up with the relief force. Borotra was an old hand at escapes – this was his third in two years. The defenders were almost out of ammunition and made plans to fall back to the keep and fight hand to hand if necessary but fortunately their back-up arrived in the late afternoon. Over 100 SS soldiers were taken prisoner. The only casualty among the defenders was Josef Gangl, who was killed by a sniper while protecting Paul Reynaud. Today, he is considered an Austrian hero. Germany would surrender within three days.

CAT BOMBS

The aircraft carrier was undoubtedly a war-winning weapon of the Second World War, but its technology was hugely demanding. A pilot had to take off from the deck of a moving ship, find an enemy ship and drop his bombs on it before returning to the mother ship. Everything is moving – sea, ship, plane, bombs – a nightmare of physics. So the American Office of Strategic Services, forerunner of the CIA, dreamed up the cat bomb. Because cats hate water and because they have an uncanny ability to land on their feet, the idea was to drop cats attached with bombs from the air onto naval targets. As the cats landed in the water they would instinctively head towards the vessels and thus detonate their explosive. This idea never got passed the testing stages as the cats would lose consciousness on their descent. Quite how the cats could have swum after a ship with a bomb attached to them in an open ocean was another imponderable of physics and could only be explained by the paranoid geeks of the OSS.

THE CHANNEL ISLANDS

On Sunday 30th June 1940 a German plane circled over Guernsey before landing on the island's airport. The local 'bobby' (policeman) scurried over to the Germans who had landed with a letter from the bailiff, 'This Island has been declared an Open Island by His Majesty's Government of the United Kingdom. There are no armed forces of any description. The bearer has been instructed to hand this communication to you. He does not understand the German language.' And so began the five-year occupation of Britain's Channel Islands, arguably the most lackluster occupation of the entire war. Strategically, the islands were worthless, but the propaganda value of having Britons within the Reich was priceless.

Following the fall of Dunkirk and anticipating invasion, thousands of islanders had already evacuated to the mainland. Boats were made ready to take as many to England as possible. Not all could, or would, leave. Among them were a handful of Jews, twelve on Jersey and four on Guernsey.

Despite Churchill's roared speeches of defiance, there was no fighting on the beaches, the streets or the hills. People got on with their lives, just as did the men and women of any occupied country, trying to maintain the fine line between independence and normality without crossing it and risking German reprisals. The British were treated gently compared to other nations, perhaps as an experiment in appeasing the British so they would listen to Hitler's 'appeal to reason' and make peace, or a taste of things to come if Britain was invaded and Operation Sea Lion worked?

Radios were confiscated, phone lines cut, spirits and petrol were banned, permits were needed for boats and an 11pm – 6am curfew was put in place. Eddie Chapman, one of the most enigmatic men of the war, was in prison for burglary. He tried to escape prison and was sent to Paris where he offered to work for the Germans as a spy, they accepted his offer. Codenamed *Zig-Zag* by the British and *Fritz* by the Germans, he would eventually become a double agent under Cecil Masterman's XX Committee. He is the only Englishman to have received the Iron Cross.

In April 1942 three Jewish women on Guernsey, Therese Steiner, Marianne Grunfeld and Auguste Spitz were in trouble. The British bobbies told the women to pack their bags and report to the police station, where they'd be handed over to the German military the next day, last stop, Auschwitz.

What is upsetting here is the absolute compliance of the police. It is no secret that the horror show of the holocaust was only possible because of the never-ending army of myrmidons who were 'just following orders'. Was there really no opportunity to give the women a heads-up? There was a whole evening of waiting – could the women not have 'escaped' police custody and found an old boat on the shore?

Police Clerk Sergeant Ernest Plevin gave an absolutely scandalous justification for the complicity of the British police: 'Police involvement in deportations was rarely more than carrying out orders given by the occupying forces.' (What else would it be!)

A 1945 British intelligence report was deeply concerned by the actions of the islands police and local authorities. The report laments they put up absolutely no protest to anti-Jewish measures, knowing full well the Jews would receive 'unpleasant' treatment in Europe. In contrast, the islanders did everything possible to protect Freemasons. Women who fraternized with occupying soldiers became known as 'Jerry-bags'; estimates for the number of illegitimate children from these relationships ranged from 80–900. Wretched slave labourers skulking around the island, of whom 700 died, would have brought the horrors of the Reich home to the locals. With all this being said, it was easy for mainlanders who weren't in danger (and modern minds) to condemn and judge when they have never been in such an excruciating position themselves. The majority of Channel Islanders acted stoically and honourably in extremely difficult circumstances.

Photographs of German soldiers parading through the streets, chatting happily to the local bobby, and perusing shops with English signage still shock and fascinate today.

THE CHANNEL WHITE WITH BODIES

In June 1940, Britain stood alone. The army had been driven out of France at Dunkirk and the next military step, it seemed obvious, was the invasion of Britain. It was an extraordinarily difficult thing to do; the last successful invasion by a foreign power took place in 1066. The point was that aerial and bombing technology had added to the terror and several of Churchill's military advisers were telling him that Germany would be bound to win the war.

In August as the Battle of Britain raged in the skies over southern Britain, there were reports of a parachute landing in the north and constant rumours that the Isle of Wight, like Jersey and Guernsey, had already been overrun by the Wehrmacht. By Christmas, America, still not in the war, was reporting in various newspapers that two German invasions had been repulsed with a loss of 80,000 men; so many that their corpses gave the Channel a whitish appearance and were being washed up all along the south coast. French hospitals were choked with wounded and the Channel itself blazed with burning oil. And none of this was true.

There were indeed casualties from an invasion scare, but they were British, not German. Reports of a Kriegsmarine break out from the Dutch coast prompted the 20th Destroyer Flotilla of the Royal Navy to investigate. They ran into a minefield, two ships were sunk and a third was damaged. The wounded were brought back to various hospitals along the east coast and the government probably believed that a rumour about a scotched invasion would sound better than a failed raid.

In early September another 'invasion' was foiled, at Sandwich Bay in Kent. This time the water was *black* with German dead, rather than white. The majority of British people had never seen a German in uniform and believed (as many people still do) that the Wehrmacht wore the Waffen SS's black uniforms, rather than the field grey they actually wore. Similar landings were reported to have happened in the west country and in Scotland; there were thousands of dead on Clacton beach alone. Some of these corpses were apparently tied up in groups of three; as diarist James Hudson noted, with or without a straight face, 'Lots of funny stories go about.' At Southend, the bodies were supposedly picked up by council rubbish lorries.

Wing-commander Guy Gibson, who led 617 Squadron's famous raid on the Mohne and Eide dams in 1943 summed up the situation very well – 'no one will ever know anyone who saw a dead German soldier, although many a man will claim to know someone else who knows someone else who buried one.'

In May 1940, AP Herbert, poet, MP and member of the Naval Reserve, called for calm –

'Do not believe the tale the milkman tells;
No troops have mutinied at Potters Bar,
Nor are there submarines at Tunbridge Wells.
The BBC will warn us when there are.'

In fact, it was in the interests of Churchill's government to give invasion rumours their head. What is common to them all is that the corpses were *German* – in other words, the invasion failed. Blitzkrieg was beaten back. This positive ethos was exactly what Churchill wanted in his desperate bid to bring the Americans into the war – Britain was far from beaten, but a little help would be nice. The icing on the cake of these stories was the weapons technology actually going on in Britain at the time – and of course, top secret – which let the world believe that they could stave off invasion for ever by setting fire to the sea.

CHANSON D'AUTOMNE

Chanson d'automne (Autumn song) is one of the most famous French poems. Written by Paul Verlaine around 1866, it was part of his 'sad landscapes' collection.

The long tears
Of Autumn's
Violins
Wound my heart
With a monotonous
Lethargy.

All suffocating
And pale when

The hour strikes
I remember
The old days
And I cry...

And I am going away
On an ill wind
That carries me
Here, there,
Just like a
Dead leaf.

This poem would do its bit for the war effort nearly eighty years later. The British, through the BBC radio broadcasts, would give the nod to the French Resistance that the time for Operation Overlord and the D-Day landings were almost at hand.

The first three lines of the poem, when played on the radio, would secretly inform the resistance that Operation Overlord was to start within two weeks, these were broadcast on the 1st June 1944. The next set of lines would tell the French that the landings would start within 48 hours, these were broadcast on 5th June at 23:15, the night before D-Day. Such a cunning and clandestine use of a poem was indecipherable to German counterintelligence.

The broadcasts were successful in informing the French Resistance that it was now time to prepare to fight. With the broadcast of this poem they began sabotage operations such as blowing up railways and blocking roads and generally hindered the enemy in any way they could.

CHARLIE BROWN

In any war, particularly one as nightmarish and devastating as the Second World War, simple acts of compassion and chivalry stand out. Rare flashes of humanity in the senseless slaughter of war are poignant reminders to us that people can defy the odds. One such incident was between Charlie Brown and Franz Stigler.

Lt. Charlie Brown was a USAAF pilot, commanding a Boeing B-17 Flying Fortress, 'Ye Olde Pub', on a bombing run over Bremen. Brown was flying in left of the formation, known as the 'Purple Heart corner' for its vulnerability. On return from the bombing run, enemy flak and fighters crippled the plane, their compass and engines were damaged and the crew did not know where they were. They could have been flying deeper into the Reich rather than returning to Britain. The tail gunner had been killed and nine other crewmen were injured. The oxygen system was damaged, causing Brown to momentarily black out; he regained consciousness just in time to stop his spiraling plane crashing into the ground.

Franz Stigler, a Luftwaffe ace with 27 victories to his name intercepted the B-17 and couldn't believe it was still airborne in the state it was in. Stigler, risking his own life, flew his Messerschmitt Bf 109 G-6 alongside the plane to see a panicked Charlie Brown and the injured crew desperately trying to make it home. Stigler hoped the plane would land, or at least head towards neutral Sweden. It became clear to Stigler that Brown was determined to reach England. He turned his plane and escorted the bomber back to Britain, accompanying it part of the way across the North Sea. Brown, still not entirely sure of the enemy pilot's intentions, ordered his dorsal turret gunner to aim at the Messerschmitt but not to open fire. Stigler gave Brown a salute and left. 'Ye Olde Pub' eventually made it back to base. The incident concerned Allied command, and the crew were ordered to keep quiet as positive sentiment for the enemy was considered dangerous. Brown himself later commenting 'someone decided you can't be human and flying in a German cockpit.' Stigler kept the incident to himself too, as he risked execution for his insubordination.

Decades after the war, Brown was desperate to track down the man who spared him and his crew. Years of searching revealed nothing until a chance letter to a pilots' newsletter came to the attention of Stigler, who was by then living in Canada. Forty years later the two men were reunited and remained life-long friends, dying a few months apart of each other in 2008.

CHEERS!

Deception has been part of the art of war since the Chinese strategist Sun Tzu wrote his book of the same name in the fifth century BC. Shakespeare makes much of Macduff's army using trees as a defence, bringing to reality the omen that 'Birnham wood shall come to Dunsinane' to defeat the tyrant Macbeth. In the real (medieval) world, Edward, Prince of Wales raised false standards to make his enemy, Simon de Montfort, believe that friends were on their way to rescue him at Evesham in 1265. In the build up to D-Day, in June 1945, inflatable tanks were scattered in various parts of northern England to confuse spotter aircraft into believing that Operation Overlord would be delivered in Norway.

The Germans had their own deception plan. They built fake airfields, including runways, buildings and 'parked' planes. The idea was to lure Allied bombers to waste their bombs on unimportant fields. As far as their real airfields were concerned, they painted bomb damage on perfectly usable buildings to make bomber crews believe there was no point in hitting them again. We must understand that bomb accuracy in the Second World War was nothing like it is today and that most bombs were dropped in relatively cloudy weather from 30,000 feet.

You cannot, however, con a conman. The Allies became wise to all this and dropped wooden bombs onto the wooden airfields, just to make a point. One German airman, who saw the funny side of all this, wanted to buy a drink for the pilot who had dropped fake bombs onto his fake airfield. The question is, would it have been a real drink?

CHIPS THE DOG

Chips, a mix of a German shepherd, collie and husky served in the United States Army, and is believed to be the most decorated canine of the Second World War. During the war, American families donated their dogs for military service and in 1942 the Wren family offered Chips, who became a sentry dog.

Among his valiant efforts was his part in the 1943 invasion of Sicily. During the assault, Chips, along with his handler Pvt. John Rowell and his men were pinned down by a machine gun nest. The dog broke cover and charged towards the nest, biting enemy soldiers and pulling a smoking machine gun from its base. Chips grabbed one of the enemy by his neck and dragged him out from his cover; the soldier and his comrades surrendered. Later in the day Chips took a further ten Italian soldiers prisoner.

Chips was also given the honour of being a guard at a meeting between Winston Churchill and Franklin D. Roosevelt. He wasn't always well behaved though. When the future president General Dwight D. Eisenhower went to pet him, he bit him. The fault can't lie completely at Chips door for this incident. He was trained to clamp down on any humans he didn't know.

In December 1945 Chips was reunited with his owners, the Wren family. Sadly, though, he would die just seven months later, probably as a result of complications from injuries he sustained during his service.

In 1990, Disney made a film on the dog's life, *Chips, the War Dog*. In 2018, Chips was posthumously awarded the prestigious Dickin Medal for his heroic actions.

CHURCHILL'S TOYSHOP

Churchill's Toyshop was the nickname for the top secret British laboratory MD1, itself part of the secret weapons development unit MI9, attached to Military Intelligence Research run by Lt. Colonel Joe Holland of the Royal Engineers. Originally based in the cellars of Radio Normandie in Portland Place, London, MD1 relocated after being bombed, to a Buckinghamshire mansion called The Firs near Aylesbury. Even – perhaps especially – during a war, the various government ministries fell over each other, bickering as to exactly who did what; and inevitably, it was all about funding. Churchill was keen to cut through the red tape and his War Cabinet controlled everything that MD1 did.

The list of inventions – some brilliant, others silly – have filled whole books and this snippet can only scratch the surface. They included the Limpet Mine, used to sink enemy ships, which contained condoms and aniseed balls as part of its components. Another invention was the sticky bomb, of which the prototype involved porridge. Churchill was impressed and told them 'Sticky bomb – make one million.' Containing nitro-glycerine, they were stuck to vehicles and were used extensively by commando units. Time pencils were delayed detonator fuses. M mines were made of cardboard. The 'Bomb, H.E. Ainslie, Aircraft, JW' was the 'Johnnie Walker', designed to travel underwater until it reached the keel of a ship, when it would explode. L-Delay fuses also allowed bomb fuses to be lit, with a delay on the explosion of over a week! The huge numbers of uncanny inventions made by the team was probably author Ian Fleming's inspiration for his character Q in the James Bond novels. Fleming was with Naval Intelligence during the war.

'CLUTTY'

We are all familiar with Q of the James Bond franchise, an earnest, white-coated boffin (played usually by Desmond Llewellyn) who has invented the most cunning and brilliant gadgets and is exasperated by Bond who appears that he could not care less. Inevitably, though, the world's most famous spy ends up using the relevant gadget to foil his enemies, stay alive and, of course, make the world a safer place.

Perhaps the closest we can come to a real life Q was Clayton 'Clutty' Hutton, a pilot in the First World War who became fascinated by magic and escapology. He once had a bet with the famous escapologist Harry Houdini that the magician could not escape from a particular trap. Hutton knew he was on to a winner because he had given Houdini's maintenance crew a back-hander to fix the bolts!

When the Second World War loomed, Hutton joined M19, the branch of the Secret Service most concerned with espionage gadgetry to do with escape and evasion. By 1942 he had written the manual, a top secret list of his inventions called *Per Ardua Ad Libertes* (Through Hardship to Freedom). It was rumoured that he set up his workshop under a cemetery so that he would not be disturbed!

In his autobiography *Official Secret*, published in the United States in 1961 because no British publisher would touch it for security reasons, Hutton spelt out the ingenious ideas that he came up with. Prisoners of war in Germany and elsewhere were allowed to receive parcels. These came in the Red Cross, but others were accepted too, once they had been checked by the camp authorities. Under bogus aliases such as the Welsh Provident Fund, the Licensed Victuallers' Sports Association and the Jigsaw Puzzle Club, M19 sent valuable 'get out of Stalag' cards which took a variety of forms. Packs of playing cards had maps hidden in them. Pilots' navigation charts were stashed inside the heels of shoes. Compasses were secreted behind buttons. Perhaps the most ingenious of all was the hijacking of the popular board game, Monopoly. The government did a secret deal with Waddingtons, the game's manufacturers, which had brilliant secrets all over the board. A full stop after 'Marylebone Station' was destined for Italy with hidden escape routes over the Alps. A full stop after 'Mayfair' was the version sent to Norway so that escapees could get to neutral Sweden. Some boards had real gold tokens (top hats and so on) that could be used as barter by escapees; and most daring of all, some of the Monopoly money was actual German currency, the Deutschmarks of which Hitler was so proud.

Q would have been proud too!

THE CODE TALKERS

In any war, there is a need for secrecy and government departments have been set up with that specifically in mind. They usually operated complicated systems of code, from Thomas Phelippes working for Sir Francis Walsingham, Elizabeth I's spymaster in the sixteenth century to the elaborate enigma device of the Second World War. But any code, no matter how complex, can be cracked. An actual *language* is infinitely more complicated.

In the United States, the Navajo code talkers are much celebrated heroes of the war and perhaps the most famous code talkers of all, their language being indecipherable to the enemy. The Navajo system was never broken by the Axis powers and they have even been immortalized in the 2002 movie *Windtalkers*. This wasn't the first use of Native Americans; as early as the First World War, the Americans realized they could use the various languages of their First Nations' soldiers to confound their enemies. The Cherokee and Choctaw soldiers were deployed in various roles in the Great War, the first use of Cherokee at the second Battle of the Somme in 1918. The US military continued to use Native American code talkers up to the Vietnam War, utilizing the languages of the Assiniboine, Comanche, Meskwaki and Seminole tribes. The Americans also used their European ancestry, employing descendants of the Basques from northern Spain. The British occasionally used Welsh!

COMFORT WOMEN

Throughout history, the 'brutal and licentious soldiery' have assumed a natural right to help themselves to local women, be they the enemy or camp followers. During the war, the Japanese imperial government forced women into sexual slavery for use by their troops in any country they occupied. The estimates for the number of girls coerced into military prostitution varies significantly between 20,000 and 400,000, based on the opinion of different scholars, Japanese and Chinese.

Women from any occupied country were at risk of coming to the attention of the Japanese soldiers but Korea and China appear to be the worst affected. Imperial troops would try to lure girls with promises of work and safety, but the girls ended up finding themselves in 'comfort stations'. If tempting them didn't work, they would simply be stolen from the streets, on one occasion even setting up a girls' school – the Huimi school in occupied China – with the specific intent of abusing the students. Disturbingly, the justification for this was that it would encourage soldiers not to rape indiscriminately. Three out of four comfort women, due to the horrific abuse they received from dozens of men daily, would not survive the war.

The subject remains controversial today with many apologists claiming that the women involved were volunteers. The Japanese government caused outrage in 2016 when their deputy Prime Minister claimed 'there were no documents confirming that the Japanese government or army forced comfort women into sexual servitude', despite previously admitting their role in the 1990s. Less than fifty of these women are still alive today, affectionately called *hadmoni* (grandmothers). Japan has set up a fund to offer these women financial assistance. At the close of the war, only eleven soldiers would be convicted of crimes against women.

COMICS FOR THE KIDS

There was even space for comics in the Nazi propaganda repertoire. The *Vica* was created in occupied France in 1940 to demonize the Allies. Only three issues appear to have been produced. The hero of the comics was a character who looks remarkably like Popeye and the first issue sees him dealing with the British secret service, as well as handling Uncle Sam and Bolshevism.

American children were bombarded too and the sales of comics went towards the war effort from January 1942 onwards. The Nazi hierarchy were invariably shown as aristocratic, with monocles and jackboots; they were always cruel. The Italians were a joke, puppets in the hands of their German masters. The Japanese (clearly *the* unprincipled villains after Pearl Harbor) were portrayed as devious and look like monkeys. Ironically, the all-American heroes, especially Captain America, were often shown as Aryan, with astonishing muscles, blue eyes and blond hair.

In Britain, at least three Fascist leaders were lampooned. The *Dandy* had Addie and Hermie (Hitler and Goering) while the *Beano* had Musso the Wop!

THE CONFIDENTIAL PIGEON SERVICE

As with so much from the war years, particularly in the murky realms of the secret services, the truth and scale of the Confidential Pigeon Service is hard to pick out. Author Nigel West wrote 'the whole point about a secret service is that it remains secret' and despite the passing of the Freedom of Information Act in Britain in 2000, a great deal of espionage information is still classified. From 1940 onwards, the British began parachuting pigeons in crates into occupied Europe. Each pigeon was accompanied by writing paper, a special pencil and instructions in various languages; it was then set free to return to their home in London with their message. They were also to have a copy of a London newspaper attached to them, to prove their British origin, although exactly how this was possible is unknown (at least to the present writer!). When Lieutenant John Randall of 1SAS was behind enemy lines in France soon after D-Day, he radioed home to say that a pigeon sent from London had been found, but without the daily paper. He asked whether this was right. Yes, he was told; it was. He sent the pigeon back, but it had not arrived four days later and no one mentioned the bird again.

The phenomenon of pigeons' ability to 'home' is still not completely understood, but is generally accepted to involve the magnetic field of the earth. MI4, who were in charge of the project, were pleased with the results and the intelligence they were receiving. By 1944 the Nazis were so concerned they began deploying their own pigeons, which would home back to the Reich as counter-intelligence, even containing a packet of English cigarettes to fool the receiver.

Thirty-one pigeons received the Dickin Medal for bravery, though they would have to keep that to themselves as our secret pigeon spies did not become public knowledge until the files were released by the National Archives in 2007.

THE COLDITZ COCK

The story of Colditz is the stuff of Boys' Own adventure. The prison for 'incorrigible' Allied officers in Saxony was the plotline for a hugely popular film *The Colditz Story* and a long-running BBC drama – *Colditz* – in the 1970s. Both were based on Pat Reid's memoirs, as an inmate himself, and the exploits caught the imagination of several generations.

The Geneva Convention insisted that prisoners of war be treated with dignity and even courtesy. It was all a far cry from the treatment doled out to civilians in concentration camps throughout Europe, but the Germans by and large honoured it. Putting determined escapees together in one place made some sense, so that not every camp was infected with them; but policing a place like Colditz was a nightmare.

There were at least 186 escape attempts, 32 of them resulting in a 'home run' in which the escapees got to a friendly or neutral destination. It was a British officer's duty to try to escape; and a German guard's duty to stop him. It was all in the methodology. Any prisoner using forged or stolen German papers and impersonating a German soldier risked a firing squad; otherwise, it was all rather gentlemanly. This changed in 1944 when a Fuhrer order specified that commandos captured behind enemy lines were to be shot on sight.

Because of its layout, the Renaissance castle at Colditz was thought to be impregnable, perched high in the Saxon mountains. But there is a difference between a castle that is difficult to attack and one that does not leak its prisoners! In the castle library was a book called *Aircraft Design* which gave an enterprising escapee like Lieutenant Goldfinch not only the idea, but a blueprint for a plane. If you cannot tunnel your way out through rock and masonry using not much more than a teaspoon, how about flying out? They built a false wall in the prison attic behind which the 'hangar' gave birth to a glider, the *Colditz Cock*. A small team of technical men, largely Royal Engineers, calling themselves the Apostles, built the thing, with a further forty taking shifts as lookouts for patrolling, nosy guards.

The aircraft's ribs were made from bed-slats. The wing spars had once been floorboards and control wires were electric cables. The 'skin' was made from cotton sheets and sleeping bags. When it was finished, the *Cock* was 19 feet from nose to tail and had a 32 foot wingspan. How the guards could have failed to find something that size and to be totally unaware of its existence is beyond belief.

The problem, of course, was how to launch the *Cock*. In the event, history intervened, either depriving the world of a flash of true genius (had it worked) or deep embarrassment (if it didn't!). The American army spoiled the fun by liberating the camp on 16 April 1945.

The fate of the *Cock* is unknown. Since Colditz effectively disappeared behind Stalin's Iron Curtain in 1946, it was never seen again. One photograph of it exists, however. It was taken by American war correspondent Lee Carson and one of the Apostles, the aptly named Mr Goldfinch, had retained his drawings. Accordingly, a ⅓ scale model based on these was flown from Colditz castle in 1993, by which time there were no guards to object!

THE COOLER

If you are of a certain age, you will remember the cult television series of the 1960s,

The Prisoner, starring Patrick McGoohan. The central character, known only as Number Six ('I am not a number; I am a free man!') is imprisoned in a surreal 'village' (Portmeirion in North Wales) and subjected to endless interrogation about what he knows. He is an agent who has fallen foul of his masters and knows too much top-secret 'stuff' to be allowed his freedom.

The writer of *The Prisoner* was George Markstein, a German Jew who fled to Britain as Hitler's grip on his native country became intolerable. And his own experiences meant that Number Six's predicament – the spy who knew too much – was not far removed from reality.

Espionage was a very impressive science. Many agents were incompetent or events overtook them, which led to their being compromised and of no further use to their handlers/spymasters. The Special Operations Executive (SOE) faced this problem by requisitioning Inverlair Lodge, a stately home in Scotland known officially as Number Six Special Workshop School and unofficially as 'the cooler', American criminal slang for solitary confinement.

Here, ex-agents were given comfortable accommodation (like McGoohan's prisoner) and, to make them feel useful, they worked behind the scenes on fictional missions which would keep them busy until the war ended. It could only ever be a temporary solution. Every Intelligence officer had signed the Official Secrets Act which meant that they had to keep their mouths shut. After the war, however, with politics changing by the week, several of them forgot that and rushed into print with their explosive memoirs.

THE CRAZIEST PILOT

Beam me up, Scotty,' became one of the best known catchphrases of the 1970s when television's Captain Kirk (William Shatner) of the USS *Enterprise*, gave orders to his chief engineer, Scotty (James Doohan) in *Star Trek*. In fact, Doohan was a genuine war hero of a terrestrial rather than extra-terrestrial war. Joining the Canadian artillery, he was sent to Britain in 1940. His first action as a lieutenant was at Juno Beach on D-Day, killing two snipers. He then led his men through a field of anti-tank mines and was later accidentally shot six times by one of his own men. One bullet hit a finger, which was amputated, four hit his leg, and one hit his chest – the impact of this being stopped by a cigarette case.

Doohan was later attached to the Royal Canadian Air Force and was noted as their 'craziest pilot', once slaloming a Mark IV Auster near RAF Andover between two telegraph poles 'to prove it could be done.'

His death, from pulmonary fibrosis in July 2005, is believed to be related to exposure to toxic substances during the war.

CROFT'S PIKES

The British Home Guard, the last-ditch call up of old men and those deemed unfit for active service, is considered peculiarly endearing to the British. This is thanks, in part, to the BBC comedy series, *Dad's Army* (1968 – 1977), which followed a group of bumbling and incompetent, but well-meaning and courageous, reservists.

The atmosphere in Britain at the time would not have been light-hearted. The threat of Nazi invasion, through Operation Sea Lion, was considered real, plausible and imminent. The volunteers were to be the last line, holding off *Fallschirmjaeger* (paratroopers) and coastal assaults in the desperate hope of buying the doomed country some time, fighting heroically to the last man. Thankfully, the Home Guard never saw combat, and the events of 1941 turned the tides of war in a different direction. However, they remained on guard, and it was possible, though increasingly unlikely as the war progressed, that the tide could turn once more. Perhaps a reasonably reliable comparison to the heroic desperation and mindset of the Home Guard is the tragic *Volkssturm* (people's storm) of Nazi Germany.

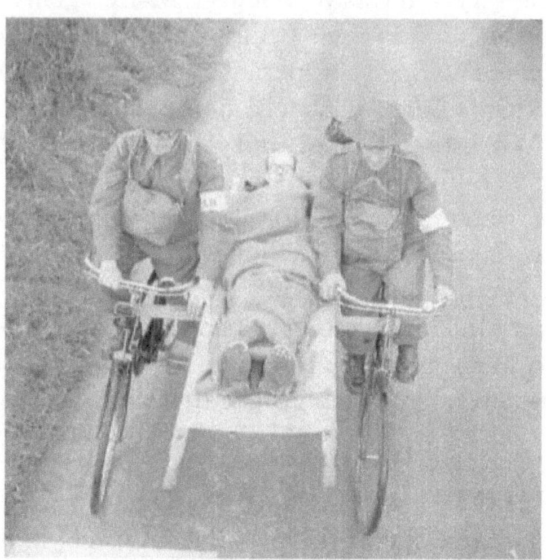

1940 was arguably Britain's most dangerous year – certainly just after the miraculous escape from Dunkirk. 1,682,000 men volunteered for the Home Guard, but there were not enough weapons, 739,000 were unarmed. In 1941, Churchill wrote, possibly tongue-in-cheek, that 'every man must have a weapon of some sort, be it only a mace or pike.' Whether or not Churchill was speaking literally about medieval weapons, he was taken at his word. A quarter of a million pikes were ordered, long steel tubes fixed with a bayonet.

The soldiers of the Home Guard were obviously unimpressed, and it is believed none were issued after protestations. Lord Croft, Under-Secretary of State for War said in the House of Commons, defending the pike, it was 'a most effective and silent weapon'. Others suggest that 'Croft's Pikes' *were* a serious suggestion by Churchill, but Lord Croft did the honourable thing and took the blame away from the Prime Minister for this foible.

The armament crisis was eventually resolved with all the reservists being properly equipped. Quite how the Wehrmacht would have reacted if they invaded Britain, being met on the shores by elderly men with pikes, can only be guessed at. For those who have seen *Dad's Army*, we can imagine the reaction of Captain Mainwaring and his men: 'We're doomed!'

THE CURSE OF THE *WILLIE DEE*

Sailors are a notoriously suspicious lot. Stories of mermaids, St. Elmo's Fire, Leviathans and the edge of the world, have been swapped in portside taverns for centuries. Old tars today are still not very happy about women serving on Royal Navy ships in the British Service.

In the Second World War a focus of this superstition was the *USS William D. Porter*, a Fletcher-class destroyer known with much affection, as '*Willie Dee*'. In November 1943, the ship was part of a convoy that was taking President Roosevelt to the high-level conferences at Cairo and Tehran. Somebody on board forgot to raise the anchor and the *Willie Dee* smacked into another destroyer as a result.

Tehran was frought with all kinds of security difficulties but these were coincidentally worsened by the activities of the *Willie Dee*. All four ships in the convoy initiated radio silence because of marauding Axis submarines. When an attack came, everybody manned battle stations and prepared for anti-sub manoeuvres. The whole thing was a false alarm – *Willie Dee* had accidentally dropped a depth charge off her stern, giving rise to the imminent attack panic.

The *Willie Dee* had to break off from the convoy for repairs as rough seas had flooded her engine room and had only just re-joined the others when near-disaster struck again. USS *Iowa* let off balloons for target practice, perhaps to impress FDR and *Willie Dee* joined in with torpedo drills. The combat crew forgot to remove the explosive charge from a missile headed right for the leader of the free world. Frantic attempts to signal *Iowa* went awry when the wrong message was sent – the incomprehensible 'WDP is breaking up'.

Roosevelt was sitting on deck in his wheelchair throughout this scare and reports exist claiming that his secret service bodyguards were firing at the incoming torpedo with their handguns! The torpedoes missed but that was hardly the point. The crew were arrested and court-martialled; Captain Dawson was sentenced to fourteen years hard labour, but the President used his power of commutation and all was forgiven.

Forgiven but not forgotten. Just in case *Willie Dee* was indeed a cursed ship, she was sent out of harm's way to the Aleutian Islands off Alaska – effectively in the middle of nowhere. On New Year's Eve, 1943, all was going well, with fireworks and merriment, when a sailor who had over-imbibed fired off a 5-inch gun, obliterating the flower garden of the local commandant.

In April 1945, *Willie Dee* took part in the battle of Okinawa. Bad enough that the US Navy had to contend with the mighty battleship, *Yamato*, and swarms of kamikaze (suicide) pilots, but the cursed ship contributed to the mayhem by accidentally straffing the USS *Luce*. The Pacific war was still raging on 10 June when a kamikaze pilot dove his plane directly at *Willie Dee*. He mistimed his attack and his aircraft ended up under the ship's keel, exploded and lifted *Willie Dee* out of the water. She keeled over and had to be abandoned although there were no casualties.

Bad luck? Gross incompetence? Deliberate sabotage? Or a genuine example of what superstitious sailors have known all along – a cursed ship. Whatever the situation, USS *William D Porter* received four battle stars for her service in the war.

DADA

The First World War destroyed the established order. Millions of men died and were wounded during a seemingly pointless conflict. Throughout Europe, the old order crumbled and extremist groups such as fascists and communists began to fill the void for the survivors of an angry and bitter generation.

Even the arts were affected, an avant-garde movement known as Dada or Dadaism began to emerge from 1916 onwards, as a reaction to the horrors of the Great War itself, and a rejection of bourgeois capitalism, colonialism and other Western constructs. Dada artists enjoyed the absurd, nonsensical and surreal. Although difficult to define, some of its main manifestations were poetry, collages, photomontages and literature.

Dadaism wasn't popular with everyone. *The American Art News* described the movement as 'Dada philosophy is the sickest, most paralyzing and most destructive thing that has ever originated from the brain of man.' Later described as a 'reaction to what many of these artists saw as nothing more than an insane spectacle of collective homicide.' Dadaism spilled over into the Second World War, even being condemned during Goebbels 'degenerate art exhibition' in 1937.

One of the most striking Dada artists was the German John Heartfield. His Anglicised name was his own choice, he changed it from Helmut Herzfeld and was appalled by the anti-British sentiment of the First World War, the cries of 'May God punish England', and the general fervour for bloodshed sweeping Europe. The same 'us vs. them' mob mentality was swirling in Britain.

Heartfield's anti-Nazi photomontages have a strikingly modern feel to them. In different pieces Goering sets fire to the world; a swastika is crafted by four bloody axes; an ape Hitler sits atop the globe in a *stahlhelm*; a starving family gratefully eat a bicycle and Hitler the butcher grins menacingly over a French cockerel.

Unsurprisingly, the Nazis were not happy with Heartfield's work and in 1933 the SS broke into his apartment in the hope of arresting him. Heartfield managed to hide in a rubbish bin, waiting for hours until they left and managed to escape first to

Czechoslovakia and, later, Britain. He earned his place as number five on the Gestapo's most-wanted list.

He returned to Germany in 1950, now partitioned into east and west, and narrowly avoided a trial for treason, because of his time in Britain, from the communist East German government.

His work is still popular and referenced. One example is the modern rock band System of a Down, who used his piece 'The Hand Has Five Fingers', as a cover for their 1998 debut album.

Though not a surrealist painting, Heinrich Vogeler's striking 'The Third Reich' from 1934 is another piece that appears to be before its time. Vogeler was not as lucky as Heartfield. A German who turned communist as a result of what he had experienced during the First World War, he emigrated with his wife to Russia. After the Axis invasion of the Soviet Union in 1941, Vogeler, along with all Germans, was deported to Kazakhstan. He died there in 1942 from illness due to the squalid living conditions he faced. The Heinrich Vogeler Museum was opened in 2004 in Worpswede, Germany.

DAWE'S D-DAY

Leonard Dawe was an old-school headmaster of the Strand School, evacuated to Effingham, Surrey, who submitted more than 5,000 crossword puzzles over the years to the *Daily Telegraph*. Like all British newspapers in wartime, the *Telegraph*'s size was reduced and its news content carefully checked by the authorities. Between 1939 and 1945, Britain came the closest it has ever been to a police state – ironic in that she was fighting against one!

MI5, responsible for espionage and security on the Home Front became suspicious of Dawe's crossword clues. In the spring and summer of 1944, the words 'Utah', 'Gold', 'Sword' and 'Juno' all appeared, as did 'Omaha' – all five were the secret code names for the various beach assaults planned in Operation Overlord, the amphibious landing which came to be called D-Day. Worse followed – on 27 May 'Overlord' itself was a solution and three days later, 'Mulberry' (the floating harbours towed across the Channel to enable landing). On 1 June (five days before the attack) 'Neptune' appeared – the Navy's code name for its part in the assault.

Dawe was interrogated by MI5 but nothing incriminating was found. Two ex-pupils of Dawe have now come forward to say that they had heard those code-names being bandied about by troops stationed near the school in the build-up to D-Day and that it was Dawe's habit to invite boys to help him devise his crossword clues.

While some readers might consider the case closed, that solution is highly unsatisfactory. In a country paranoid to the point of obsession, where 'careless talk costs lives', how feasible is it that squaddies would have known those codes, talked openly about them and that schoolboys would have found the random names so compelling as to pass them on, unwittingly, to Dawe?

DEALING WITH THE DEVIL

Some Germans today, appalled by their country's recent past – or perhaps in denial over it – refer to Hitler as 'the man who made the Volkswagen'. In fact, although Hitler promised the 'people's car' as a cheap, efficient mode of transport for all civilians, it was not produced as such before the Reich was destroyed. In the 1940s, the KdF Wagen, as it was originally called, was used entirely by the armed forces. It was only after the war that the car was built on a massive scale, helping to rebuild the shattered German economy and becoming one of the world's most popular automobiles.

To some people, extolling the virtues of a machine built by a regime like the Nazis is abhorrent, but it does not end there. The industrial giant I.G. Farben, which claimed to make dyestuffs, was a corrupt cartel keeping its prices high and competition out. During the war it supplied the Wehrmacht with 85 per cent of its explosives and nearly all synthetic materials that kept the Nazi war machine rolling. Before the war, it had negotiated lucrative deals with the United States, Britain, France and Japan. Auschwitz, by 1944, was turning out oil and rubber products through the slave labour available there and elsewhere. In August 1945, the company's directors were put on trial for what amounted to war crimes but the eventual prosecution was dropped because the Americans realised that they needed German industrial muscle to counter the Cold War expansionist threat of Soviet Russia.

A subsidiary of Farben, Bayer, gave the world aspirin but it also produced Zyklon B, the cyanide capsules used to kill millions in the death camps. Prior to that, IBM had developed a punch-card system that allowed Nazi authorities to set up the equivalent of databases to hunt for the 'undesirables' that filled those camps. While the majority of German newspapers got out of the country as the war loomed, if not earlier, the Associated Press stayed, contributing to the Nazi propaganda of the *Volksischer Beobachter* and *Der Sturmer*. Krupp had been making German weapons since before there was a Germany (1871) – they willingly contributed to the Nazi war effort too. As did Hugo Boss, himself a passionate Nazi, who made SS uniforms using the camps' slave labour.

Sam Pivnik was a survivor of Auschwitz. Thirteen when the Germans invaded his native Poland, he survived the ghetto, two death camps, a death march and the mistaken bombing of the SS *Arcona* by the RAF in the spring of 1945. Years later, when John Kennedy was President of the United States, Pivnik saw a photograph of the man walking arm in arm with Werner von Braun, the Nazi who had devised the V2 missiles unleashed on Britain during the war. Von Braun was one of many former Nazis who had been embraced by the west because of his technological know-how, rather as many of today's international businesses once worked for Adolf Hitler and made a great deal of money out of him. 'A mass murderer,' said Pivnik, 'walking arm in arm with the leader of the free world.'

As President Kennedy might have said – 'Go figure.'

DEAR HITLER

Mohandas Gandhi, the Indian revolutionary, is one of the most famous faces in history. His non-violent resistance to British imperialist rule sent shockwaves through the world and helped crumble the last remnants of colonialism. History better remembers him by his honorific title Mahatma (venerable).

In the 1930s, Gandhi was clearly disturbed by the events unfolding in Europe. Two curious letters were written by Gandhi and posted to Hitler.

The first letter of 23 July 1939 reads:

Dear friend,

Friends have been urging me to write to you for the sake of humanity. But I have resisted their request, because of the feeling that any letter from me would be an impertinence. Something tells me that I must not calculate and that I must make my appeal for whatever it may be worth. It is quite clear that you are today the one person in the world who can prevent a war which may reduce humanity to the savage state. Must you pay the price for an object however worthy it may appear to you to be? Will you listen to the appeal of one who has deliberately shunned the method of war not without considerable success? Any way I anticipate your forgiveness, if I have erred in writing to you.

I remain,
Your sincere friend
M.K.Gandhi

A second, longer letter in 1940 is a much more direct and imploring than the first. In it, Gandhi demonstrated the values, perhaps somewhat naively given the recipient, of pacifism and non-violent resistance.

The letters never reached Hitler, having been intercepted by the British. Even with this in mind, we must take into account Hitler's appetite for war, the countless appeals for sanity since his rise in 1933 and his views on race and 'sub-humans.' It would be extremely surprising if he had any time to entertain the ideas of a Hindu ascetic, though he did in fact later support the creation of an Indian Waffen-SS unit, led by Subhas Chandra Bose, though this was most likely out of pragmatism.

This tragically optimistic correspondence was dramatized in the 2011

THE DEATH MATCH

An American book in 2001 and a Russian film in 2012 have highlighted this bizarre sporting event. As Andy Dougan wrote in 2001, 'If ever soccer was a matter of life and death, then it was here.'

Many of the details of the infamous 'Death Match' are unfortunately hard to unravel due to the layers of legend it has attracted via Soviet propaganda. What is known is that the Ukrainian FC Start, from Kiev, was made up of former professional footballers, now working in an occupied bread factory. On 6 August 1942, Start played a *Wehrmacht* team at Zenit Stadium in front of 2,000 people. SS Soldiers and police dogs would have been intimidating to the players, and it was rumoured that the referee was an SS Officer who went into their changing room to tell them to throw the match. He ignored SS fouls and discounted some of Start's goals. These accounts were later denied by the players. FC Start went on to win the match 5 – 1 and the Germans demanded a rematch three days later, which FC Start won again 5 - 3. The Soviet propaganda machine eventually spun their own yarn and the legend grew. Whatever the truth of it, and whether it was linked to football, eight players would soon be arrested by the Gestapo and five would be murdered by the SS within a year.

DEATH RAY

It was not just the Nazis who had a penchant for wonder weapons, miraculous inventions so powerful they'd change the course of the war and bring all other nations into submission. The Japanese were in on it too, having hopes for a death ray.

Since 1924, some scientists had been boasting of their ability to build a death ray. But it was Nikola Tesla in 1934 who stated in an interview with Time Magazine of the potential of wiping out entire squadrons of planes and armies 250 miles away using 'teleforce.' Tesla made contact with the US military, who weren't particularly interested in his claims – but the article made the Japanese wonder whether it could be done.

After the war, documents confiscated by the US military showed a laboratory in Noborito had been working on this potentially deadly weapon. Development had begun on a device named 'Ku-Go': a large magnetron which created powerful microwaves. It was planned to beam radiation at enemies, killing soldiers and destroying equipment. Fortunately the project floundered. The end of the war stopped the research.

Unlike the lethal death rays of popular science fiction a decade or so later, the Japanese version was not as dangerous. At the peak of research, a focused beam could kill a rabbit from 1,000 yards away - assuming it would stay still for five minutes.

The British themselves dabbled with the idea of a death ray under the guidance of Sir Henry Tizard, Robert Watkins Watt and other academics before finding it unfeasible. This may have been a blessing in disguise, as they developed the game-changing concept of radar instead.

THE DEFECTOR

Martin James Monti was one of thousands of Americans who felt the draft. The United States might have dithered at the outbreak of the war in Europe, but the unprovoked attack by the Japanese at Pearl Harbor changed all that. Monti was from St Louis, Missouri and he joined the US Air Force as a cadet in 1943.

The next year found him as a second lieutenant based in Karachi, India, at a time when the whole of the sub-continent was still part of the British Empire. On 1 October 1944, Martin Monto suddenly went AWOL. He got to Cairo and on to Tripoli in Libya. The fighting here was long over, a combined force of British and American troops having forced Rommel's Afrika Korps off the coast. From there, Monti travelled north to Naples in the wake of the Allied armies who were closing in on Bologna. The Fascist dictator Benito Mussolini was on borrowed time by now. His ally Adolf Hitler advised him to pull back north of the River Po and the collapse of Italy and the fall of Mussolini were only weeks away.

Monti reached the 354th Air Service Squadron amidst the chaos and told them that he was a pilot from the 82nd air group. Oozing charm and confidence, he persuaded the 354th to let him test fly an F-5E Lightning, a version of the P-38 used for aerial reconnaissance and photography. He took off into the sun and literally vanished off the radar. Two hours later, in fact, he landed his hijacked aircraft near Milan in enemy territory. The Italian Social Republic was actually run by the Germans by this time and Monti, with an Italian name but mid-western American papers and accent, was taken prisoner.

So far, so odd, but it got odder. With the war's end, prisoners were released and Monti was back in Milan to re-join the American forces. But he was wearing an SS uniform, given to him, he said, by Italian partisans who had helped his escape. 1945-6 was a time of payback. Europe was in ruins, the Red Army was already squaring up to the West and there were, despite everybody's sense of exhaustion, scores to settle. Accordingly, Monti was court-martialled for desertion and the theft of a plane. He was sentenced to fifteen years in prison, but this was quashed as long as he re-enlisted as a private in the army. The media at the time had him down as an 'eager beaver' who longed for action rather than languishing in India, rather as hundreds of Americans had enlisted before December 1940 posing as Canadians to join the war effort.

But the case of Private Martin Monti did not quite add up. Facts were clouded with doubt; timelines did not fit. In 1947, the FBI turned up at Monti's army base in Florida and interviewed him. They discovered that he had made between ten and twenty broadcasts over the radio under the name Martin Wiethaupt, complaining about the Allied bombing of civilians. He had joined the SS as *Untersturmfuhrer* (second lieutenant); the uniform he had worn on his return to the fold was his own!

Monti faced trial again in 1949, but this time nobody was in a lenient mood. A huge case was presented involving witnesses who included former SS officers who offered testimony that the American had voluntarily enlisted in their ranks. To the astonishment of the prosecution, Monti pleaded guilty. He was sentenced to 25 years in prison and given a fine of $10,000 ($110,000 today). Two years later, he hit the headlines again, claiming that he was coerced into the guilty plea on advice from his counsel to avoid a death sentence. He was paroled in 1960 (so much for 25 years!) and lived quietly until his death in 2000.

What is weird about Monti's behaviour is the timing of the whole thing. There were any number of Italians and Germans in inter-war America who had doubts about where their loyalties lay. Some of them were openly Fascist but what could have motivated Monti to defect to the enemy so late in the war? It was common knowledge by October 1944 that the Italian war effort was in serious trouble. Even if Monti did not believe the British propaganda he would have read in Karachi, once he reached Naples he must have realised that Mussolini's Fascist state was dead in the water. What did he hope to achieve in the twilight of the war? If it was not defection, but some clever undercover plan of deception and subterfuge, again, what was the purpose? And why did Monti not explain himself? One of the mysteries lost to time.

DEGENERATE ART EXHIBITION

One of the apparent enemies of the Reich was modern and abstract art, which must have been culturally threatening to the Nazis. Between July and November 1937 they ran a 'Degenerate Art Exhibition' in Munich showing off 650 works of art they had confiscated.

The idea of this exhibition was to run parallel with an exhibition showing off 'proper' art in the 'Great German Art Exhibition.' Things didn't quite turn out as Hitler and Goebbels had expected; the 'degenerate' exhibition was a raging success with over 2 million people attending, at the same time the 'Great German' exhibition was considered mediocre by critics, with only half the number visiting it.

Hitler saw himself as an artist but his dreams were shattered by his being turned down (twice) by the Viennese School of Art before the First World War. His watercolours, mostly of buildings in Vienna and elsewhere, are not bad, but there is no real creativity or artistry about them. To him, new forms of artistic expression – the new realism of Paul Klee and Wassily Kandinsky – were 'the sick production of crazy people.' There was even a German phrase for this, ironically borrowed from Yiddish, *Meshuggism*, the cult of insanity.

DESMOND DOSS

Desmond Doss was a celebrated hero of the war. Born in Lynchburg, Virginia in 1919 to a Seventh-day Adventist family, the man was deeply religious. His beliefs meant he was classified as a conscientious objector during the war. Refusing to carry a weapon when signing up for the army in April 1942, he assumed he would be trained as a combat medic, only he wasn't.

His initial relationship was tense. His comrades didn't trust a soldier who wouldn't carry a gun. Many of them bullied him and tried to make his life as difficult as possible in the hope of making him leave, breaking his nerve, or even getting him court marshalled, but Doss refused to go. Ultimately, he stuck to his principles and was transferred and became an army medic with the 77th Division.

Despite refusing to kill, in battle Doss earned the respect and admiration of the men for his courage and selflessness. Fighting in the Pacific theatre, he received two Bronze Star medals for exceptional valor in assisting his comrades. He saw action at Guam, Leyte and Okinawa.

At Okinawa, his division was fighting to take the 350ft high Maeda Escarpment, a rock face known by the Americans as Hacksaw Ridge. After finally securing it, the soldiers were startled by a vicious Japanese counterattack. The fighting was hard and bloody, not all the men managed to escape when the order to retreat was given. Those who could withdraw did so - except Doss. The medic charged back into combat, scurrying among the wounded, dying and dead to save as many lives as he could and carry them to safety. He refused to retreat until every soldier with a chance was away from the fight. As many as 75 soldiers survived thanks to the medic. He did this despite being injured four times in this battle. He was badly wounded by a grenade, and shrapnel tore through his leg. While struggling on, he was hit by a sniper's bullet in the arm. Even after making it to safety, he gave up his litter for another wounded man. He was evacuated on 21 May 1945, aboard the USS *Mercy*.

Doss was one of 431 servicemen to receive the Congressional Medal of Honor. Throughout his life his golden rule, in fact, *the* Golden Rule from many of the world's religions was, 'do to others what you would have them do to you' (Matthew 7:12). Doss died in 2006. Mel Gibson's 2016 movie *Hacksaw Ridge* is based on the man's extraordinary life.

THE DICTATOR OF BRISTOL

Bristol is not known for its exotic wildlife. Sharing the honours with Liverpool as *the* part of western Britain, its wealth came from the slave-trade and the import of raw cotton. In the nineteenth century, it became forever linked with industrialisation and the ship-building genius of Isambard Kingdom Brunel.

But an even greater icon once graced the city and he can still be visited today. He is an adult male gorilla or silverback and peopled called him Alfred. He arrived at Bristol Zoo in 1930, at a time when few people had ever seen an animal like this. Used to endless wildlife programmes as we now are, thanks to television and the equally endless outpourings of David Attenborough, we are rather blasé about such things, but in the Thirties, Alfred was a sensation. Queues formed around the block to gawp at him in his cage and the press kept up a running commentary as he grew to maturity with a story on his 'first shave'!

When the Blitz hit London and other major cities in the autumn of 1940, a decision had to be made about zoo animals. They were expensive to keep at a time when money had to go to the war effort and the paying public were not inclined to risk queuing when death was raining from the skies. Many animals were put down. In the case of Alfred, however, he was neither destroyed nor evacuated, but remained stoically in his cage and became known as the dictator of Bristol, the city's answer to the human dictators who were bent on destroying Europe.

The soldiers stationed in the city loved him and postcards were sent to troops anxious for news from home, travelling as far as the United States, Australia and New Zealand. The fan club was not mutual, however – Alfred hated the thud of marching boots and let the passing troops know about it, snarling behind his bars and beating his considerable chest. By 1945, he was the official mascot of Bristol and when he died three years later, was stuffed and put on display in the city's museum and art gallery. In 1956, somebody broke in and stole Alfred, much to the horror of Bristolians. Whether through shame or the problem of keeping a seven foot animal somewhere under wraps where no one would notice him, he was returned three days later!

The case of the stolen dictator was finally solved in 2010 when one of the kidnappers made a deathbed confession. It was long overdue – the real age of the dictators had come to an end a long time before.

DIE GLOCKE

Die Glocke (the Bell) was a groundbreaking Nazi invention in the closing stages of the war, supposedly worked on from a secret base in Poland's Wenceslas mines. Die Glocke, one of countless *wunderwaffen* (wonder weapons), allowed its operators to travel into space, using gravity-defying technology to reach as far as the Moon and even Mars. The bell-shaped craft, three metres in diameter, was powered by a secretive 'red mercury' substance. After the war, it was captured by US forces and taken back to America. Observers of the famous 1947 Roswell Incident state the crashed UFO they saw was Die Glocke. It could even manipulate time.

Of course, this is all nonsensical. Despite imaginative conspiracy theories involving Antarctic bases and alien races – the first mention of Die Glocke was actually from 2000, sixty-five years after the war ended. Oh, and there is no substance known as 'red mercury'. We owe our current speculation of Die Glocke to the Polish journalist Igor Witkowski, in his book *Prawda o Wunderwaffe*.

It's likely that Die Glocke was dreamt up from a confused rehash from the 1960 occult book *The Morning of the Magicians* by Louis Pauwels and Jacques Bergier, which thought up similar concoctions. It is believed, in turn, that the *The Morning of the Magicians,* and the subsequent imaginative theories, was actually inspired by the famed science-fiction writer H. P. Lovecraft.

THE DIRLEWANGER BRIGADE

Oskar Dirlewanger is one of those historical caricatures who, if we didn't know he really existed, we could easily assume was fictional - a character from a horribly grim story. Dirlewanger is in this book because his actions were so vile that they were enough to even appall his Nazi comrades in the SS.

He was a veteran of the Great War and had been awarded the Iron Cross for his actions. After the signing of the Treaty of Versailles, he took part in the failed Kapp Putsch of 1920. He joined several *Freikorps*, the brutal paramilitary forces made up of veterans, and joined in the crushing of Communist uprisings that occurred during the interbellum years of the Weimar Republic.

With the rise of Hitler and his *Sturmabteilung*, he saw a cause which matched his own views. He joined the brownshirts in 1932. Two years later, he was convicted of abusing a 14-year-old girl and sentenced to two years in prison. He was released in time to take part in the Spanish civil war, as part of Germany's Condor Legion.

Dirlewanger appealed personally to Heinrich Himmler to join the Waffen-SS, and thanks to friends in high places his wish was granted. Obersturmfuhrer Dirlewanger was even given command of his own unit, which was named after him.

The Dirlewanger Brigade was, at first, made up of 'honourable poachers' -- those convicted for poaching, whose invaluable skills in the wild and flouting of the law would make them ideally suited for the unit. Over time convicted prisoners from all walks of life would join up as an alternative to prison to 'redeem' themselves in the eyes of the Reich. The SS, with their bizarrely paradoxical code of honour, were disgusted by the unit.

Dirlewanger and his men were in their element fighting 'bandits', usually unarmed civilians far from the battlefront. Rape, looting, indiscriminate slaughter and general terrorizing of the local population, often while drunk, was where this unit excelled. One such 'anti-partisan' action reported 386 'bandits dead' and, an ominously vague, 294 'bandit suspects finished off'.

The SS proper, for reasons best known to themselves given their own actions, were outraged by this unit. They sought to put Dirlewanger on trial to answer for his crimes, but friends in high places made sure this didn't happen.

The unit took part in crushing the Warsaw Uprising, joined by Ukrainians and Cossacks. They went house-to-house, slaughtering those within, and murdering the patients of a hospital. The nurses who survived were sent, naked and bleeding, running into the streets.

With the vengeful Red Army pouring towards Germany, Dirlewanger's men were forced to fight at the front. Fighting actual soldiers was something they were pitifully inadequate at, and the unit crumbled in the face of resistance. Many deserted or defected, and the unit all but ceased to exist. Dirlewanger himself was injured and removed from the front, vanishing soon afterwards.

He was arrested on 1 June 1945 under a fake identity while hiding in a remote hunting lodge. While interned, he was recognized by concentration camp survivors. Within a few days he was dead, officially of 'natural causes.' Some say he was beaten to death by Polish camp guards, others that he escaped and took part in all sorts of imaginative escapades. Authorities dug up his body in 1960 to put that nonsense to bed once and for all.

THE DISAPPEARANCE OF DOCTOR DEATH

A number of guards, commandants and especially doctors, have been given the grim sobriquet 'Dr. Death', but one who probably escaped retribution was Dr Aribert Heim, who became a physician in Austria's labour camp at Mauthausen in 1941.

Mauthausen was never an extermination camp, but it does hold the record of all concentration camps with 31, 318 executions logged in the *totenbuch* , the death book that the Nazis meticulously kept. Heim carried out gruesome operations on the inmates rather as Josef Mengele did at Auschwitz and literally held the power of life or death of thousands in his hands. By 1942, he had been transferred to Oulu in Finland, where his ghastly work continued. He was captured by the American army in March 1945 but soon released as no-one knew at that stage of his career at Mauthausen.

On 9 December 1946 twenty-three doctors, including one woman, were put on trial at Nuremberg charged with war crimes and crimes against humanity. Heim was not among them because, like so many other Nazis, he had slipped under the radar and was working as a gynaecologist somewhere in Germany.

In 1962, however, all that came to an end. The previous year there had been huge world-wide publicity as Adolf Eichmann, a leading player in the Holocaust, was caught, put on trial in Israel and executed. Everyone was looking harder at older German men with dodgy backgrounds and Heim thought it was time to vanish. He converted to Islam (totally at odds, of course, with Nazi doctrine) and took the name Tarek Hussein Farid. Despite the occasional letter to family and friends in Europe, Heim had, to all intents and purposes, disappeared and no-one knew exactly where he was.

Fast forward to 2007 when a book was published called *The Secret Executioner*. In it, the author, a former Israeli Air Force Colonel, Danny Baz, claimed that a clandestine organisation known as The Owl, tracked Heim down on the Californian island of Santa Catalina and executed him. The Simon Wiesenthal Foundation, set up after the war to hunt down such ex-Nazis has dismissed Baz's claim as fantasy.

THE DISLOYAL LEGIONS

The Free Arabian Legion was the idea of Amin al-Husseini, a Palestinian leader and anti-imperialist. The Legion was to be a *Wehrmacht* unit of Arab volunteers; Palestinians, Iraqis and Tunisians. Al-Husseini led the Arab revolution in Palestine in 1936 and fled the British once they had suppressed it. He hoped to secure the backing of Hitler for an Arab homeland and to overthrow the colonial powers of Britain and France. Hitler agreed to this in 1941 though an attempted overthrow of British rule in Iraq failed. At its height, the unit contained 20,000 men. Sonderverband 287 had three battalions fighting in Tunisia against the Allies' Operation Torch. Others fought in the Balkans.

There is nothing 'free' about those units and, bearing in mind Hitler's obsession with race and the fact that Germany, Italy and Vichy France had occupied all of North Africa, it is difficult to know what the legion thought it would have achieved had Germany won the war. British imperialism would simply have been replaced by the Reich.

The second 'Disloyal Legion' was the Indian, known as the Tiger Legion, a unit within the Wehrmacht, made up of volunteers, Indian POWs and expatriates. The idea was devised by Subhas Chandra Bose, seeking Germany's aid in securing India's independence from the British Empire. Hitler recognized the 'Free India Government' and helped set up a military unit.

The legion reached a maximum size of 3,000 men but they were not deployed in much frontline fighting and most Germans were oblivious. At the close of the war, the Indian Legion attempted to find sanctuary in neutral Switzerland, but were handed over to the Allies, who returned them to India to face charges of treason. Most were released after short prison sentences.

THE EDELWEISS PIRATES

Internal opposition to Hitler's Nazis after 1933 was as rare as it was unwise. Those who disagreed with National Socialism and could leave, did so. Others toed the party line. Very few were brave enough to put their heads over the parapet, but, perhaps oddly, some who did were children. Brainwashing of the young was vital if Hitler's Third Reich was to last for a thousand years. Every boy over ten had to join the Hitler Youth (*Hitlerjugend*) run by Baldur von Schirach. Every girl joined the league of German Maidens (*Bund Deutsche Madel*). In both organizations, hearty songs were sung, survival techniques learned and there was total and unswerving devotion to the Fuhrer.

The Edelweiss Pirates were not an organisation as such, but reactionary groups of young German people opposed to Nazi rule and who refused to take part in the Hitler Youth. These disaffected youths, aged between fourteen and seventeen, were anti-authority and the Edelweiss Pirates was a collective term for the various gangs, which included groups such as 'The Travelling Dudes' and 'The Navajos' (note the American influence). A loophole in the law meant that they were exempt from the HJ, having left school but were too young for conscription into military service. Their activities were wide ranging but did include anti-Nazi activities, attacks on government officials and sheltering deserters and escaped POWs. At first considered just a nuisance, the Gestapo became suspicious of the Pirates, describing them as 'riff raff – throwing their weight around'.

Punishments for those found to be members were harsh, ranging from beatings, having their heads shaved to being publicly hanged, six of them on a single day in October 1944.

ENEMY AT THE GATES

If you have seen the excellent 2001 movie, *Enemy at the Gates*, you will be familiar with the broad brush strokes of the story. Stalingrad was a 'do or die' situation for Stalin's Red Army, as it was for von Paulus's Wehrmacht. It became the greatest killing ground in Russian history, and marked, perhaps, the beginning of the end for the Third Reich.

With modern, sophisticated weaponry and mass destruction from the air, the Second World War was not one in which personal heroics were common. But there were exceptions and in a killing ground like Stalingrad, the rivals stood out. Allowing for their different time and nationalities, they could have been Hector and Achilles of the ancient Greek world, from Homer's epic poem, *The Iliad*.

With the Wehrmacht was Erwin Konig, a world-class sniper who seemed to be everywhere in the grim street fighting in Stalingrad. Whenever a Russian soldier popped out of cover, even for seconds, he ran a huge risk of meeting one of Konig's bullets. His opposite number was Vasily Zaytsev, who became a 'hero of the Soviet Union' with his 225 kills, including 11 at Stalingrad. In the duel between these two, Zaytsev won, catching the weak sunglint on Konig's scope and shooting him in the head. Rather as heroes had done on battlefields for centuries, the Russian took Konig's scope and identity papers as souvenirs.

The problem with this apparently straightforward story is that Erwin Konig probably did not exist. He is not in any official Forces records (although it is true that many of these were destroyed at the end of the war); neither was there any sign of the daughter he was supposed to have; nor have the documents lifted from his body ever come to light. We only have the word of Vasily Zaytsev himself. And the Soviet authorities under Stalin, as before that time and since, have been all too eager to create good stories for propaganda purposes.

THE ENIGMA OF ENIGMA

Although little known in his own lifetime, Alan Turing is now a well-respected and admired hero of the war. There is much to say on Turing, but essentially he was a British scientist and mathematician who joined the British government's code-breaking department in 1938. His genius helped to finally crack the seemingly unbreakable 'enigma code' used by the Germans to communicate encrypted messages. The cracking of this code saved countless lives and was a great boost to the Allied war effort. Turing's work also included electronics and he is considered to be the father of modern computing. For his crucial role in the war effort, he was given a knighthood by King George VI though his classified work remained secret. Turing was only one of several boffins working at the top secret government department at Bletchley Park, but his eccentricities earned him the nickname 'prof'. He wore a gas mask to ward off hay fever (from which he suffered in the first week of every June) and chained his favourite tea-mug to railings to prevent it from being stolen. He was also a superb long distance runner and sometimes ran the forty miles from Bletchley to London for a top secret meeting.

And what happened to this man who served King and Country so diligently? Turing was homosexual and in 1952 his house was burgled. During the course of the investigation it became clear the perpetrator was a former lover and both men were tried for 'gross indecency' as homosexuality was a criminal act. Turing was given a choice of prison or probation, on the condition he accepted injections to reduce his libido. Turing chose the latter. These injections would render him impotent and his conviction meant he lost his security clearance and barred him from working with the British government's intelligence agency, which was his passion. Turing took his own life in 1954 and was 'pardoned' under the queen's prerogative of mercy in 2013.

ESCAPE PLAYING CARDS

An ingenious plan was dreamed up by the United States Playing Card Company working with the Operation of Strategic Services and British Intelligence. They made 'map decks'. When the conventional-looking playing cards were soaked in water, the layers could be peeled apart to reveal useful maps from prisoner of war camps across Europe. They were top secret and there is no record of exactly how they were made.

It is believed that only two decks still survive; one in private hands and the other in the International Spy Museum in Washington DC.

Cards providing a totally different kind of escape were also available in wartime. In the first weeks of the war, when the Blitz was expected in Britain but had yet to happen, Black Out playing cards were all the rage. The variety of designs included a silhouette of an Air Raid Precaution warden (silhouettes of aircraft were used to familiarise the public with them) and 'A Black Out View of Piccadilly' – a black square.

THE ETERNAL JEW

The Eternal Jew is one of the most despicable monstrosities to come out of the Nazi propaganda machine based on a book of 265 photographs supposedly showing Jewish antisocial types and behaviour. The 1940 movie was the brainchild of Goebbels as Minister of Propaganda and Enlightenment and was intended to stir up feelings of disgust and hatred towards Jews. Cinema was as old as the century and it was powerful and popular; for many it was the only gateway for ordinary people to life outside their own environment. Previously, there had been movies which were sympathetic to the Jews and it is likely Goebbels insisted on countering this. A 1936 British film of the same name shows the unjustified oppression of Jewish people. The Nazi version was directed by Fritz Hippler, Goebbels' head of film in the Ministry, who would try to distance himself from it when confronted by the Allies after the war. He claimed the film had no connection with the Holocaust. The screenplay was by Eberhard Taubert, an anti-Semitic lawyer known as *Anti* in Nazi circles.

The title itself comes from the medieval tale of 'The Wandering Jew'. In this, a Jew is cursed with immortality and forced to walk the earth until the second coming of Christ.

This bizarre movie is stomach churning to a modern audience and an unforgiveable manipulation of the truth. Essentially, the viewer sees a montage of real life footage from ghettoes. Over this the narrator, actor Harry Giese – acting as though it was an animal documentary – violently and insistently condemns the lifestyles of the Jews, comparing them to an epidemic disease or rats that must be annihilated. The filmmakers deliberately filmed the most destitute people or those with physical deformities. Their ill looks, torn clothes and desperate situation are portrayed as proof of the filth of Jewish culture. The fact that these people are in this state because the Nazis took them from their homes, ruined their careers and put them in the ghetto in the first place seems completely lost! The messages of the film are also contradictory and confusing; on one hand the subjects are poor, work-shy and lazy – and on the other they are mansion-dwelling tycoons in charge of the world's economy, sipping champagne in the 'decadence' of Berlin in the days of the Weimar Republic.

Another infuriating concept of the film is the idea of Jewish people 'mimicking' and 'assimilating' with their 'hosts'. The narrator laments that many Jews are so Germanised they are almost impossible to tell from other people; unlike their ghetto kin who show their true nature. This is a ludicrous catch 22; on one hand they are demonized for staying isolated and not taking part in German culture and on the other they are attacked for not being loyal to their own roots and making an effort to integrate with their 'host' country. *The Eternal Jew* can only be shown in Germany today in specified educational establishments and under strict rules.

EXECUTIVE ORDER 9066

After the Japanese attack on Pearl Harbor in December 1941, the American government had decisions to make. By definition, the United States was a vast polyglot society. There were Jews in America and there were Germans, Frenchmen, Englishmen, descendants of every European and most world races, including the Japanese. Executive Order 9066 declared that all Japanese-Americans were to be relocated from the West Coast in case they were on the side of the enemy. Despite the fact over 60% were American citizens, in total around 127,000 people were forced from their homes and made to live in one of ten internment camps. The Land of Liberty's hope was to combat the 'yellow peril' and the fears of collaboration and sabotage.

Outraged, 5,000 of those interned renounced their citizenship – though this was declared void by a federal judge. The camps themselves were similar to those in Britain that housed 'aliens' rounded up in 1939-40 by Defence Regulation 18B – anyone of German, Austrian or Italian descent. They included fairgrounds and racetracks, holding up to 18,000 inmates. All education and welfare was provided by the US government. The camps remained open until 1946 even though Order 9066 was suspended in December 1944. A 1948 law compensated those interned for financial loss and a 1998 act of Congress awarded payments of $20,000 each to the 73,000 survivors as compensation for the violation of their liberties. The legality and morality of Executive Order 9066 is still debated to this day and the anniversary of the signing of the Order is commemorated by Japanese Americans as a Day of Remembrance.

THE EXORCIST

In 2006, Father Gabriel Amorth, an official exorcist for the Vatican, announced to the world that Hitler and Stalin were possessed. During the radio interview Amorth explained that the men were under the influence of the devil.

As a result, Pope Pius XII (Eugenio Pacelli) during the war, attempted a 'long distance' exorcism of the brutal dictators; Amorth explained why this didn't work.

'It's very rare that praying and attempting to carry out an exorcism from a distance work. Of course you can pray for someone from a distance but in this case it would not have any effect. One of the key requirements of an exorcism is to be present in front of the possessed person and that person also has to be consenting and willing... However I have no doubt that Hitler was possessed and so it does not surprise me that Pope Pius XII tried a long distance exorcism.'

However, Amorth also believed wholeheartedly in the satanic evil of Harry Potter and yoga. His favourite film was *The Exorcist,* which he thought was accurate but a bit heavy handed on the special effects...

EXPLOSIVE RATS

Explosive rats was the idea of Britain's Special Operations Executive (SOE). This often eccentric organization – 'Winston's wizards' they were sometimes called – was set up by Churchill himself to 'set Europe ablaze'. SO1 were the daredevil agents who parachuted behind enemy lines, linking with local Resistance groups and causing chaos with sabotage and as much disruption as possible. SO2 were the boffins, working out of Bush House in London and Woburn Abbey in Bedfordshire, to devise ingenious 'black propaganda' to cause maximum confusion and doubt in the Third Reich. Dead rats would be filled with plastic explosives and then placed near boiler rooms. The SOE assumed the Germans would throw the rats into the boilers to get rid of them and thereby cause an explosion.

The rats never saw action, being discovered by the Germans before they could be used. The Nazis were so panicked by the idea that any rat could be a bomb that they showed them to military experts and organized searches. This time wasting of military effort meant that the SOE considered it a success.

The source of the dead rats came from a London supplier, who was led to believe they were being used for University experiments.

FACES OF THE REICH

Werner Goldberg is one of the most famous faces from the war years. He was born in Konigsberg, Germany, in 1919. Later in his life his uncle became a zealous member of the nascent Nazi party. In 1938, Goldberg joined the Reich Labour Service, and by September 1939 he was a soldier taking part in the invasion of Poland.

Goldberg was handsome, and he was astonished to find that his official military photograph had been sold by the *Heer*, the German army, to the *Berliner Tagesblatt* newspaper. He was described as 'the perfect German soldier' and his *stahlhelm* adorned head was soon being used for recruitment posters throughout the country.

There was just one little issue with the Reich's new golden boy; he was half-Jewish. Goldberg was a 'first-degree *mischling*' in the parlance of the Nazi justice system. In 1940 he was dismissed from the *Wehrmacht*, as were all 'first-degree' *mischling*, on Hitler's orders, and spent five dangerous years trying to stay alive. Goldberg and his father were the only members of his family to survive the war. Goldberg himself died in Berlin in 2004.

That wasn't the end of the debacle though. In 2015 a Russian war monument in Tobolsk to the 'defenders of the motherland for all time' bizarrely, somehow, used Goldberg's face for the etching! This was later changed.

The embarrassing foibles kept coming. *Sonne ins Haus* (Sun in the Home) was a Nazi-backed magazine. A 1935 edition features a cute 'Aryan' baby wearing a bonnet on the front cover. The face of this shining example of Aryan youth was, naturally, a Jewish girl named Hessy Levinsons Taft.

Taft's parents, Jacob and Pauline, had taken her to have a photograph taken when she was a year old, as most parents would who could afford it, and thought nothing more of it. But they were later astonished to find their baby daughter's photograph on the cover of the magazine, the winner of a competition hand-picked by Joseph Goebbels! The parents were horrified and contacted the photographer, telling him they were Jewish. The photographer admitted he knew. He discovered Goebbel's beautiful Aryan baby competition, and surreptitiously entered Taft's photograph to mock it and 'make the Nazis ridiculous'.

The Nazis never uncovered the truth. The family was able to escape Germany, eventually ending up in the United States. This story came to the world's attention in 2014 when Taft donated the *Sonne ins Haus* magazine to *Yad Vashem*, the World Holocaust Remembrance Centre.

THE FAITH AND BEAUTY SOCIETY

The place of women in Hitler's Reich was, for most people, seen as a retrograde step. From 1933, women in medicine, the law, the media and the professions generally were expected to step down in favour of men. Anti-Nazi propaganda posters showed downtrodden frauleins kneeling before black-uniformed SS men, lovingly lacing up their boots! A woman's role was to bear the children who would carry on the Reich into the future. Mothers were given bronze, silver and gold awards for child bearing. Part of this concept was the notion of perfect Aryan womanhood – the beautiful, blonde-haired, blue-eyed Valkyrie of German Teutonic mythology.

In 1938, the Germans created the Faith and Beauty Society. This voluntary organisation was the bridge between the League of German Maidens and womanhood. The Society was open to girls aged seventeen to twenty-one in preparation for their future lives as perfect mothers. Activities ranged from home economics such as cooking and sewing, to sports, dancing and gymnastics. The girls also volunteered in the community, helping mothers raise their children and supporting the troops. Around 400,000 people took part.

The idea backfired slightly because of the overt sexuality of these girls. Just before the Society was founded, in the 1936 Nuremberg Rally, nearly 900 girls of the League of Maidens were maidens no more!

THE FALCON HAS LANDED

Sparrowhawks, Ma'am.' This was the famous solution suggested by the Duke of Wellington to Queen Victoria when she was worried about the hundreds of sparrows flying around the Crystal Palace in 1851 and the mess they would make on the fee-paying public below.

But birds of prey came to the county's rescue more recently. In the war years, the military and the secret service routinely used homing pigeons to carry messages from one part of the country to another, avoiding the use of telephones and radio frequencies. There was genuine concern that the enemy were doing the same and various pigeon centres were identified in Paris, Lille, Cherbourg and Angers.

So the British set up the Special Falconry Unit, using birds to intercept and kill 'enemy pigeons'. The Germans were also believed to have a Falcon Destruction Unit, a group of snipers poised to bring pigeon-hunting falcons down. No one seemed to be clear how a falcon could tell an enemy pigeon from 'one of ours' and the rate of 'friendly fire' must have been high.

If you are wondering why MI5 kept all this secret until it released the relevant files in 1999, perhaps it is because the whole notion is so laughable. Did these people not have a war to fight?

FANTA

Coca-Cola was originally a medicinal pick-me-up invented in America in the nineteenth century by John Pemberton and marketed by Asa Candler. Its exact composition is a closely-guarded secret, but it contained caffeine, kola nuts and coca leaves. The one billionth gallon of Coca-Cola syrup was made by the company in July 1944.

Coca Cola had a factory in Germany run by Max Keith but syrup from the United States, hostile to the Third Reich and setting up a trade embargo in 1940, became difficult to source. To keep the factories in operation, Coca Cola had a meeting to discuss a new name, with 'Fanta', the German for imagination, being the winner.

This new drink was made from a slapdash assortment of by-products and ingredients – Keith called them 'leftovers of leftovers' – that were available to Germany and was described as 'a light-coloured beverage that resembles ginger ale' it was actually whey and apple pomace The popularity of Fanta is unclear, but it was often used to flavour food when other flavourings were a luxury and a recipe for *Fantakuchen*, Fanta cake, is still popular.

It is perhaps unfair and incorrect to call Fanta a Nazi drink, though it did develop as a result of and in response to wartime activities. Fanta was discontinued after the war but was relaunched in 1955 and is now one of the world's most popular soft drinks. Either way, the updated recipe means the drink we know today would be unrecognisable to that enjoyed by the *Wehrmacht*. Except, that is, for the special 75th anniversary brew sold in Germany. Its glass bottles were of 1940s design and the contents included whey and apple pomace. An advertisement claiming to bring back the taste of the 'good old times' was removed for fear of causing offence!

FIDO

In the often-confusing history of the Second World War, Fido was a French pilot who parachuted into England in July 1943. He was working for the German Secret Service (SD) and his mission was to steal a British plane and take it back to Germany. John Masterman, the head of the XX Committee, turned him and he never did fly back.

But Fido was something else too, nothing to do with the French aviator. It was all about the weather, which has done more to disrupt military operations than any enemy action in history. FIDO stood for Fog Investigation and Dispersal Operation or Fog, Intensive Dispersal Of (acronyms have a foaflore of their own!).

Britain had a particular dense fog that hovered over cities, which, combined with industrial output from hundreds of factory chimneys caused smog, a potentially lethal pollution that often caused large numbers of deaths. Londoners called them 'pea-soupers'. It was the RAF that was most concerned with this. Ground troops and even ships could cope with most fogs, but aircraft, before the advent of advanced navigation systems, flew by vision; a pilot had to see where he was going.

From 1943, a dispersal system had been worked out, spraying the air with calcium chloride using a 100ft pipe fitted with downward-pointing nozzles. As part of the country's efforts to stop the feared German invasion of 1940, Churchill's government set up the Petroleum Warfare Department with plans to set fire to Britain's beaches to deter landing. Two pipelines ran each side of a runway spraying out fuel. When an aircraft was due to land, men would run along the pipeline with flaming torches. The vapour ignited and the fog dispersed. The first test was not carried out until 1942, at Moody Down near Winchester and it was expensive, burning 450,000 litres of fuel an hour.

Fido's success was limited. It was a brave pilot who would land his aircraft between two walls of fire!

FIFTH SYMPHONY

'V for Victory' became one of the most famous and enduring symbols of resistance to Nazi occupation throughout the war. Vs and V graffiti were plastered everywhere. Colonel Britton, the voice of the European service called for people to 'Splash the V from one end of Europe to another.' Colonel Britton was in fact Douglas Ritchie, an assistant news editor at the BBC, whose identity was a closely guarded secret until the end of the war.

It dawned on Ritchie that the four opening notes of Beethoven's fifth symphony were extremely similar to the Morse code for V (dot-dot-dot-dash). It became his theme song and listeners copied the sound however they could.

This piece is further fitting when you consider that Beethoven was German, and gradually went deaf. He used the vibrations of sound to understand music. Of his fifth symphony being a symbol of resistance, it was said by Victor de Laveleye, a Belgian exile broadcasting from London, that the theme would remind the enemy that they were 'surrounded, encircled by an immense crowd of citizens eagerly awaiting his first moment of weakness, watching for his first failure.'

FIRE HEDGEHOG

There were many weird and wacky technological inventions put forward during the war. A Soviet contribution to this was the Fire Hedgehog. 88 PPSh-41 submachine guns were strapped into the bomb bay of a modified Tupolev Tu-2 aircraft giving the impression of the needles of a curled up hedgehog. Upon approaching a concentration of enemy forces, the bomb bays would open and let rip a salvo of 7.62mm bullets.

It is unclear whether the weapon was ever used, and if so to what effect. But in principle – despite running out of ammunition in five seconds – the weapon could be devastating to a concentration of people on the ground.

Like most of the weird and wonderful weapons of the war, it was not so much whether the concept was effective, but simply that research and development was focused onto more resourceful and tried and tested ideas.

FLIGHT 19

5 December 1945, five Grumman TBM Avengers led by Commander Charles Taylor took off from their naval base at Fort Lauderdale, Florida. They never returned. The US Navy's report on this mystery said that their disappearance on that clear day was for 'reasons unknown': the legend of the lost patrol was born.

The training exercise in which they vanished involved flying 56 miles east into the Atlantic to practice bombing. They should then have travelled east a further 67 miles, in the direction of the Bahamas, before turning north for 73 miles and finally completing their triangular route by flying 120 miles back to base. Upon losing contact, a Martin PBM Mariner was deployed to find them. This did not return either.

The exact cause of their disappearance remains a mystery, though experts generally agree it was down to a faulty compass, a lack of navigational training, or the incompetence of Taylor.

Flight 19 would come to contribute greatly to the legend of the Bermuda Triangle, or 'the Devil's Triangle', in which countless planes and ships would disappear. Experts have dismissed claims that there is anything odd about an arbitrary triangle stretching roughly between Florida, Bermuda and Puerto Rico. Although there have, of course, been disappearances, considering the sheer volume of traffic in the area, the triangle does not have a peculiar number of incidents. Others have stuck to their guns, claiming that there is a disproportionate number of unexplained events, with some even suggesting that the Bermuda Triangle is proof of extraterrestrial activity, while others equally rationally blame the lost island of Atlantis.

FLYING TANKS

As a weapon to replace the horse in battle, the tank was second to none. The name given as a cover for a bullet-proof armed vehicle running on its own caterpillar tracks in December 1915 was first used in warfare, at Cambrai two years later. Improved and modified as time went on, the tanks of the Second World War were battle-winners and spelt the end of conventional cavalry warfare.

Bearing in mind that aerial warfare also came of age in the twentieth century, ideas were being bandied about of machines combining the two - a 'flying' tank that could be dropped from the sky into the middle of a battle. The most highly developed form was Russia's Antonov A-40, designed by Oleg Antonov, which, theoretically, worked!

Existing armoured vehicles, especially jeeps, were routinely dropped by parachutes from aircraft, especially by the SAS and other commando units who operated behind enemy lines. The problem was that such machinery was often damaged on impact with the ground and the crews dropped moments later would often be a long distance from their vehicles.

Antonov's wings were a work of genius, linked to the turret, so that the tank commander could tilt them in the same way that he turned the vehicle left or right. In the end, it was decided that, tactically, the expensive flying tank was not much of an improvement on the conventional type, which would free up the necessity of cargo aircraft/bombers that could be used for other things.

FOO FIGHTERS

'Where there's foo, there's fire' was a catchphrase of an American cartoon character, Smokey Stover and the term caught on for what US airmen also called 'krautballs'. The same paranoia that produced the phantom Fifth Column in Britain also produced ever more lurid notions about Nazi technology. Some of this was, of course, based on fact. Both sides in the war were trying to perfect jet technology and ever more powerful bombs; the ghastly results were the V1 and V2 'doodlebugs' that rained on Britain in 1944 and '45 and the flattening of Hiroshima and Nagasaki in August 1945. It was no coincidence that the Nazi the Americans most wanted to meet at the end of the war was the rocket scientist, Werner von Braun who went on to lead the US space programme during the Cold War.

On 13 December 1944, General Eisenhower's headquarters (SHAEF) in Paris held a press conference to describe a new weapon that had been observed by American airmen. They looked like Christmas tree decorations, silver spheres that appeared either singly or in clusters. If they *were* weapons, no one could quite work out what they did. In a report in the New York *Herald Tribune* the next month, the 'balls of fire' had become red, flickered on and off and flew along the wingtips of American aircraft. In Britain the *Daily Telegraph* thought they were orange and they appeared *under* planes' wings with dull flashes of light. The differing physical characteristics should have been clue enough that the whole thing was suspect, but human nature loves nothing better than the inexplicable.

Unfortunately for anyone trying to sort fact from fiction in the world of air technology, on 24 June 1947, civilian pilot Kenneth Arnold reported seeing 'saucer', 'disc' or 'pie-plate' craft in the sky as he flew over Oregon's Cascade Mountains. The flying saucer legend was born and a world made hysterical by the atomic threat of the Cold War became gripped by UFO mania. That meant that test pilot Randolph Schriever's claim in 1952 that the Luftwaffe had developed these crafts as early as 1941 must be called into serious doubt. So must some of the claims made by Rudolf Lusar in a book on Germany's secret weapons, published in 1957.

As for the Foo Fighters, what were they? It is possible that they were freak atmospheric conditions, rather like St Elmo's Fire, electricity in the air that had been witnessed by sailors for centuries. They could have been ball lightning, which some physicists contend is a genuine phenomenon. What is most likely is that they were tricks of the imagination of men exhausted by flying too many nerve-wracking missions.

FRAULEIN HITLER

Wouldn't it have been better if Hitler was a woman? He'd be less angry, more compassionate and easier to talk to. This was what some British spies thought. Their plan was to sneak oestrogen into his food to make him less aggressive. Poison was ruled out as it would be discovered by Hitler's food testers. Oestrogen however is tasteless and the effects would not be instant, allowing for a continuous campaign of feminising. The plan was never realised but the British claimed they were perfectly able to carry it out. We will never know, but it's amusing to think how things could have been different if Hitler found himself developing breasts, having to buy a büstenhalter and feeling a bit emotional.

All in all the idea was nonsensical. Dyed in the wool Nazi females like Ilse Koch and Irma Grese, both sadistic concentration camp guards, were every bit as vicious as their male counterparts, so feminism does not guarantee niceness! Bearing in mind the Nazi opposition to women in high places (only the superb film maker Leni Riefenstahl kept her position working for Goebbels' propaganda unit) even the Fuhrer would have been removed had the oestrogen worked.

The vague background to all this is that it is just possible that Hitler was bisexual or even homosexual. His sexual appetite seems to have been small, especially in comparison with Goebbels and Goering and his relationships with women were largely platonic – his mistress Eva Braun and his niece, Geli Raubal. There were rumours that Hitler and Rudolf Hess were lovers, but actual evidence is non-existent.

As this book goes to press, an American woman, asked for her opinion as to whether the next President could be female said, 'No. What if she had hot flushes? She could start a war in ten seconds!'

FUEHRER GLOBE

Hitler's Globe, officially the Columbus Globe for State and Industry Leaders, was one of two globes (or more, depending on the source) made specifically for him, the other being made for the Nazi party as a whole. Made in the 30s, this globe would have probably been of little interest to people, until Charlie Chaplin's 1940 film *The Great Dictator* lampooned him and his possession. This film was controversial, for although Chaplin was an Englishman, the film was American and the United States were at that time neutral.

A famous part of the film sees Chaplin portraying Adenoid Hynkel, leader of Tomainia, and is clearly based on Hitler, silently playing with the globe, fawning over it and gently dancing with it, as if the whole world was his. The globe eventually bursts and Hynkel is heartbroken.

Reported to be almost as big as a car, Hitler's Globe moved with the Nazis from their old Reich Chancellery to the new one, where it remained until the Soviets arrived in April 1945.

One globe, which allegedly belonged to the dictator, was taken from the 'Eagle's Nest' in Berchtesgaden by the American John Barsamia. His loot returned with him to America, where he kept it for sixty years. When it was sold at a San Francisco auction in 2007 it reached $100,000. As for *the* globe, its fate is unknown.

What is as mysterious as the disappearance of the globe itself, are the countless conspiracy theories regarding its whereabouts. It doesn't seem that Hitler had any particular fondness for it, and why this single item has become so notorious, lying at the centre of some truly outlandish claims, and holding such a fascination for so many conspiracy theorists, is unclear.

FUKURYU – THE CROUCHING DRAGON

Fukuryu is Japanese for 'crouching dragon', but what was the word applied to? *Kamikaze* divers of course. As the Americans closed in on the Japanese Empire, the idea for these suits was to beat back any American invasion of Japan itself, which would have to come by sea. The suits allowed the wearer to breathe underwater and a 15kg mine would be placed on US ships via a 5m bamboo pole. Weighed down by their suits and 9kg of lead, the divers would walk along the seabed for hours undetected and place their mines on the hull of an enemy vessel, probably killing themselves in the process. The war ended before the Fukuryu could be widely implemented – a thousand specialised suits were ready and a further eight thousand on order – and the only deaths appear to be from suit malfunctions in training.

The divers' suicide missions must be seen as part of the eastern mentality that produced the *kamikaze* (divine wind) airmen, who deliberately ploughed their aircraft into enemy ships. No one in other armies, even the younger fanatical elements of the Waffen SS in the war's closing stages, accepted so resolutely that a cause was worth dying for.

THE GAULEITER OF THE BAHAMAS

In the 1930s, Britain had mixed views on Adolf Hitler and the Nazi party. On the one hand, wily old politicians like David Lloyd George, a former prime minister, were impressed by the Führer and the economic 'miracle' he was presiding over in war-torn Germany. Some members of the House of Lords, such as Brockett and Londonderry were, to say the least, non-comital about Nazi policies. Prominent politicians like Lord Halifax at the Foreign Office, did not want to bomb the Ruhr, once the war had begun, because it was private property! Still others, like the charismatic MP Oswald Moseley and the dour Admiral Barry Domville, were openly Fascist, praising both Hitler and Mussolini as saviours of their respective countries. Men like Winston Churchill, demonising these leaders as tin-pot dictators, were very few and far between, 'in the wilderness' on the fringes of events.

The position of the Royal Family was also surprisingly dubious. By definition, the Windsors had, until 1914, been the Battenbergs – the line of royal descent had been bound with Germany since the arrival of Geroge I in 1714 – and many of the titled courtiers around the king were either pro-German (such as the Duke of Buccleuch) or anti-war, or both. Even as late as February 1940, by which time the war had been raging for six months, Buccleuch was writing that the war would 'play into the hands of Soviet Russia, Jews and Americans'.

The abdication crisis of 1936 threw a spanner into the royal works. Obsessed with protocol and tradition, the rest of 'the firm' were appalled when Edward, Prince of Wales, a tennis-playing and not very bright playboy, fell in love with Wallis Simpson, an

American divorcee. On all counts she was unsuitable as a future queen. She was divorced (which the Church of England could not countenance). She was a commoner with not even noble, yet alone royal blood. *And* she was American. Despite the fact that the Americans had fought with Britain in the First World War, there was no 'special relationship' then; there had been more wars against them than with them. But 'Eddie Windsor' would not be swayed. Determined to marry Simpson, he made an emotional plea-cum-explanation over the radio to his astonished people and abandoned the throne, passing it to his younger brother who became George VI. There is little doubt from what we know, that George's wife, Elizabeth (still known, affectionately in Britain as 'the queen mother') was pro-appeasement and a fan of both Neville Chamberlain, the prime minister, and Lord Halifax. It is likely that the new king was too.

Edward VIII had abdicated on 10 December, making his the shortest reign since that of Edward V in the fifteenth century. He and Mrs Simpson (now the Duke and Duchess of Windsor) moved to Austria and France where they were married and spent some time in Portugal where there was a ludicrous plan, run by the spymaster Walter Schellenberg, to coax the ex-monarch over to the German side. Nothing came of it and the Windsors were only delayed for a few hours. In 1937 Edward was the official guest of the Führer in Berlin and photographs of the pair, smiling and shaking hands, were beamed around the world.

In the end, probably to keep him out of harm's way, Churchill sent the Duke to the Bahamas as governor of the island. He had returned to Britain shortly before war began, but his position was thought to be untenable.

Was Edward, Duke of Windsor, a Nazi? Probably not, but there are many things relating to the Second World War, the Royal Family, and senior politicians, which are not yet – and perhaps never will be – in the public domain. The jury is still out. As Edward once said to Patrick Balfour 'I never thought Hitler was such a bad chap.' How enigmatic is that?

GELI RAUBAL

Geli Raubal was born on the 4 June 1908, the daughter of Leo and Angela, Hitler's half-sister. When Angela became widowed in 1928, Hitler invited her to become a housekeeper at his residence, the Berghof in Obersalzburg. Her daughter came with her. Geli would move into Hitler's Munich apartment with him the following year.

All evidence suggests Hitler became infatuated his niece, stating: 'a girl of eighteen to twenty is as malleable as wax. It should be possible for a man, whoever the chosen woman may be, to stamp his own imprint on her. That's all the woman asks for.' According to Patrick Hitler, his American nephew, Geli affectionately called him 'Uncle Alf.'

As Hitler rose to power, he would often bring Geli with him. Her presence was a surprise to the high ranking officials at the solemn meetings he was attending. Ian Kershaw, the English historian, has noted 'for the first time in his life (if we leave his mother out of consideration) he became emotionally dependent on a woman.' Hitler became possessive of his new pet, dismissing his personal chauffeur Emil Maurice, upon discovering the two were having a relationship. Maurice was an early Nazi stalwart, having joined in the Beer Hall Putsch and having been incarcerated alongside the future Fuehrer in Landsberg Prison. The jealousy was mutual. Geli was herself troubled by a seventeen-year-old girl called Eva Braun who had recently caught Hitler's eye.

Geli Raubal gradually became little more than a prisoner. Her hopes of escaping to Vienna, the site of Hitler's failed art career, were dashed when he forbade it. On 18 September 1931 there was a heated argument between them. He was informed the next day that his niece had shot herself with his Walther pistol, though it was said that an optimistic hand-written letter was left unfinished on her writing desk.

Hitler was devastated with the turn of events, declaring she was the only woman he had ever loved. Afterwards her Obersalzburg room was left untouched, and a portrait of the doomed girl hung at the Chancellery in Berlin.

Countless speculations have arisen since the event. Local papers and political opponents scandalised the story, and there have been theories bandied about involving pregnancy, murder and violence. An SA officer, Wilhelm Stocker, claimed many years later that '[Geli] admitted to me that at times Hitler made her do things in the privacy of her room that sickened her, but when I asked her why she didn't refuse to do them, she just shrugged and said that she didn't want to lose him to some woman who would do what he wanted.' Though such allegations must always be taken with a very large pinch of salt.

A coincidence worth noting now is that of Bernhard Stempfle, a Catholic priest, die-hard Nazi, and alleged co-author of *Mein Kampf.* Despite being one of Hitler's inner circle, he mysteriously fell out of favour with him, being deported to Dachau concentration camp, and then murdered in the woods. It is widely believed that Stempfle knew too much about the Fuehrer's past and personal life.

Whatever the truth of it, Geli Raubal's death was quickly covered up and any hope of knowing what really happened during this enigmatic episode is now lost.

THE GERMAN GLANCE

Der Deutscher Blick was a glimpse of sanity in Hitler's Third Reich. The greeting 'Heil Hitler' replaced 'Guten tag' (good day) as a social convention, first with the Nazi Party and later across Germany and German-occupied territories. Originally, 'heil' meant 'salvation', as in *heiliger* (holy) and its use was required by law. It was also used in national institutions like schools and colleges, always accompanied by the extended, rigid right arm salute. Contrary to popular myth, heel-clicking was not part of this ritual; that was associated with the old Prussian officer class of the army.

The German glance preceded 'Heil Hitler' and sometimes made it unnecessary. Sceptics and opponents used it, checking right, left and behind to ensure that no one was within listening or viewing distance. Their subsequent conversations could then be carried on as normal, as though the whole country had not gone mad!

THE GHOST ARMIES

The USA's 23rd Headquarters Special Troops had one objective; 'tactical deception'. Their mission was to confuse the enemy as much as possible via the art of illusion. To that end, many of its members were actors, artists and sound engineers. Their most famous work was the creation of 'ghost armies'. Over 1100 men were ordered to create vast numbers of props; inflatable tanks and rubber aircraft to give the impression of a vast concentration of forces, thereby fooling the Nazis that a particular place was to be the location of a particular attack. Over twenty of these operations were carried out, perhaps the most famous being on the English coast in preparation for D-Day.

They blasted out the sounds of moving troops into the countryside via amps which could be heard from miles away and communicated misleading Morse code and radio messages, copying the codes of real fighting units and even using the idiosyncrasies of individual radio operators.

Amusingly, they would also drive trucks around in a loop, giving the impression to any watching enemy that huge numbers of troops were being transported through the area. The unit was incredibly successful; ultimately they caused mass confusion for the enemy, convincing them that the Allies were much more powerful than they were. It is estimated their tricks saved tens of thousands of lives. The story remained classified until 1996.

THE GHOST PLANE

On 8 December 1942, just over a year after Pearl Harbor, the US military in the Pacific detected unusual activity on their radar heading towards them. Two fighters were scrambled to investigate, but upon intercepting the plane they were confused to see it was one of their own, a Curtiss P-40 Tomahawk, but with markings that had not been used for a year. As they flew alongside the mysterious aircraft, they noticed it was riddled with bullet-holes, had no landing gear and the bloodied pilot was slumped in the cockpit. He had just enough energy to smile and wave at the interceptors, before plummeting to the ground and crashing.

At the crash site there was no sign of the pilot but they did find a diary, which suggested the plane had travelled from the island of Mindanao in the Philippines 1,300 miles away. The Americans were lost for words. Who was this mysterious pilot? How did he launch without landing gear and fly when unconscious? Where had he been for the last year? And what happened to his body?

As with most tall tales, this should be taken with a very large pinch of salt. The story of 'the Ghost Plane' is one of those urban legends where the setting, characters and theme change but the essential story remain the same. At first the story seems quite convincing, perhaps even frightening – but there is no documented source for it.

The tale actually comes from a collection of war stories told by Robert Lee Scott Jr. in *Damned to Glory*, published in 1944!

G.I. JOE

Many grown-up boys may remember having owned at least one or two G.I. Joes from when they were children (Action Men in the UK). The manly action figures with their various uniforms and weapons and flicking eyes have been popular for decades. However, their namesake was a hero of a completely different calibre.

In October 1943, the invasion of Italy was raging as the Western Allies fought to establish footholds on the continent. The British 56th London Infantry Division had taken the village of Calvi Vecchia. But their capture of the village was unreported. In the midst of the chaos and confusion of battle, air support had been requested to bomb the village. It was believed that the enemy was still defending it. The only hope for the villagers and the British soldiers alike was GI Joe, a pigeon. Taking the urgent message, Joe set off for the air base and managed to cover twenty miles in an incredible twenty minutes! The message to call off the attack arrived just in time, because the bombers were preparing to launch. It is estimated that Joe saved over 1,000 lives that day.

Joe retired after the war, with 24 of his pigeon comrades to Fort Monmouth in New Jersey. In 1946 he was awarded the Dickin Medal for gallantry, his citation stating '*the most outstanding flight made by a United States Army homing pigeon in World War II.*' He was the first recipient of the Dickin Medal who was not British.

GLASMINE 43

War has always given a spur to technological advancement. Soldiers fight, politicians talk, nurses heal; but their success ultimately comes down to the boffins on their side. On a very basic and oversimplified level, it's boiled down to the evolution of oneupmanship. In ancient times cavalry could smash infantry, so spears were developed to stop cavalry; spearmen controlled battlefields, so archers were used to break up their ranks, and so on. Originally this was thanks to the efforts of smiths and armourers, latterly engineers and technicians evolved to take over the new concepts.

So it continued into World War 2. The war that began with the use of horses, biplanes and rifles, would, after only six years, end with tanks, jets and atomic weapons.

A useful means of denying territory to soldiers was the land mine. But land mines were becoming increasingly easy to deal with, using metal detectors and flailing chains on the front of tanks, so this too had to be countered.

The answer was the Glasmine 43, a mine housed in glass. Not only would this be undetectable, but it has the benefit of saving on precious metal, which was needed elsewhere. Glasmine 43 was effective because it was relatively simple: a glass jar containing *Sprengkörper 28*, a 200 gram explosive, atop which a lighter is placed, beneath a pressure plate. When the pressure plate was depressed, the plate broke the igniter and set off the explosion.

Eleven million of these mines were laid throughout the war. Many remain undetected in the ground to this day, such as at Vogelsang Military Training Area. Conflicts of today involve cyber-attacks, drone strikes and use of disinformation. Where it will go next can only be guessed at.

THE GLEIWITZ INCIDENT

The Gleiwitz Incident started the war. The Nazis were ready and eager to invade Poland, but as part of their propaganda, they wanted to manipulate the truth and justify the invasion. Although Hitler expected Britain and France to do nothing to defend Poland, he wanted the world to think it was the Poles who were the initial aggressors. This was achieved on 31 August 1939. Under instructions from the Gestapo, Nazi soldiers, led by Alfred Naujocks, dressed up in Polish uniforms and attacked a German radio station called *Sender Gleiwitz*. Once inside they broadcast a provocative anti-German message.

> 'People of Poland! The time has come for war ... Unite and smash down any Germans, all Germans, who oppose your war!'

To make the attack look more convincing, the Gestapo murdered a local and several prisoners from Dachau's prison camp, poisoning them with lethal injections before riddling their bodies with bullets, and dressed them up as saboteurs, leaving their bodies at the scene as 'proof' of the incident. The codename for this was the rather grisly 'Canned Goods' and the idea was dreamed up by Heinrich Himmler, head of the SS, his second-in-command Reinhard Heydrich and Heinrich Muller, the Gestapo chief.

The next day Germany would invade Poland and the Second World War would begin. Hitler referred to the incident when justifying the invasion claiming that there had been 'an attack by regular Polish troops on the Gleiwitz transmitter'. Unconcerned that it was a lie, he confided in his commanders, 'The victor will not be asked whether he told the truth.'

'GOD WITH US'

The relationship between Nazi ideology and Christianity is muddled. While some leaders such as the neo-pagan Himmler were indeed atheists and wanted to abolish the church, many more believed in a 'positive' Christianity which could evolve and adapt to distance itself from the religion's Jewish parentage. Catholicism was greatly harassed by the Nazi party, with thousands of priests being arrested. While Pope Pius XI (Achille Ratti) had been protesting against Nazi excesses inside Germany since at least 1937, his successor, Pius XII (Eugenio Pacelli) has gone down in history as 'Hitler's Pope', remaining mysteriously silent over the Holocaust even though he knew what was going on.

It is probable that the Nazi leadership simply had other things to worry about than to risk discontent among the predominantly Christian German population. The Wehrmacht continued to have '*Gott Mit Uns* (God with Us)' on their belt buckles as had the German army since its creation in 1871, unlike the SS who had 'My Honour Is Loyalty' stamped on theirs.

Hitler himself seems to have had an even more confusing personal relationship with spirituality. At the age of four he was reported to have been saved from drowning by a priest. This story was known to the locals, but Hitler never spoke of it himself. It is also claimed that Hitler wanted to be a priest when he was younger. He was certainly a choirboy in his home town of Linz and the ritual of the Catholic Mass appealed to him. He mentioned God and faith in his speeches, though whether his words were what he personally believed or just for his audience is still debated.

Ultimately, it can be conjectured that hostility towards the Church was more due to the fact it detracted from loyalty and worship of the Nazi ideology. What would have happened to Christianity if Germany had won the war is unknowable and can be only the stuff of alternative history.

THE GOLD OF THE NORTH

Amber is a fossil resin from extinct coniferous trees and is found mostly in the clays of the Oligosene system. It is particularly common in Eastern Germany and was known in the eighteenth century as the gold of the north. An entire chamber, lined and decorated with amber, was built in Prussia in 1701 by Andreas Schlüter to enhance the Charlottenburg Palace in Berlin nearly two centuries before Germany came into existence.

The 'eighth wonder of the world' was visited by the Russian Tsar Peter the Great in 1716. Peter was one of the great reforming rulers of Russia, bringing his backward, almost medieval kingdom kicking and screaming into modernity. Frederick Wilhelm of Prussia would much rather have the man as an ally than an enemy and gave him the amber chamber as a gift. It was deconstructed, slab by slab, and rebuilt in the Catherine Palace, St Petersburg.

Fast forward to June 1941. Operation Barbarossa was the end result of Hitler's expansionist foreign policy in the east. He had recently built an alliance with Stalin's Soviet Union in order to destroy Poland, but that objective achieved, it was time to achieve his *lebensraum* (living space) further east. St. Petersburg was now Leningrad, renamed in honour of the father of the Soviet State and Hitler, who saw himself as an art connoisseur, wanted the amber room to come home to Germany.

Once again it was dismantled and reconstructed, this time in Koningsberg Castle and was on public display for two years. In 1945, however, the intense Allied bombing of Germany, by British and American aircraft, day and night, saw the medieval fortress collapse into rubble. And with it, the amber room vanished.

One man obsessed with what happened to it was General Kuchumov. It was under his watch that the room had been taken from Leningrad four years earlier and he was not about to let it happen again. But the general had no luck. There was no obvious signs of amber in the ruins of Koningsberg, so a host of conspiracy theories emerged. Some claimed the whole edifice had been smuggled on board the Wilhelm Gustaff, a German merchantship that was sunk with a huge loss of life in 1945. Others believed that the room lay in the myriad secret tunnels underneath Koningsberg Castle. Yet more pointed to Czech salt mines and the existence of the fabulous room under some musky lagoon. When the Soviet authorities destroyed the ruins of Konigsberg in 1968 the amber room vanished forever.

But not quite. Two men who, like Kuchumov, became obsessed with the search for the room died in suspicious circumstances. Georg Stein, an ex-German soldier and historian spent years investigating the chamber's disappearance. He was murdered by disembowelling in 1987. General Yuri Gusev, head of Russia's Foreign Intelligence Unit, was looking for it also when he was killed in a suspicious car crash in 1992.

Was the truth simply that Stalin's own bombers, rather than those of the Allies, had destroyed the amber room? The Soviet Union, before its collapse in the 90s, was all about reputation and saving face. Is that why Stein and Gusev died?

If you want to see the amber chamber today, you can. In 1979 it was reconstructed from original drawings and photographs in the Catherine Palace and the room officially opened in 2003.

THE GOLD TRAIN

In the panic of spring 1945 as the Third Reich collapsed, there was a scramble among the Nazi high and middle command to salvage what they could of the loot taken during the war. Most of this – gold, silver, paintings, antiques – had belonged to Jewish families across occupied Europe. Rumours abounded from those months that there was an entire freight train loaded with such goodies, but mostly gold bullion bars, that vanished somewhere en route to or from the east (the stories vary).

The most persistent legend says that the train, heavily armoured against attack, disappeared inside the Owl Mountains, then in Germany, in a top secret project called Riese (giant). Over the past five years, there have been serious investigations by archaeologists and geophysicists in tunnels near the Polish town of Wlabrzych. The latest in-depth investigation – by Andreas Richter and Piotr Koper – has revealed ... precisely nothing. The dig has cost $37,000 to date, a virtual money pit; but Richter and Koper refuse to give up, intending to start again in September 2016.

The legal ramifications of who exactly owns the gold – if it exists – would be horrendous, with court cases dragging on for years.

GOLIATH

Despite its name – and it's even worse in German (*Leichter Ladungstrager*) – the Goliath was tiny, standing 1ft tall and 4ft long. The tank was in fact a tracked mine, originally a French invention, but hijacked by the Germans after the Wehrmacht captured the prototype in 1940. The idea of the remote controlled gadget was to send it to attack tanks, destroy bridges and carry out general demolition. They were designed to be expendable, blowing up with their targets. They were even used in the defence of D-Day but repeated shelling cut their command cables. The weapons weren't particularly successful, having a top speed of just 6 miles per hour and hindered by their attached cables, they were also prone to getting stuck easily. American GIs often found the captured or abandoned goliaths amusing, posing with them for pictures. There are a number of them in various military museums around the world.

THE GRAN SASSO RAID

If there was any moment of the war meant for Hollywood, it was the daring Gran Sasso Raid under Operation Eiche (Oak). The only problem was, it was the Germans who carried it out. In July 1943, after the invasion of Sicily and the bombing of Rome, the Italians deposed the dictator Benito Mussolini and the king, Victor Emmanuel III, had the former Il Duce arrested and moved throughout the country. Unknown to his captors, the Germans, led by SS Captain Otto Skorzeny, were keeping an eye on things. The SS cracked a coded message to discover that their ally was being held at the guarded and fortified Campo Imperatore Hotel, deep within the Appenine mountains, high on a bleak ridge. On 12 September, around 100 SS and Paratroopers launched a daring glider raid to rescue him. They landed on the mountain and overwhelmed 200 guards of the Carabinieri without a shot being fired. A relieved Mussolini was told, 'The Fuhrer has sent me to set you free', to which he replied, 'I knew my friend would not forsake me.' He was then flown from the mountain base to a military airport, and from there to Vienna where he received a hero's welcome at the Hotel Imperial.

It was a late triumph for the Germans, though Mussolini was ruler now only in name, as the header of the Reich's puppet government, the Italian Social Republic. Skorzeny came to be regarded as the 'most dangerous man in Europe' and even Churchill was impressed by the raid.

The escapade ultimately did Mussolini no good. Trying to escape in a private's overcoat in the last days of the war, he was arrested by Italian patriots who shot him and his mistress, Clara Petacci, at an Esso petrol station in the Piazzale Loreto in Milan.

The Campo Imperatore Hotel claims that the room in which Mussolini stayed has been untouched since the Gran Sasso Raid itself.

THE GREAT DICTATOR

Charlie Chaplin's 1940 movie *The Great Dictator*, remains one of the world's most influential works of cinema. The brave film is a famous parody of Hitler and fascism and was made at a time when America was still neutral. There seem to be two theories as to Chaplin's inspiration. The first is that he discovered that Hitler had placed him on his 'kill-list' for being a 'disgusting Jew acrobat'; even though, ironically, he admired the man's talent. The Nazis believed Chaplin to be Jewish as he never denied it. He was in fact English, born in the hardship of working class London.

The second theory is that Chaplin was shown a copy of the Nazi movie, *Triumph of the Will*, Leni Riefenstahl's masterpiece, a ground-breaking piece of chest puffing, showing the full might of the Reich through rallies and marches at Nuremberg. A friend of Chaplin's was so overwhelmed by the movie he said the American people must never be allowed to see it or they would lose their resolve. Chaplin found it pompous and hilarious and wanted to mock it.

The Great Dictator follows Chaplin as two doppelganger characters, a persecuted Jewish barber and a megalomaniac ruler (Adenoid Hynkel). The film is funny and poignant and a famous hope-filled speech where the barber pretends to be the dictator in front of a crowd at the end and has had a change of heart, is still moving and surprisingly relevant to a modern audience.

Famous for his silent movies, this was Chaplin's first 'talkie' and was both a commercial and critical success one of the greatest movies of all time. Hitler saw it, his responses ranging from bursting out in tears to finding it funny, depending on the source.

The film, banned, in all Nazi-occupied countries, remained unavailable in Germany until 1958. A copy was said to have been smuggled into the Balkans where a Wehrmacht audience either left the cinema in disgust or fired bullets at the screen.

THE GREAT PANJANDRUM

The Great Panjandrum was a British creation designed to break through the Nazi defences in Normandy. Essentially, it was two ten foot wheels joined by an axle, the wheels lined with seventy rockets and the centre filled with explosives. As the rockets were lit, the plan was for the Panjandrum to propel itself along the beach at speed, looking like a huge Catherine Wheel, roll into the German fortifications and create a giant explosion, allowing tanks to pass through.

It was the brainchild of the Department of Miscellaneous Weapons Development, also known as the 'wheezers and dodgers.'

The weapon was taken to Westward Ho! in Devon, but the experiment didn't quite go to plan. The Panjandrum flew out of control, almost knocking down the cameraman and a group of VIPs and ended with observing soldiers and civilians running for their lives. At least an excited dog enjoyed the event, chasing after a stray rocket. Fortunately the testers had changed the explosives with sand for this experiment, much to the relief of the people of Westward Ho!. Needless to say, it was never used in action.

Something very like it featured in a *Dad's Army* episode on television, but the device used there was operated by remote control radio.

The phrase was first used in an 1820 novel by Maria Edgeworth and came to mean a pompous, self-opinionated expert.

GREMLINS

Many of us may know of Gremlins because of Joe Dante's 1984 movie, but they were around long before then. They were even said to be involved in World War Two, generally causing mischief and being a nuisance.

During the war, British pilots began to complain of tiny creatures, referred to as gremlins, with a knack for planes, causing aircraft malfunctions, errors, faults and all sorts of headaches. During the Battle of Britain, there were so many reports of these creatures causing plane problems that the Air Ministry put serious time and effort into investigating the phenomena. Workplace posters were put up, advising employees of the various dangers gremlins were apparently involved with. Germans and American pilots later became their victims too. Many crewmen swore blindly they even saw them, menacingly clambering over cockpits or sitting on wingtips.

American aviator Charles Lindberg, in his 1953 book *Spirit of St. Louis* said he met them while flying. He wrote that he was surrounded by several of the creatures, and he was amazed by their advanced technological knowledge. Luckily for Lindberg, he stated these gremlins were friendly, helped him, and reassured him he'd be fine.

Our modern notion of gremlins is thanks to famous children's author Roald Dahl. Dahl himself had served in the RAF and believed he had also been a victim of the gremlins funny business. His book *The Gremlins* was published in 1943 for Walt Disney.

So what was all this about? It must have been a combination of hallucinations caused by the planes high altitudes and the stress of combat that lead to such imaginative scamps.

Perhaps the gremlins were helping in ways the pilots couldn't fathom. By taking the blame for the countless technical issues a pilot faced, the blame was diverted away from the army of factory workers, technicians and engineers who may have actually been at fault.

'GUNG HO!'

One of the most iconic photographs of the war is the picture of six marines raising the US flag on Mount Suribachi after the battle of Iwo Jima. The Pulitzer Prize winning picture had such an impact it was immortalised into a statue at the Marine Corps War Memorial in Arlington, Virginia, unveiled in November 1954.

It has been claimed the picture was staged, but as with most things, the truth is more complicated than that. Joe Rosenthal was the Associated Press combat photographer.

He died at the age of 94 in 2006 and was always annoyed by the allegation. In an interview, his colleague Hal Buell explained how it came about. There was an earlier photograph taken by a Marine photographer, Sgt. Lowery, but his equipment was damaged during a firefight. Afterwards, the soldiers were ordered to replace the flag as it was too small and erect a larger one. Rosenthal was on site to witness this, and as the first flag was being lowered the second flag was being raised. With seconds to decide he chose to capture the latter. Sgt. Lowery's picture was fine, but didn't capture the imagination of its viewers in the same way as Rosenthal's.

Rosenthal did stage a photo, asking a group of celebrating Marines to stand around the flag in what is now known as the 'Gung-Ho!' picture. The film was sent to Guam to be developed and soon after to the American newspapers. The flag-raising picture was so impressive some thought it was staged. When Rosenthal was asked if it was, he replied 'Yes', believing they were referring to the Gung-Ho! version. Immediately, he realised the confusion and corrected his answer for the journalists. Hal Buell said it was too late 'the correction never catches up with the error. Joe spent the rest of his life defending what was alleged as a phony picture.'

The whole story formed the plot of *Flags of Our Fathers* directed by Clint Eastwood in 2006.

GUSTAV SIEGFRIED EINS

Intelligence and communication were war-winners between 1939 and 1945. The British Secret Intelligence Service (SIS) began to use 'wireless' in 1938 and during the war there were 48 clandestine shortwave radio stations in Britain, broadcasting in 14 languages. The first, in May 1940, was codenamed G1 and was in response to a similar set-up in Berlin run by Josef Goebbels' Ministry of Propaganda and Enlightenment, which ran stations like Radio Caledonia, Welsh National Radio and, ironically, Christian Peace Movement.

The first of the Germans to front the British G1 service was Dr Carl Spiecker, an anti-Nazi who had earlier operated against the Reich from Paris. But the real brains behind the broadcasting network was 'Tom' Sefton Delmer (whose name was actually Dennis), an Australian journalist brought up in Germany. His German was impeccable and he coined the term 'black' propaganda for subversive deception to fool the enemy. Delmer himself described the difference between white and black propaganda, saying it was a bit like spitting in a German's soup before shouting 'Heil Hitler!'

GS1 (Gustav Siegfried Eins) was a right-wing station that used (for the time) bad language and appeared to stand one hundred per cent behind the Fuhrer. As Delmer wrote to his boss, Leonard Ingrams, 'We want to spread disruptive and disturbing news among the Germans which will induce them to distrust their government and disobey it.' GS1's first broadcast, two weeks after the event, covered Rudolf Hess's bizarre flight to Scotland, which was being officially ignored by Churchill's government. To add to its authenticity, Delmer hired a German actor and crime writer, Peter Seckelmann, to voice *Der Chef* (Hitler's nickname among his staff in the 1930s) and a journalist, Johannes Reinholz, as his heel-clicking Number Two. If it all sounds like an episode of the 1980s sitcom *'Allo! 'Allo!*, we have to remember that the 1940s was a different decade and people in desperate, terrifying situations relied on radio – *any* radio at times – as a lifeline. Seckelmann went to live with Delmer and his wife at The Rookery in Aspley Guise within a stone's throw of the secret code and cypher school at Bletchley Park. *Der Chef* was supposed to be an old-school German, disapproving of the hypocrisy and rumoured degeneracy of the Nazi elite. The whole thing was carefully orchestrated to sound like a private conversation in a pub rather than a broadcast to potential thousands.

With its outspoken attacks on 'that flat-footed bastard of a drunken old cigar-smoking Jew, Churchill', the Gestapo believed that Gustav Siegfried Eins was a genuine station and tried to work out what the name itself meant.

In the end, the station closed, after over 700 broadcasts, because Sefton Delmer went too far. In one programme, *Der Chef* described witnessing an orgy. The script got to the desk of Sir Stafford Cripps, who was so appalled by the idea that he wrote to

Anthony Eden, the Foreign Secretary, on 12 June 1942, that he objected to 'such filth being allowed to go out of this country. If this is the sort of thing needed to win the war, I'd rather lose it!'

Cripps' heart was in the right place, but he clearly had no grasp of black propaganda at all. Gustav Siegfried Eins came to an abrupt end on 11 November 1943 when the Gestapo were heard storming the station, screaming at *Der Chef,* 'I've finally caught you, you pig!' before killing him in a crescendo of machine-gun fire. The sound engineer handling the woofers and tweeters spoke no German and misunderstood his cue, playing the massacre twice in a row.

Gustav Siegfried Eins – so good, they shot it twice!

HAKENKREUZ

The swastika remains, perhaps forever, as a symbol of terror and oppression. All of the values of order, law and authority twisted and gnarled into something grotesque and nightmarish. The sight of the swastika, even after all these years, gives us the mental image of Hitler, his legions and all their odious apparatus. But we must, if we can, at least try to remember that the symbol is much older and more powerful than Nazi Germany.

The word swastika itself comes from the Sanskrit word, roughly translating as 'good luck' and is over 7,000 years old. The English first began to use the word in the 1870s.

The peculiarity of this symbol is the contrasting use of it in East and West. In the West, for all obvious reasons, the swastika is now anathema – even today it is still illegal to display it in Germany and several other countries. In the East however, it remains to this day a force for good and a sign of auspiciousness. It is sacred to Hinduism, Buddhism and Jainism.

German archaeologist Henrich Schliemann found the symbol at the sight of the ancient city of Troy. Schliemann was taken by the symbol, and over time it was slowly transformed into a symbol of 'remote ancestors', the so-called Aryans, and the pseudo-history and unscientific absurdity poured forth from there.

The symbol *was* sacred in the West, and believed to be closely associated with the Viking god Thor, or perhaps Odin, the All-father. But Hitler's use of it, and the SS's use of 'Nordic runes' (actually made up by the nonsensical new-age mystic Guido von List around 1908), has nothing at all to do with the untainted earlier historic period.

The swastika, known as the hakenkreuz (hooked cross) in German was destined to become the symbol of the Nazis. Hitler himself designed the red and white flag on which the hooked cross would sit. 1935 was the year Hitler's standard became the official flag of Germany.

Many academics and authors were appalled by the bizarre appropriation of this ancient symbol. One notable example was Rudyard Kipling. He loved the swastika and many of his books featured them, before the Nazis sullied it. Another was J. R. R. Tolkien, himself of German descent, who was disgusted by the blatant distortion and twisting of Germanic folklore. A planned 1938 German translation of *The Hobbit* was halted when Tolkien was dismayed to receive a letter from the publishers, asking him to prove his Aryan ancestry. It wouldn't reach Germany until 1957. Tolkien described Hitler as a 'ruddy little ignoramus' and was generally disgusted by the whole insanity of the conflict, referring to those who designed as the atomic bomb and bought the war to a cataclysmic end as 'lunatic physicists'.

The symbol was also beloved by the Native Americans. In 1940, four tribes from Arizona officially renounced the symbol in response to the link with Nazi aggression.

With all this in mind, the symbol remains benevolent in the East, and Western misunderstandings of its usage has led to countless protestations and outrages. As an example, an unbelievably ludicrous article from *The Daily Telegraph* in 2017 featured an elderly man who was outraged that the design of the soles of his imported slippers looked a bit like swastikas (they didn't). 2005 saw Prince Harry give the tabloids front-page fodder when he dressed as a Nazi for a fancy-dress party.

One question remains: can the West ever reclaim the ancient swastika, and look beyond its brief abduction as a symbol of evil? And if it can, should it? Or should it belong to the histories, as a stark reminder and warning of the shadow of the past? Perhaps this is a question best left to the sages and scholars among us.

HERMANN'S A GERMAN

Hermann Goering is best known as one of the Nazi high command and head of the *Luftwaffe*, but he was something of a diva too. A fighter pilot in the First World War and recipient of the coveted 'Blue Max' medal for bravery, Goering joined the infant Nazi party in Munich in 1923 and quickly became indispensable to Hitler, responsible for the Four Year Plan, part of Germany's economic revival in the late 1930s. He was fond of elaborating and personalizing his uniforms to make them as fabulous as possible. He was also obsessed with rewarding himself with medals. This amused Hitler so much that he was known to make jokes about Hermann, awarding the man medals from gold and silver paper to wear with his pyjamas.

Official records show that during the First World War, before there was a Nazi Party, Goering received eleven awards and three during the Weimar years when the Nazi Party was growing. During the twelve and a half years of the Reich, he awarded himself no less than twenty-eight decorations and gleefully accepted a further thirty-two from Germany's allies or occupied countries. Contemptuous opponents of the Nazis ridiculed such over-dressing with the term *gold fasanen* (golden pheasant).

According to Rochus Misch, who was a telephone operator in Hitler's bunker under the streets of Berlin, one of his favourite jokes went as follows. 'One day, Mrs. Goering came into the bedchamber and found her husband waving his Field Marshal's baton over his underwear. "Hermann, darling, what are you doing?" she enquired. "I am promoting my underpants to overpants!"'

HIBAKUSHA

'Now I am become Death' says the Hindu Holy book, the Bhagavad-Gita, 'The Destroyer of Worlds'. Dr. Robert Oppenheimer, one of the leading physicists behind America's atomic bomb programme, the Manhattan Project, quoted this to describe the impact of the weapon he had helped to create

On 6 August 1945, Colonel Paul Tibbets of the United States Air Force flew his B-29 Superfortress, Enola Gay, over the Japanese city of Hiroshima and dropped a uranium fission bomb equivalent to 20,000 tons of TNT. Sixty percent of the city was flattened (later aerial photographs show a ghostly wasteland) and there were 80,000 dead in minutes. Worse destruction was caused by the bombing of Tokyo in March, but nothing had the dramatic impact of Hiroshima. For a single plane to cause so much devastation was unbelievable. Three days later, Nagasaki received the same treatment, using a more advanced plutonium bomb. The casualties were about half those of Hiroshima. Despite some opposition from his High Command, Emperor Hirohito surrendered. In a broadcast to his people over Japanese radio, he said 'We have resolved to endure the unendurable and suffer what is insufferable.'

Those who suffered most were the hibakusha, literally, 'a person affected by a bomb'. Robert Louis Stevenson had no idea how right he was when he wrote in the boys' adventure story, *Treasure Island*, 'Them's that die will be the lucky ones'. The bombs of August caused horrendous physical and mental problems for the survivors. A total of about a quarter of a million died from radiation sickness as well as the bombs themselves and various forms of cancer are linked to this.

What is grim is that the hibakusha were despised and discriminated against by the Japanese themselves. They were not given jobs in the years ahead. Would-be in laws objected to their sons' and daughters' marriage partners in case radiation were to be passed on to succeeding generations. To the West, Japanese culture had always appeared odd, but the psychological effects of being the only country in the world to have suffered the atom bomb are still on-going.

It even finds its way into popular sci-fi culture today. Godzilla is a monster bent on destruction, smashing its way through cities with ease. And Godzilla was created as a result of nuclear warfare. If you are a fan of horror films, you will almost certainly have heard a piece of music linked to all this. Written by the Polish composer Krzysztof Penderecki in 1960, it is called 'Threnody to the Victims of Hiroshima'.

HIGH AS KITES

A modern mind may think that a soldier in the Second World War had to be on drugs to do what they did, and there is every chance they were. The *Wehrmacht*, issued millions of tablets to their soldiers, one of the most common being the appropriately named pervitin. This was actually methamphetamine, often known today as crystal meth. Over thirty-five million tablets were issued in a four-month period alone. The Nazis were happy to hand out drugs including alcohol and opiates, on the condition that their military objectives were met.

A book published in 2015 – *Der Totale Rausch* (Total Rush) revealed that the drug was first issued in 1937 to combat stress and fatigue. Field Marshal Erwin Rommel – the Desert Fox – was believed to have been a daily user.

The Germans noted that soldiers on methamphetamine were more alert, confident and daring and were not affected by pain, hunger, thirst or sleep deprivation as much as their sober counterparts. As the war was turning, the Nazis were working on a pill to turn their soldiers into super-humans and to 'boost their self-esteem.'

Alcohol abuse was also rife, with fighting, insubordination and 'unnatural sexual acts' resulting from the excesses of the men. It wasn't just the fighting men who caved in to addiction; by the end of the war four times as many doctors were addicted to morphine than at the start of it.

Ironically, recreational drugs in Germany before the war were regarded as a Jewish perversion, but Pervertin became a rival to Coca-Cola, the American drink and was available in chocolates for civilians.

HITLER THE HYPNOTIST

During the Munich crisis of 1938, Duff Cooper, First Lord of the Admiralty, wrote that Hitler had 'cast a spell' over Neville Chamberlain, the British Prime Minister. 'I was completely horrified,' Alexander Cadogan, Permanent Secretary at the Foreign Office said, '... more horrified still to find that Hitler has evidently hypnotised [Chamberlain] to a point.' Neither man was impressed by Hitler's intellect nor his oratory; there had to be something all the more weird about the influence he was able to exert over people.

Several people referred to the famous Hitler stare. He had a habit – or was it a conscious psychological ploy? – of looking into someone's eyes for far longer than was usual. It cowed politicians, soldiers, journalists, friends and enemies and gave the impression that the Fuhrer could read minds or at least knew more about a situation than anybody else.

Arguably the most weird notion in this book and the most difficult to explain, is why millions of intelligent and decent Germans, not to mention Nazi followers in other countries, fell under such delusion for as long as they did. This can have had nothing to do with Hitler's own animal magnetism in that relatively few ever met him. The answer probably lies in the mob mentality and the madness of crowds.

HITLER THE INVINCIBLE

Adolf Hitler believed he was guided by divine providence, being nudged along like a 'sleepwalker' by a higher power that was protecting him. Winston Churchill had a similar line of thought for himself – he had his own experiences that shaped his worldview, and he would even be ordained into the Ancient Order of Druids.

With a figure as controversial and divisive as Hitler, it was not odd that he was the target of multiple assassination attempts. What is odd, bearing in mind how many of them there were, is that all of them failed.

There are too many to list here, and whole books have been written on this subject, but it is believed the dictator survived over thirty plots from the 1930s up unto 1944. Living through every one of these increased the man's paranoia and suspicion, but also cemented his belief in divine providence – surely one must have the favour of the gods to dodge death so many times?

All the attempts failed; lone gunmen, the German military, Poles, the NKVD and the SOE. Many more ideas didn't get past the planning stage, such as the odd plan to return the imprisoned Rudolf Hess to Germany, hypnotized, to finish off his leader! Perhaps the most well-known of these plots was the July 20 plot, where Claus von Stauffenberg and his Wehrmacht conspirators attempted to blow up Hitler during a meeting. This would have probably worked if it wasn't for a last minute change of venue, and the suitcase containing the explosive being accidentally kicked away. This close call was made famous by the 2008 film *Valkyrie* starring Tom Cruise. The bomb detonated, Hitler escaped with a shattered eardrum and a few other minor injuries. He was furious and his vengeance was swift, decimating swathes of German commanders in response.

Interestingly, the British didn't particularly want him dead – the reason for this is that in his final years Hitler was so incompetent and was making such disastrous military decisions that they feared him being replaced by someone more cunning and competent who could lengthen the conflict. Then, of course, there is the glaringly obvious reason not to have killed him before the end of the war. If he *did* die before the war's end, he could have become a martyr. In a similar vein to the stab-in-the-back myth of World War One, fanatical elements might have fought even more fiercely, convinced that Hitler somehow would have turned the tide once more if he was alive. No doubt we would still be bombarded in this day and age with lurid conspiracy theories.

Mussolini and his mistress had been humiliatingly hanged from an Esso petrol station on 28 April 1945 and no doubt a similar fate awaited Hitler. Deep within Berlin's *Fuehrerbunker*, he decided to end his own life. His wife of one day, Eva Braun, joined him by taking a cyanide pill. Hitler probably shot himself. With a twist worthy of *Macbeth*, the dictator who it seemed no living man could kill, finally died on 30 April 1945 by his own hand.

The Soviets soon conquered the *Fuehrerbunker* and this is where things get murky. Stalin, for reasons best known to him, stated that Hitler hadn't died there and was being sheltered by the Allies in Spain or South America – despite overwhelming evidence to the contrary. Experts believe this was done as part of a state sponsored disinformation campaign. But it is unclear what Stalin would have got out of it. Perhaps he genuinely believed it, perhaps he was trying to stir up distrust of the capitalists and imperialists whose temporary alliance with him would soon be severed.

Stalin's response has not helped historians. Theories of Hitler's survival have lived on, growing and exaggerating in the telling. He could be in Spain; more reckon Argentina is theobvious choice; even a secret Antarctic base has been bandied about -

and it's said that he's still alive. Not bad for a man over 120 years of age!

HITLER THE POET

As well as being a soldier, painter, author and violent oppressive dictator, Adolf Hitler was also a poet. One of his poems, *The Mother* from 1923 is a tribute to his mother who died in 1907 and it's an interesting glimpse into the mind of a man who was usually consumed with hatred.

'When your mother has grown old
and with her so have you,
When that which once came easy
has at last become a burden,
When her loving, true eyes
no longer see life as once they did
When her weary feet
no longer want to bear her as she stands,
then reach an arm to her shoulder,
escort her gently, with happiness and passion
The hour will come, when you, crying,
must take her on her final walk.
And if she asks you, then give her an answer
And if she asks you again, listen!
And if she asks you again, take in her words
not impetuously, but gently and in peace!
And if she cannot quite understand you,
explain all to her gladly
For the hour will come, the bitter hour
when her mouth will ask for nothing more.'

Hitler's admiration for motherhood is seen throughout his earliest art. His painting 'Mother Mary and Holy Child Jesus Christ' shows an idealised bond.

There is no doubt that young Adolf was his mother's favourite. He looked like her and detested his father who he described as vicious and violent. Mothers had a special place in Nazi ideology, although, paradoxically, women did not.

HITLER'S AMERICAN

The name Henry Ford is synonymous with American enterprise and conveyor-belt mass production, making the motor car not only *the* symbol of twentieth century America but a must-have gadget bought by millions around the world. The Ford Motor Company used slave labour drawn from French prisoners of war at its German subsidiary in contravention of the Geneva Convention's Article 31 that banned such employment. Before the Americans entered the conflict, Ford supplied the Reich with military equipment, declining an offer to work with the British Royal Air Force.

He believed that all modern wars, including the Second World War, had been deliberately started by 'financier warmakers', his euphemism for the Jews. Even baseball had its problems, according to Ford – 'too much Jew'. The company produced a newspaper, *The Dearborn Independent* throughout the 1920s focussing on *The International Jew*, a series of articles written by Theodore Fritsch, a well-known anti-Semite in Weimar Germany. Heinrich Himmler was impressed by Ford – 'one of our most valuable, important and witty fighters'.

He was even praised by Hitler in his book *Mein Kampf* – 'only a single great man, Ford [who] to [the Jews'] fury still maintains full independence [from] the controlling masters of production.' The respect was mutual, both Hitler and Ford keeping photographs of the other on their office desks. In 1938 the American was awarded the Grand Cross of the German Eagle medal, which he refused to return when Germany declared war on the US.

At the Nuremberg trial of leading Nazi war criminals in 1946, the ex-Hitler Youth leader, Baldur von Shirach, claimed that Ford's *International Jew* (although he did not write it himself) turned him and many others into anti-Semites.

HITLER'S JEW

Eduard Bloch was a Jewish doctor from Linz, Austria, who was the Hitler family's physician, caring for Hitler's mother when she had breast cancer. Hitler was extremely grateful for this and referred to Dr Bloch as a 'noble Jew', even sending him a postcard and a picture he had painted. On his mother's death, the doctor would later recall the young Adolf was 'the saddest man I have ever seen.'

In 1939, the Nazis took over Austria in the *Anschluss* (Union) and the Reich's anti-Semitic policies kicked in. As the persecution intensified, Bloch wrote a letter to the Fuhrer. Hitler arranged his protection under the Gestapo, the only Austrian Jew to receive it. In a later biography, Bloch would say of the young child Adolf, that he remembered a modest, polite, boy with such a good mother, he could not understand how he turned out the way he did. By that time, and, again, thanks to the Fuhrer, Bloch and his family had emigrated to America.

Historians debate to what degree Bloch's part in Hitler's life had in shaping his anti-Semitism, either encouraging or discouraging it. In the memoirs that Bloch published shortly before his death from stomach cancer in June 1945, he said of the young Hitler, 'What dreams he dreamed, I do not know.'

HITLER'S MISCHLING

Ernst Hess was one of the handful of ordinary German people that Hitler personally became involved with. Although Hess was a Protestant, his mother was Jewish so he was officially a *mischling* (mixed blood). Ernst Hess had served in the First World War and had been the commander of Hitler's unit, the 16th Bavarian Reserve Infantry, known as the List Regiment.

There can be no doubt of the effect of the First World War on Hitler's mindset. Hitler was commended for his bravery in battle and his loyalty to his mischling commander clearly caused confusion.

When the Nazis first came to power, Hess was allowed to continue in the law (he had become a judge after the war) by virtue of his war record, but the Nuremberg Laws of 1935 removed all *mischling* from office by declaring them full-blooded Jews. He was forced to resign from his position in 1936 and was beaten up outside his house. Tragically his mother and sister were ordered to be removed to Theresienstadt concentration camp, wrongly believing the 'protection' also covered them. His sister, Berta, would be murdered at Auschwitz though her mother would escape to Switzerland. When Hess was summoned to appear before the SS in June 1941 he produced the letter of protection he received from Hitler. He was told it had been revoked in May and he was now 'a Jew like any other.' He would spend the remainder of the conflict as a slave labourer in Milbertshofen concentration camp near Munich.

Ernst Hess survived the war and become a successful business man. He was offered back his role as a judge but not could bring himself to work with his ex-colleagues who had been part of the Nazi legal system. He died in Frankfurt in 1983.

HITLER'S WOMEN

In the carefully constructed propaganda surrounding Adolf Hitler, beautiful girls and blond, blue-eyed children were always caught by the camera at the front of the crowd, cheering wildly and beaming adoringly at their Fuhrer. To the girls, he was 'der schone

Adolf' (handsome Adolf). It was all part of the cult of leadership adopted by other dictators like Mussolini and Stalin; but nobody did it better than the Nazis.

Hitler's private life was very different however. Most people today see the man as the epitome of evil, a megalomaniac with no redeeming features, a sociopath who was utterly immune to other people's suffering. While all this is true, it does not begin to plumb the depths of his psychosis and leaves us guessing about his sexuality.

There were those who hinted that the young Adolf was homosexual and that one of his lovers was Rudolf Hess, his 'Hesserl', who was one of his earliest supporters. There is no evidence of this and by virtue of what he did, a balanced, rational approach to Hitler's psyche is probably not possible. He certainly adored his mother, the plodding, religiously inclined Klara Poelzl and looked like her. He was her favourite child – 'mother's darling' – but he let her down by not joining the priesthood as she had hoped but trying to become an artist instead.

There were four women rumoured to have been romantically linked with Hitler. The first was Maria Reiter, known as Mimi, who attempted suicide in 1928 when the Nazi party had been reborn with Hitler as its leader and the bully-boys of Ernst Röhm's SA still dominated. Maria was a 16-year-old shop assistant from Oberzalzberg and Hitler was thirty seven. He promised to marry her but his mission for Germany got in the way. Depressed and lonely, she tried to hang herself but her brother-in-law cut her down in the nick of time. She went on to marry SS Hauptsturmfuhrer Georg Kubisch who was killed at Dunkirk in May 1940. Mimi told her story to *Stern* magazine in 1959 and she died in 1992.

It was the second relationship, however, that shone a spotlight on the future Fuhrer's private life. In 1931, Hitler was still only the leader of a fringe political party regarded as a joke by most Germans. On 19 September of that year, his niece, Geli Raubal, was found dead in Hitler's apartment at 16 Prinzregentenplatz in Munich. She had shot herself with Hitler's pistol. The image that the Nazi leader had carefully cultivated was that of a 'man alone', wedded to the concept of a German revival after the disaster of the First World War; his private life was on hold because Germany must come first. Yet here was a possible mistress so unhappy with the new messiah that she had killed herself. Geli had been seeing Hitler's chauffeur-bodyguard, Emil Maurice and 'Uncle Adolf' was furious, flying into one of his legendary rages. The jury is still out on exactly what the Hitler-Raubal relationship was, but it may very well have been sexual. He certainly had a private shrine to the girl in his Munich flat, as witnessed by the film-maker Leni Riefenstahl, with flowers around a bust of her. It took him months to recover from his loss.

Very different was Unity Mitford. One of a nightmarish brood of daughters of David Freemantle-Mitford, 2nd Baron Redesdale, the fact that her middle name was Valkyrie gave a hint as to her Teutonic leanings. Tall, blonde and just as eccentric as her father, she drifted to Munich in 1933, the year that Hitler took power, and became a much-photographed member of his circle. She fell madly (how else?) in love with him and probably saw herself as Frau Fuhrer. Whereas the Nazis deliberately excluded women from serious political discussion, Unity spoke loudly, usually extolling the virtues of Britain, at every gathering she went to. On the day that Neville Chamberlain's Britain declared war on Germany, Unity sat on a bench in the appropriately named

Englischer Garten in Munich and put a bullet in her head. The calibre was small, however, and she did not die. Hitler sent his best doctors to treat her and she was sent home via Switzerland. She died in 1948, never having recovered from her suicide attempt, still declaring her love for the man who had murdered six million Jews.

Eva Braun never discussed politics, which may be why she lasted so relatively long. The daughter of a Munich teacher, she was tall and athletic, without much of a brain and little in the way of ambition. She was a semi-professional dancer, but shy and quiet, in many ways the perfect partner for a politician who veered towards the autocratic. 'A highly intellectual man,' he once said, 'should have a primitive and stupid woman. Imagine if I had a woman to interfere with my work.' Both Goebbels and Goering introduced Hitler to Nordic beauties but the Fuhrer was not interested. Eva, known to her servants as 'E.B.', stayed in the background at Berchtesgaden, keeping out of the way while Hitler talked politics with the great and not so good of Nazi Germany. Not until 1943 was she allowed to go to Berlin and they would never be seen together in public. He treated her abysmally, taking her for granted and she too, like the other three women in Hitler's life, attempted suicide.

And she finally succeeded in typically Wagnerian style. Hiding in the bunker under the streets of Berlin while Russian shells devastated the streets, Hitler married Eva Braun and they committed suicide together. On that last day when a servant referred to Eva with the usual 'grädiges fräulein' (gracious lady) she smiled and said, 'You may now safely call me grädiges Frau!' (In other words, Mrs Hitler). Although details are unclear, Hitler probably shot himself in the head and Eva swallowed poison.

All four women linked with the Fuhrer attempted suicide. Why? The American Office of Strategic Services (OSS), forerunner of the CIA, carried out a study of the dictator while he was still alive and came to the conclusion that he was an impotent homosexual with a faeces fixation. But then, to paraphrase someone else in a rather different context, 'they would, wouldn't they?'

HOBART'S FUNNIES

The disastrous Allied raid on Dieppe in August 1942 highlighted the many dangers and obstacles to coastal invasions of the mainland and it fell to General Alan Brooke, Chief of the Imperial General Staff, to find a better way. His solution was to create a new unit, the Specialized Armour Development Establishment, under Major General Percy Hobart.

Despite the implications of the nickname 'Funnies', Hobart's modified tanks were effective. They included the Duplex Drive, which was an amphibious version that could operate on land and provide cover and support to the infantry; they were used on all five beachheads of D-Day with varying degrees of success.

The 'Crab' was a converted Sherman tank fitted with metal chains which would flail the ground and clear safe passages through minefields. The 'Crocodile' was a Churchill tank fitted with a flamethrower which could reach up to 120yds, a devastating psychological weapon, particularly effective at clearing out bunkers and fortifications. Another modification which was excellent at destroying fortifications was the AVRE (Armoured Vehicle Royal Engineers). This tank was equipped with a mortar, providing speed and range that infantry mortar teams could not compete with; it fired a 40lb bomb known as a 'flying dustbin'. The 'Bobbin' was equipped with a roll of reinforced matting which it could lay out in front of itself, to create a path for vehicles which may struggle on the beach or soft terrain. There were various other tanks which could fill trenches, move troops and bridge gaps but one of the most unusual is the 'CDL' (Canal Defence Light), equipped with a strong searchlight that would be used to light up night time battles and dazzle the enemy. Altogether, fourteen different gadgets were built and used; later modifications of some of them were still in use in the Gulf War and Iraq.

HOLMAN PROJECTOR

The Holman Projector was an anti-aircraft weapon used by many British ships and was an impressive piece of improvisation. Several different designs were made but they followed similar lines. It was designed by a machine tool manufacturer, Holmans. A 4' 6" barrel would hold a tin. Inside the tin was a bomb. The bomb's safety pin was held in place by the tin until the bomb was in the air. The weapon used compressed air or high pressure steam to fire the projectile at the enemy. It's main advantage being it was very cheap to build and easy to install.

It was intended to assist the Royal Navy and the Merchant Navy, who were being terrorized by German air attacks during their crucial supply runs. The idea being the bombs could, at the very least, deter low flying attackers and force them to climb to higher altitudes where their attacks would be less accurate.

As an effective anti-aircraft weapon, the Holman Projector was a failure, though one ship did in fact shoot down two enemy planes with it. Its limited range of around 200 yards made it nearly impossible to hit enemy aircraft. A test demonstrating the weapon, witnessed by Winston Churchill, failed because the testers forgot to bring any ammunition! The men improvised and fired off some beer bottles, and an amused Churchill quipped that it would at least 'save on cordite'.

However, as a source of amusement for its users, it was invaluable. As the barrels were smooth-bore, they could be filled with anything. Curious gunners found potatoes were particularly good missiles to fire. Nearby vessels even conducted play fights with them!

THE HONOUR RING

Heinrich Himmler was obsessed with Germany's Teutonic past and one of his many quasi-medieval ideas was the SS *Ehrenring*, the Honour Ring. Nicknamed *Totenkopfring* (The Death's Head Ring) it was given to the men of the SS, a personal gift from Himmler himself. Carved with the grinning skull of Death (itself an old Prussian design) and runic symbols such as the swastika, the hagal and the sig, the ring was inscribed with Himmler's signature, the date of issue and the recipient's name. Recipients had to have three years' service, providing that their careers were 'impeccable' and the ring was to be worn on the third finger.

When an officer died, his ring was supposed to be returned to Wewelsburg Castle where it was to be stored in a sacred chest. As the tide of war turned, Himmler ordered all the Honour Rings be returned and blast-sealed into a nearby hill. By 1945, 14,500 such rings had been sent back. With the fall of Wewelsburg Castle, the rings met different fates; some were kept by their holders, others were lost and the rest were no doubt taken by Allied soldiers as souvenirs. The rings remain a sought after item by war memorabilia collectors and copies appear everywhere. As well as the Honour Ring, those who pleased Himmler could also receive Honour Swords and Honour Daggers.

The Reichsfuhrer wrote of them that they were 'a reminder at all times to be willing to risk the life of ourselves for the life of the whole'.

THE HORIZONTAL COLLABORATORS

The inhabitants of countries occupied by the Germans during the war faced a stark decision – capitulate or die. Once the French army surrendered, it was left to civilians to cope as best they could. Vichy France openly collaborated, even contributing to the roundup of dissidents like gypsies (today's Roma) to be sent to concentration camps. The free French army under Charles de Gaulle was in Britain waiting for D-Day and the chance to win back their homeland.

With the liberation of France in 1944, over 20,000 thousand distraught women were arbitrarily and publicly humiliated and attacked by mobs. They were often stripped, spat at and had their heads shaved simply for having relationships with German soldiers. After this they would then be paraded through the local town on the back of a lorry or on foot. What level of degradation the girls received was based purely on the whim of the mob. Those attacking them were often no more innocent then those they were punishing, often naïve teenage girls caught up in the excitement of the war and being seduced by German soldiers, as English girls were by the Americans. Many were prostitutes or single mothers who had no option but to work with the Germans. One woman received this treatment just for being a cleaner for the Reich. Parisian prostitutes were kicked to death for 'collaborating' with the enemy. Allied soldiers would use the same girls themselves, buying their services with food and supplies.

Stories spread that French girls, heartbroken by the loss of their *Wehrmacht* beaus, took to becoming snipers, shooting at Allied soldiers, though this was dismissed by the British high command as 'latrine rumours'.

Pictures of young French girls with their German lovers, dressing up in their boyfriends' uniforms don't invoke any anger or disgust, and it could easily happen anywhere (and did). Equally, pictures of these same crying girls being stripped and abused to the amusement of the grinning crowd doesn't sit easily as justice.

It is difficult today to understand or judge the French. Traditionally, the Germans were the enemy. As Prussians they had humiliated them in the Franco-Prussian War of 1870-71. At Versailles the French were bent on vengeance after the First World War. Yet in the 1930s, the French government was soft, guilty of appeasement and ready, it seemed, to cosy up to Hitler. After suffering years of tyranny during the occupation, attitudes of the mob are perhaps understandable. The victims had no trials, no one to speak for them, and doubtless many girls who had no part in any of it would have been caught up in the hysteria. To this day, there has never been a complete investigation into what is still, to Frenchmen, a

THE HORTEN HO 2-29

The Horten Ho 2-29 was a prototype Nazi stealth bomber, the result of years of experimentation to find newer, more deadly technology. With its 'flying wing' design it resembles modern stealth bombers and in 1944 it must have looked bizarre as it was so far ahead of its time. Goering, as head of the Luftwaffe, had demanded much from his engineers and designers in the escalation of technology the war required. High levels of advancement were deemed essential in any future *Luftwaffe* aircraft. The plans for the Horten Ho 2-29 were put forward by the brothers Reimar and Walter Horten, and Goering approved its development.

The sleek design of the prototype flying wing meant it would be difficult to detect by enemy radar and would have been capable of bombing raids before being intercepted and could have potentially made a significant impact.

A successful test flight was made in December 1944 (a glider version was flown in the previous March) but, as with many of the Nazi super-weapons, it was too little too late. The Allies were closing in on Germany by then. There is only one surviving copy of the Horten Ho 2-29, currently undergoing complete restoration for the Smithsonian National Air and Space Museum in Washington DC and even to this day, scientists are not quite sure how technical aspects of its design were overcome in the 1940s.

HUMAN TROPHIES

It reads like the stuff of nightmares and has been interwoven with fiction and urban legends for centuries: the taking of human trophies. American GIs in the Second World War had a particular contempt for the Japanese: they were the aggressors, and perceived as a brutal, savage and barbaric race. Fighting with the Japanese was always fierce, and the loss of friends and comrades would have further demonized the enemy. Old-fashioned ideas and propaganda portrayed this particular enemy as sub-human. Tragically, this led to a similar attitude to that which saw to the obliteration of the native Americans.

It was claimed many years after the war, when the bodies of Japanese soldiers were repatriated from the Mariana Islands, that half came back without their heads. We should always tread lightly with stories such as this, but it was said that GIs would decapitate enemy corpses and boil the heads until only the skulls remained. They would then use the skulls as camp decorations or ashtrays or have them sent home as trophies. Teeth, arm bones and ears were also popular souvenirs.

The Japanese were outraged when a letter-opener made from a soldier's arm bone was given to President Roosevelt as a present. The US authorities eventually stepped in to stop this macabre practice, ruling that the taking of skulls was in violation of the Geneva Convention.

There is photographic evidence that this gruesome practice occurred but, just as tales of the crimes of Axis soldiers were inflated so that the truth of their actual offences became blurred, the scale of this dark chapter in American history, and the degree of involvement of those alleged to have participated, is unclear.

Experts today believe that acts of cruelty and inhumanity may flourish in any quarter of the globe, when authorities demonise specific demographics and distance themselves from groups considered 'other'. Consequently group-punishment and arbitrary revenge may become tolerated.

'HURRAH FOR THE BLACKSHIRTS!'

The events of the Second World War, the exposure of the Holocaust and awareness of Nazi atrocities destroyed for ever the credibility of Hitler's Third Reich. Before all this, however, many people in Britain, from senior politicians to the man in the street, were impressed by Hitler's bold policies, impressed by the economic recovery of Germany and some of them shared the Nazi antipathy towards Jews. The Marquis of Tavistock, for instance, wrote at the time –

'We should not forget that even in our boyhood the German Jew was a byword for all that was objectionable ... Indeed, there may be a bit of Hitler even in ourselves ...'

Viscount Rothermere was Harold Harmsworth, a British business tycoon and owner of the *Daily Mail* newspaper; and fourteen others. He was an anti-communist and a supporter of Nazi appeasement. He admired Hitler and wanted to avoid war with the Reich, using his newspapers to spread his personal views. He was a supporter of the maverick politician Oswald Mosley who had set up the British Union of Fascists, complete with Mussolini-style black uniforms. Rothermere himself wrote a piece titled *Hurrah for the Blackshirts.*

'Because Fascism comes from Italy, shortsighted people in this country think they show a sturdy national spirit by deriding it. If their ancestors had been equally stupid, Britain would have no banking system, no Roman law [?] nor even any football [?] since all of these are of Italian invention.'

Ignoring the fact that Rothermere was wrong about Roman law (never a British system) and football (common to all European countries), his support for Fascism was trotted out to thousands of readers whose education was limited and who probably believed every word he wrote.

Rothermere travelled to Berlin to meet Hitler in person in 1934. MI5 papers released in 2005 show us that he wrote to Hitler several times, congratulating him on his illegal annexation of the Sudetenland and encouraging him to invade Romania in 1939. All this is at odds with the book he wrote that year, *My Fight to Rearm Britain* as the war clouds gathered. If this was a *volte face,* it was a little late – Harsmworth died in 1940, two months after the beginning of the Blitz.

I LOVE LUCY

Lucille Desirée Ball was a dizzy, red-headed comedienne who was a child model and chorus girl before gravitating to B-feature movies and television. Between 1951 and 1973, she was a hit in a variety of shows, all featuring her own effervescent character with or without her straight man, first husband Desi Arnaz.

In 1942, then in her early thirties, Lucy was driving home from the MGM film lot in Hollywood where she was working on the movie *Du Barry is a Lady.* It was then that she started hearing music. Her car had a radio but it was not switched on and she realised to her horror that the sound was coming from her mouth. For a while, she kept the information to herself, believing she might be going mad. In the end, she told her story to a man who, on the big screen at least, could be guaranteed to keep a secret – the 'silent' comedian, Buster Keaton. Keaton had an explanation – he had a friend with a similar problem and it was caused by fillings in the teeth.

The next time Lucy heard the sounds, she was again alone in her car, but the sound was not music, it was morse code. By now, thoroughly unnerved, she told her bosses at MGM and they, equally alarmed, passed the whole thing over to the FBI. The Federal Bureau of Investigation was (and is) responsible for law enforcement in the United States, but during the war, its remit included counter-espionage and sabotage. As a result of their enquiries, the Feds uncovered a Japanese spy ring and several arrests followed.

Is all this true? Or does it belong in the Boston Herald Rumor Clinic category? Scientifically it is just about feasible that the metal in a tooth cavity could pick up a radio wave, but whether it did and whether the FBI were able to carry out the work they did, remains conjecture.

I WAS HITLER'S MAID

Pauline Kohler was one of an unknown number of Germans who was overheard making a disparaging remark about the Fuhrer. Such paranoia was not confined to Nazi Germany – in Britain too, defeatist comments and gripes about Churchill landed people in gaol.

In the Third Reich, however, punishments were harsher and Pauline found herself interrogated, tied to a chair naked, by the Gestapo, before being sent to Buchenwald, the camp near Weimar. Even as early as 1940, the place was notorious for its routine torture of prisoners and the grim work carried out in the camp's munitions factory.

Pauline survived and ended up working as a maid for a Gestapo officer, who abused her on a daily basis before his wife intervened, pulling strings and got the girl a job as a domestic at the Berghof, Hitler's idyllic retreat in the Bavarian mountains, near Salzburg.

To her horror, she found that the Führer was every bit the monster she had heard recent mutterings about. There was a 'rape dungeon' in the house's cellar and the whole place was littered with sadistic pornography. High-ranking Nazis were frequent visitors.

None of this surprised Hitler's enemies, inside Germany and elsewhere. The trouble was, it was all fiction. Pauline Kohler wrote '*I was Hitler's Maid* (retitled '*The Woman Who Lived in Hitler's House*' for the American market) in 1940. The book was an immediate best seller translated into seven languages, even Chinese! *Hitler's Maid* is an excellent example of black propaganda and the real author was probably Robert Collier, who rattled the whole sordid nonsense off on an upright typewriter in just two weeks. Pauline's face, on the original cover of the book, the terrified victim and martyr, is actually a photo-edit of four women put together!

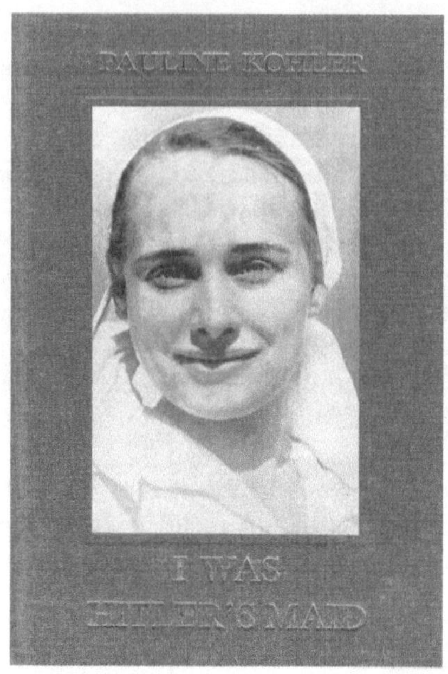

ICE CREAM

Despite various attempts by the Italians and the Arabs to claim to have developed ice cream as an exotic dish, no one did it like the Americans. The Knickerbocker Glory was named after a Dutch family who settled in the States, the name itself being hijacked by Washington Irving for a stage comedy. Rocky Road was developed by William Dreyer as an attempt to console those who lost money in the Wall Street 'crash' of 1929. The 'Doughboys' of 1917-18 had ice cream as part of their staple diet, while their 'Tommy' comrades in Britain only ever regarded it as a seaside treat in the height of summer.

In the Second World War, the GIs fighting their way east through the forest of the Ardennes made ice cream in their helmets using snow and the chocolate bars they were given in their rations. In the air, the crews of B-52s took their own ice cream with them, in the freezing cold compartments of the rear-gunners. At altitudes of 15-18,000 feet, custard froze and was churned by a combination of engine vibration and turbulence to make a delicious concoction.

Even in the Pacific, the US army were well provided with the stuff in their desperate battles with the Japanese. An ice cream barge in the South Pacific produced 38 litres of the stuff every seven minutes and could store up to 7,600 litres.

And in the British war effort? Because of the internment of so many Italians under Defence Regulation 18B, ice cream parlours all but disappeared. Those not interned had to make do with carrots on lolly sticks!

THE ICE SHIP

One of the more bizarre ideas from the British Establishment in the war was a gigantic aircraft carrier made of ice. Britain's Royal and merchant navies were being devastated by German U-boats, in the treacherous North Sea, carrying vital supplies to Soviet

Russia. There was a call to see what could be done to protect ships from torpedo attacks.

An eccentric scientist, Geoffrey Pyke, rose to the challenge. He had led an extraordinary life, having been a prisoner in Germany during the First World War and had invented motor-cycle/sidecar ambulances for use in the Spanish Civil War. Pyke suggested the building of a 2000ft long aircraft carrier, made from ice and weighing 2 million tons. The project was named Habbakuk, after the Biblical prophet. Churchill was impressed by Pyke's plans and development began. Ice wasn't as impenetrable as Pyke first envisaged but an ingenious alternative was made, a mixture of sawdust and woodchips added to it in what is now known as Pykrete. This mixture was much stronger and durable than normal ice, slower to melt and easy to repair.

Testing continued and issues with melting and warping were overcome. Although the ship wouldn't be indestructible, it could be repaired in combat and it would take such a huge and sustained effort from the *Kriegsmarine* to destroy it that they would be unlikely to risk exposing their own units to counterattacks.

In the end, the plans were scuppered. The sheer amount of resources needed to construct and maintain the carrier was deemed unacceptable. The fact the ship would only manage a top speed of six knots and the construction of a suitable rudder proved difficult to overcome. Pyke remained what he had always been, a critic of the Establishment he was trying to help. One of his typically abrasive memos reads 'Chief of Naval Construction is an old woman. Signed Pyke.'

IF DAY

Fur traders settled along the Red River in Canada before 1763 and the area was protected by the army at Fort Garry. A settlement quickly grew up around it and it became Winnipeg city in 1879, growing into a fine mini-metropolis as befits the capital of Manitoba. It has churches, schools, hospitals, lumber yards and factories, a thriving and successful icon of western knowhow and ambition.

Then, at 5.30am on 19 February 1942, all that came to an end. Air raid sirens wailed in the darkness of the morning, the radio crackled with the shocking news that the Wehrmacht were entering the town and nearly 4000 of them, helmeted and jackbooted, strutted up the streets and squares, bringing terror in their wake. The local garrison at Fort Garry fought back, but they were hopelessly outnumbered and by 9.30am the maple-leaf flag over the fort was lowered and a swastika ran up the ropes instead.

Books were dragged out of the library and burned in the street, exactly as the Nazis had done in Germany when they seized power. Posters were slapped up on walls and lamp posts telling the locals what they could and could not do. Anyone failing to obey would face harsh reprisals. In the shops Reichmarks were already replacing dollars at the payment counters.

The odd thing about all this, horrified observers noticed, was that there was no devastation. They had heard the siren, but they had not heard – or seen – aircraft. They had heard the guns, but no buildings were lacerated by shrapnel; no glass had been broken. Above all, there were newsreel cameras everywhere, recording it all for posterity.

Enter the German High Command in the form of J.D. Perrin, at the Great Winnipeg Victory home Corporation. The whole thing was a stunt using film extras and cobbled together uniforms, to be shown in cinemas across Canada exactly what to expect if Canada did not take its responsibility to the war effort seriously. An astonishing $3million was raised in war bonds.

And the day's casualties after all the sound and fury of slaughter? A soldier sprained his ankle, and a woman burnt her hand making toast in the morning's blackout!

INSTRUCTIONS FOR SERVICEMEN

The Germans have pleasant beer and excellent sausages, but they are a people prone to hysterical fits if they don't get their own way. Attractive women might be spies, and the rest are generally big, fleshy and fair-haired. Give instructions to them in a firm, military manner – they're used to it and some of them are already planning World War 3. Oh, and the Schnapps is to die for.

This is some of the 'advice' given to the British army in a pamphlet issued to them in 1944 by the Foreign Office, *Instructions for British Servicemen in Germany*. The book is a practical guide to soldiers advising them how to, and how not to, behave when in the country. The book assumes the final victory of the Allies and some of the advice is sound, some accidentally hilarious, and some is clumsily and crudely stereotypical.

Equally fascinating is *Instructions for American Servicemen in Britain* (1942). This advice includes reminding US readers the British aren't the Redcoats of 1776. The Brits like their privacy and don't enjoy small talk. The American and British versions of the English language are very different, colloquialisms and phrases may not translate, their bum is a backside, for example, so be careful not to create any 'boners'. The Brits are fiercely proud of their odd system of pounds, shillings and pence – they don't understand the superior decimal system - so don't mock their 'funny money'. The British are also bitter about being paid much less than GIs, so don't rub it in. Remember the British, despite their reserved nature, are tough. After all, the English empire and its language weren't spread around the world by a bunch of 'panty-waists'.

Both these books and others are a charming glimpse into the past. The *Instructions for British Servicemen in Germany* pamphlet became a best seller in Germany when the Bodleian Library republished it as a book in 2007.

Perhaps some of the messages in these books still ring true, such as the advice 'be firm and just, but don't be soft'.

JANIS PINUPS

Janis Pinups was the last of the Forest Brothers, an underground resistance movement in the Baltic states, to come out of hiding. During the war the Baltic states had been placed in a unique position: they were conquered by the Soviet Union as part of the Molotov-Ribbentrop Pact, were then invaded by the Axis as part of Operation Barbarossa, were then retaken by the Soviet Union as the Germans were forced to retreat, and remained occupied – without any substantial Allied opposition – until 1991.

Pinups, a native of Latvia, was conscripted into the Red Army in 1944. He was knocked unconscious during a battle, and upon waking, found the battlefield abandoned, and no sign of his comrades. Pinups, a devout Christian, believed God had saved him.

The price of desertion was death and Stalin even punished his soldiers who had surrendered during the war with further imprisonment when they returned home. So Janis Pinups would spend the next fifty years in hiding from the Red Army, living in the wild and an underground bunker. Only his siblings knew he was alive, helping them on their farms under cover of night. Over the long years, his brothers died and he had to stop visiting his sister after neighbours became suspicious of the stranger visiting the farm at impolite hours.

Latvia gained independence in 1991, but the Soviet military continued to have a presence in the country. It was only in 1995, after fifty years, that Pinups surrendered himself to local police. He moved in with his sister until his death in 2007.

THE JERICHO TRUMPETS

For anyone who has ever seen a war movie, no sound is more memorable than the famous wail of a plane hurtling to the earth, trailing black smoke before disappearing behind trees as it is shot down. Real dog fights may not have been quite so noisy. The most dreaded plane of the war was the stuka (dive bomber) or Junkers Ju 87, which was equipped with 'Jericho trumpets', propeller-driven sirens, they had no practical purpose and their usage was purely psychological. The horrible noise of these trumpets had a great effect on enemy morale and would scare and disorient those on the ground as the planes made their dive onto their target. A vital ingredient of *blitzkrieg*, the stukas' effectiveness lessened as the war progressed and there was a problem for the pilots who flew them. Such was the speed of the dive that some of them briefly passed out, occasionally with fatal results. The enemy became used to the noise so the Jericho trumpets were phased out. However, the noise was so memorable that the movies, often using real war footage in their action scenes, would frequently use stukas as the iconic terror of the skies.

JOHN R. MCKINNEY

John R. McKinney was an American soldier whose exploits read like the stuff of Hollywood action heroes. He single-handedly fought off 100 Japanese troops during the Philippines campaign.

The citation of his Medal of Honor, which was awarded to him by Harry S. Truman in 1946, read as follows:

'He fought with extreme gallantry to defend the outpost which had been established near Dingalan Bay. Just before daybreak approximately 100 Japanese stealthily attacked the perimeter defense, concentrating on a light machinegun position manned by three Americans. Having completed a long tour of duty at his gun, Pvt. McKinney was resting a few paces away when an enemy soldier dealt him a glancing blow on the head with a saber. Although dazed by the stroke, he seized his rifle, bludgeoned his attacker, and then shot another assailant who was charging him.

Meanwhile, one of his comrades at the machinegun had been wounded and his other companion withdrew carrying the injured man to safety. Alone, Pvt. McKinney was confronted by ten infantrymen who had captured the machinegun with the evident intent of reversing it to fire into the perimeter.

Leaping into the emplacement, he shot seven of them at pointblank range and killed three more with his rifle butt. In the melee the machinegun was rendered inoperative, leaving him only his rifle with which to meet the advancing Japanese, who hurled grenades and directed knee mortar shells into the perimeter. He warily changed position, secured more ammunition, and reloading repeatedly, cut down waves of the fanatical enemy with devastating fire or clubbed them to death in hand-to-hand combat.

When assistance arrived, he had thwarted the assault and was in complete control of the area. Thirty-eight dead Japanese around the machinegun and two more at the side of a mortar 45 yards distant was the amazing toll he had exacted single-handedly.

By his indomitable spirit, extraordinary fighting ability, and unwavering courage in the face of tremendous odds, Pvt. McKinney saved his company from possible annihilation and set an example of unsurpassed intrepidity.'

McKinney died in 1997, and it remains a mystery why Hollywood has not snapped up his incredible story.

JUDY THE DOG

Judy the Pointer was born in the Chinese city of Shanghai in 1936. She escaped from her kennels and lived on the streets for half a year until an incident with Japanese sailors meant she was returned home.

Later that year crew of the gunboat *HMS Gnat* bought Judy, with the dog becoming the ship's mascot. Life aboard the vessel was not always plain-sailing. The Chinese cooks didn't take to her, and her falling out of the boat and being rescued had to be covered up as a training exercise. Judy broke the heart of the mascot for *HMS Ladybird*, a male, as his feelings for her were not reciprocated.

Despite these hiccups, Judy proved herself countless times as an invaluable member of the crew. She alerted the sailors to an impending pirate attack, could hear enemy aircraft before her human shipmates to warn them of the danger, and saved Chief Petty Officer Charles Jeffery from a leopard.

She was married to a French pointer named Paul, who was serving on the gunboat *Francis Garnier*. A wedding celebration was held in Hankou, and after the consummation with Paul, the French Pointer, Judy became pregnant.

With the outbreak of war in 1939, Judy and many crewmates were transferred to *HMS Grasshopper*. This vessel was sunk in the South China Sea in 1942 after being attacked by Japanese aircraft. Judy was saved from the wreckage and the crew ended up on an uninhabited island. Always useful, she dug out a freshwater spring for her comrades, an act which the crew stated saved their lives. Leonard Walter Williams, a British seaman said, 'Judy was a saviour then. She was a marvellous life-saver.'

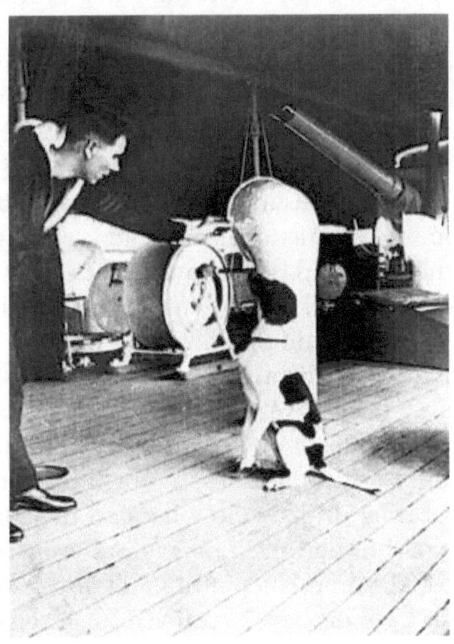

The group were rescued from the island by a Chinese junk. From there, they trekked hundreds of miles towards Padang in Sumatra, but could not be evacuated before the arrival of the Japanese army. On 18th March, they were taken as prisoners of war. Judy became the only recorded canine POW of the Second World War. For three brutal years Judy suffered with her crew, surviving on scraps, living in the unforgiving harshness of the jungle and at the mercy of brutal Japanese guards. She befriended Frank Williams, a young British sailor who shared his rice rations with her.

The Prisoners of War were ordered to board *SS Van Warwyck*, where they would be transferred to Singapore. But the Japanese refused to allow Judy to follow her comrades. Her friends, though, refused to leave her and smuggled her on board the vessel in a sack. The following day, *SS Van Warwyck* was torpedoed by a British submarine who were unaware the ship was full of Allied POWs. Five hundred of the 700 crew died, but Judy was among the survivors. She was reunited with her friend Frank Williams at the next POW camp.

In 1945 Judy was sentenced to death, but escaped, only reappearing once her captors had gone. The camp was soon liberated.

With the war over, her friends helped smuggle her to Liverpool in England. In 1946 Judy received the Dickin Medal. Her citation read, 'For magnificent courage and endurance in Japanese prison camps, which helped maintain morale among fellow prisoners and also saving many lives through intelligence and watchfulness.'

She accompanied Frank Williams to Tanzania and died there in 1950. Judy's medal and dog collar are now on display in London's Imperial War Museum.

JUST NUISANCE

Just Nuisance was a Great Dane from Cape Town, South Africa, and is remembered as the only dog to be officially enlisted into the Royal Navy. Nuisance served with the crew of *HMS Afrikander* from 1939 until 1944.

The dog was sold to Benjamin Chaney, who moved to Simon's Town to run the United Services Institute. The Great Dane became friendly with the locals and liked to sleep on the gangplank of docked ships. Being a 6ft long Great Dane, this earned him the nickname 'Nuisance' from the sailors trying to walk around him.

Nuisance enjoyed trains, and constantly travelled. His liberal use of the railways without paying his fares meant he was soon in trouble. Railway authorities contacted Chaney and warned him the dog would have to be put down if Nuisance didn't stop his anti-social behavior. Naval Command were having none of that. They officially enrolled Nuisance into the Royal Navy, meaning he now had free rail travel. He was given the forename of 'Just' and his official occupation was 'bone crusher'. Nuisance's religion was listed as 'Canine Divinity League (Anti-Vivisection)' and he was promoted to Able Seaman in recognition of his unofficial service prior to joining the Navy.

Just Nuisance never went to sea and took on only those jobs he wanted. He picked and chose, excelling at escorting drunk sailors back to their bases. Like many sailors, his career was not squeaky clean, he fought other dogs, went absent without leave, and refused to leave a pub at closing time His punishment, tongue-in-cheek, for sleeping on a Petty Officer's bed, was to have his bones removed for seven days!

A car accident in 1944 meant Nuisance was discharged from the Navy. He died later that year, having been put down on the advice of a veterinary surgeon. Nuisance was buried with full military honours, even receiving a gun salute and the playing of the Last Post.

A statue in Jubilee Square of Nuisance continues to watch dutifully over the docks of Simon's Town to this day. Simon's Town holds an annual dog parade where a lookalike is selected and an exhibition in the town's museum ensures the memory of this beloved dog is never forgotten.

THE KATYN MASSACRE

The German invasion of western Poland on 1 September 1939 sparked World War Two. On the 17th of the same month, in collusion with the Germans, the Soviet Union invaded eastern Poland, after Stalin had successfully concluded negotiations to end hostilities with the Japanese. By mid-October Poland was crushed, and the Nazis and Soviets met in the middle, shaking hands and smiling for the cameras. Tens of thousands of Polish military were taken by the Red Army as prisoners of war, deep within the Soviet Union. This was war, there was nothing untoward about that.

In 1941, with Operation Barbarossa having now turned Germany and the Soviet Union into bitter enemies, the Polish government-in-exile operating from London decided to bury the hatchet with Stalin and agreed to help form a Polish army attached to the Red Army. This was where things got awkward.

Now that they were allies, Polish general Wladyslaw Anders asked for the release and return of 15,000 Polish officers to join the new army. Stalin hesitated. In December he finally responded, claiming that the Polish POWs had already been set free, but had wandered off into Manchuria (!) and that nothing had been heard from them since. Anders was disturbed by this account, but there was a war on, and he had no choice but to take the Soviets on their word.

If we take this as an isolated incident, this then becomes a mind-boggling case of Nazi Germany being, in some sense, the good guys. In 1942, as the eastern front raged, locals told the Axis forces about the site of a massacre committed by the Soviets. The

Germans investigated and discovered thousands of Polish dead; soldiers, police officers and intelligentsia, all executed and piled on top of each other, many in Polish military uniforms – and the uniforms were fresh, they would have been killed very soon after being captured. The German investigation revealed that the slaughter took place in 1940. Stalin, with his usual flexibility of the truth, replied that the thousands of dead Poles were builders and workers who were in fact killed by the Germans. The Red Cross stepped in and their findings agreed with the German version of events.

For a man like Joseph Goebbels, this was music to his ears – there could be 12,000 dead. The discovery of the massacre was filmed, propaganda was pounded out, and international journalists descended. *Here* was a demonstration of the barbarism of Bolshevism, and proof of the threat to Western civilization posed by the Red Hordes. The hypocrisy and audacity of this propaganda coup is breathtaking in the light of the Nazis' brutality and appalling cruelty, all brought to the world's gaze a few years later.

The Polish government-in-exile were understandably outraged, and their own investigation into what happened was stonewalled by the Soviets, so on 25 April 1943 diplomatic relations ended. Stalin simply set up his own Polish government-in-exile made up of sycophants and yes-men.

This embarrassing incident was difficult for men like Churchill and Roosevelt. They had to balance honouring their commitment to their free Polish allies with keeping Stalin and the Red Army onside. The alternative was to risk turning the war into a three-way conflict. In the end, pragmatism won over idealism; and the Western leaders responses to the brutality of the Soviet Union became ever more uncomfortable and dismissive.

After the war a US inquiry found the Soviets responsible for the massacre. Once again Stalin stuck to his guns, and the Polish government, now a communist puppet-state deep behind the Iron Curtain, supported his version of events.

It was not until the 1990s that Russia revealed documents exposing the truth, that there were in fact up to 22,000 victims – even more than Goebbel's estimate. In 2010 the Russian government did the honourable thing and officially denounced the Katyn Massacre and put the blame at the door of Stalin and the Soviet Union.

Monuments to the massacre can be found in Britain, Russia, Ukraine, Canada, Austria, South Africa, the United States and, of course, the homeland of the inconvenient victims, Poland.

THE KILTED KILLER

Tommy MacPherson was a Scottish commando with the Queen's Own Cameron Highlanders. Having been captured in the Italian campaign and having won the Military Cross, he was dropped into occupied France with a French lieutenant on 8 June 1944. Their mission was to support the French resistance and conduct sabotage and guerilla operations against the enemy. Bizarrely, MacPherson jumped into occupied territory wearing his kilt under his Denison smock. One of the local Maquis (Resistance) waiting for him was horrified and ran to his leader – 'Chef, chef, there's a French officer and he's brought his wife!'

MacPherson was a prolific saboteur and carried out many successful operations blowing up railway bridges. On one occasion he delayed a *Panzer* column heading for Normandy to repel the Allied beachhead; a three-day journey for the tanks ended up taking two weeks. His actions became so enraging to the Nazis that they placed a 300,000 franc bounty on his head, earning him the nickname 'The Kilted Killer.'

One of MacPherson's most daring actions was driving a Red Cross vehicle through enemy lines and convincing a *Wehrmacht* Major General in charge of 23,000 men to surrender. The German soldiers were pulling back and the Maquis held a vital bridge. So, with his usual plucky spirit, MacPherson pretended he had a vast army with him and had the power to order the RAF to annihilate his soldiers if the Germans didn't capitulate. The Major General agreed. MacPherson himself later commented, 'The clincher was when I told him that I was in contact with London by radio and could at any time call up the RAF to blow his people out of sight. In truth, the only thing I could whistle up was Dixie, but he had no way of knowing that.'

THE KINDERTRANSPORT

The *Kindertransport* (children's transport) programme is one of Britain's proudest moments. After *Kristallnacht* (night of broken glass) on 9-10 November 1938 the situation for German Jews was becoming dire. These two days saw 267 synagogues destroyed, 100 people killed and 30,000 sent off to concentration camps. As the eyes of the world turned to what was happening in Germany, Jewish and humanitarian agencies appealed to Britain for help. The British government agreed to take unaccompanied children and put out a BBC appeal for foster homes. The first train left for Britain on 1 December 1938, and journeys from Germany continued until 3 September 1939, the day that Britain and France declared war. The last *Kindertransport* from outside Germany came from the Netherlands on 14 May 1940, when they surrendered to the Nazis.

A number of unassuming people became heroes in this operation. Nicholas Winton, 'the Englishman of Wenceslas Square' got nearly 700 children out of Czechoslovakia. Wilfred Israel kept the British government informed of the activities following *Kristallnacht* and Rabbi Solomon Schonfeld brought 300 children from Austria.

Once in Britain, the children were looked after until they were chosen to be fostered by new families. Although more could have been done and it could never be enough, at least it was *something*. These children would probably never see their families again and most settled in Britain after the war to start new lives. In the end 10,000 children's lives were saved.

One of them wrote later, 'I have the greatest admiration for England and the English people. They were the only country that took us in. To my dying day, I will be grateful to this country.' There are statues and memorials to the children in the railway stations they used, from Friedrichstrasse in Berlin to Liverpool Street in London.

KISKA ISLAND

The summer of 1943, a year and a half since the Japanese had woken a sleeping giant with their surprise attack on Pearl Harbor. The United States of America was on the warpath, and the war was going in their favour. However the Japanese still held two of their islands, Attu and Kiska, in the Aleutians off Alaska, which they had captured the previous year.

Under Operation Cottage, the US and their Canadian allies launched an amphibious attack on Kiska from opposite sides of the island. A pre-invasion bombardment peppered the island, warships fired off 330 tons of shells, the Eleventh Air Force dropping 424 tons of bombs.

34,426 soldiers landed and fought inland through the fog for two grueling days. 'Intense days of fighting followed', but this wasn't the Japanese defenders, it was the Americans and Canadians shooting at each other, mistaking each other for the enemy. By the end, the Allies suffered 313 casualties at the hands of the Japanese ghosts.

The Japanese had actually evacuated two or three weeks before the attack. The only inhabitants were a group of dogs, who had been left behind and greeted the troops when they landed.

KNITTING FOR ENGLAND

'Genevieve' was one of that brave little band of female agents parachuted behind enemy lines by SOE, the Special Operations Executive set up by Churchill to 'set Europe aflame'. Her real name was Phyllis Latour Doyle and she used the knitting skills she had learned as a girl to create secret codes. Such messages took about thirty minutes to send, so Phyllis kept on the move, sending a total of 135 in the runup to D-Day to keep the Allies informed of German troop movements.

The Belgians specialised in knitters in their Resistance organisations. Who would suspect a granny sitting on a park bench, clacking away with a pair of needles? Knitting is actually a binary system, with easily identifiable v (a knit stitch) or o (a purl) as the two symbols. Either a knitting pattern or the finished garment can easily be read by an expert. Everybody was at it – in the States, Elizabeth Beatty knitted codes for communists in the Soviet Union until 1945. In Britain, knitting patterns were banned in the post in case they carried secret codes.

Knitting for troops at the front, however, was a well-established support. Wives and mothers had been doing this for generations and governments encouraged it. As one American poster put it – 'Remember Pearl Harbor, Purl Harder!'

KUGELPANZER

The Second World War was a time of great innovation and technological advancement. Some inventions were groundbreaking, others were dismal failures, and some were simply bizarre.

The Kugelpanzer (Ball Tank) is one of the mysteries of the war. Next to nothing is known about it. The most widely accepted theory is that it was a prototype created by the Germans and had been shipped to Japan, presumably as part of their dubious Axis alliance, when it was captured by the Soviets at Manchuria in 1945.

What was the purpose of this tank? It was shaped as a ball, with a track either side of an eye slit, which leads to the conclusion it was a prototype reconnaissance vehicle. Its armour was 5mm thick, and the strange vehicle was to be fitted with a machine gun - in Germany an MG34 or MG42, although in Japan it would have had a Type 96.

Similar ideas had already been conceived, particularly during the First World War, such as the One-Wheeled-War-Tank, the Treffas Wagen, the Tumbleweed Tank and the Tsar Tank. Clearly there was an appetite for Ball-Tanks, but these have never come to a practical fruition.

The Kugelpanzer is still on display at Kubinka Tank Museum, Moscow Oblast, Russia and continues to intrigue experts and enthusiasts to this day.

KURT GERSTEIN

Kurt Gerstein's story is one of the enigmas of the war. He was either an SS war criminal, a heroic whistleblower, an inside man, a frightened liar – or some combination of them all.

Born to a Lutheran family in Munster, Germany in 1905; his mother died when he was young, and his father was a judge. He joined the Nazi party in 1933 and struggled to reconcile his religious faith with the movement. A performance of the play *Wittekind*, which attacked Christianity, offended Gerstein so much he spoke out and was beaten up for his troubles. He was arrested in September 1936 and imprisoned for five weeks when he was found in possession of anti-Nazi pamphlets which he had hoped to distribute. That led to his being expelled from the party. But thanks to his father the judge, who had friends in high places and who was able to pull some strings, Kurt was reinstated on 10 June 1939.

Around this point things get murky, and experts and investigators start to disagree.

According to some sources, Gurstein found out his sister-in-law, Berta Ebeling, had died mysteriously in a psychiatric ward. Gurstein had heard rumours of the euthanasia program and joined the SS to go undercover and find out more. Other experts aren't convinced, stating that the chronology of his joining the SS and his sister-in-law vanishing cannot be verified, and she may in fact have been alive when he enlisted.

Now an undercover spy, or proud member of the SS, he was assigned to the Waffen-SS 'Hygiene Unit', where he contributed greatly to projects to provide safe drinking water and deal with vermin issues. With the coming of the Final Solution, the murder of all Jews, his role would change. He was soon involved. For example, one of his tasks was to ensure the efficient and timely delivery of Zyklon B to Auschwitz. He would later witness the horrors of the camps for himself.

He claimed he was appalled by what he saw and made efforts to inform foreign diplomats and religious leaders. According to him, he wanted to pass on the truth to the wider world, which was at the time ignorant of the scale of the murders. His appeals for help fell on deaf ears.

In April 1945, Gerstein surrendered himself to the French. He said he did this because he wanted the world to know what had really happened. His statements to the French authorities gave vital and accurate information about Belzec – but other evidence was problematic. He grossly over-exaggerated some claims, stating 25,000,000 had died, and claimed to witness events that didn't happen.

For reasons that remain uncertain, Gerstein hanged himself while in custody in July 1945. Perhaps he was overcome by grief at his failure to stop the Holocaust, and his inability to pass on his warnings to foreign powers; perhaps he was terrified of being tried as a war criminal; perhaps he was murdered - we can only conjecture. In August 1950, a denazification court found that Gurstein was indeed a war criminal – a subsequent campaign saw him pardoned in 1965.

So was Kurt Gerstein a war criminal? Was he a martyr going undercover to expose the death camps? Was he a man whose conscience had caught up with him, and who tried to jump ship in the last month of the war? It is likely we will never know the truth. The man remains a mystery, with supporters and detractors arguing their own opinions, but with little proof of what sort of individual he truly was.

LADY DEATH

Lyudmyla Pavlychenko was a female sniper in the Soviet Red Army and not only has one of the highest confirmed kill counts of all time, but remains the most 'successful' female sniper in history. She was born in the Ukraine just before the Russian Revolution and became a crack shot at a local rifle club while working at a munitions factory. She also obtained a degree in history from Kiev University, specialising in the seventeenth century Cossack leader, Bohdan Khmelnytsky. At the outbreak of what the Russians call the Patriotic war, she was posted to the 25th Rifle Division. Throughout the conflict she racked up 309 confirmed kills, including 36 enemy snipers and probably many more.

She was one of 2,000 female snipers and made her first kill using a Tokarev SVT-40 semi-automatic with 3.5x telescopic sight. She became a 'Nazi hunter' and would spend hours, sometimes days, watching over enemy positions from her camouflaged hideout, waiting for the perfect shot. In two and a half months, she claimed 187 kills.

Pavlychenko was wounded by a mortar in 1942 and due to her fame the Soviets used her as part of their publicity machine. She was sent on a tour of the Allied nations and was the first Soviet citizen to be welcomed by an American president. She was appalled that one American journalist commented that her uniform made her look fat and her skirt was too long. She also visited Canada and Britain, accepting donations from Coventry factory workers to pay for X-ray units for the Red Army. She paid her respects at the ruined cathedral in the city. On her return to Russia, she trained other snipers until the end of the war.

Pavlychenko would be immortalised, not only featuring on Soviet postage stamps but the focus of a song by the American folk singer Woody Guthrie during the war itself and the 2015 film, *Battle of Sevastopol*.

THE LAMBETH WALK

Viral hits don't belong solely to the age of YouTube and the Internet. *The Lambeth Walk* is one of the most memorable songs of the wartime era, from the 1937 West-End hit *Me and My Girl*. The song inspired its own dance craze, a strutting cockney jig made famous by the hilarious Lupino Lane.

The Lambeth Walk craze swept the nation, with even King George VI himself joining in with the famous 'Oi!' and it crossed the Atlantic. Britain's paranoid Mass Observation Unit, which reported on the morale of the country, even devoted a chapter of their 1939 book to it. The song was popular in Germany too, much to the lament of die-hard Nazis.

The Ministry of Information used it for their own ends. One of their number, Charles A. Ridley, mockingly edited Leni Riefenstahl's bombastic Nazi masterpiece, *The Triumph of the Will*, by humorously cutting the film. In his edit, *Lambeth Walk –*

Nazi Style, the legions of soldiers are shown marching in time to the song. Their SS goose-steps fall perfectly in time with the music. The uncredited film was distributed to newsreel companies to do with as they pleased.

Joseph Goebbels, the Nazi Minister of Public Enlightenment and Propaganda saw Ridley's cut. It is reported he was so furious that he stormed out of the room, kicking chairs, shouting and swearing. As a result, Ridley earned a place on the *Sonderfahndungsliste G.B.* colloquially known as the Black Book, a list of people to be exterminated if Britain was conquered.

Perhaps the legacy of the song is perfectly summed up in *The Times* newspaper in 1938, 'While dictators rage and statesmen talk, all Europe dances — to The Lambeth Walk.' Take that, Gangnam Style!

THE LAST CRUSADE

Anyone who has seen *Indiana Jones and the Last Crusade* may be surprised to know it's not too far removed from real events. German medievalist Otto Rahn believed that the Holy Grail, the cup from which Jesus drank at the Last Supper, was not only real but has survived and was guarded by the heretical Cathars of medieval France. He became obsessed with the legends of the Grail, Parsifal and the Nibelung cycle of poems, exactly the same pseudo-history which fascinated Hitler and Heinrich Himmler, head of the SS.

Rahn's book, *Crusade Towards the Grail* came to the attention of Himmler and they met in person. Rahn became a member of the SS and was funded to continue his search. He may have soon regretted the attention, as not only was he homosexual, and punished with three months as a prison guard at Dachau but he was possibly Jewish too. 'What was I supposed to do?' he asked, along with millions of other Germans. 'Turn Himmler down?' He resigned from the SS in 1939 but Himmler was devastated by the historian's failures and gave him a choice: suicide or execution. Rahn chose suicide and was found lying, frozen to death in the Tyrol Mountains, six months before the start of the war.

THE LAST TOJO?

Nakamura Teruo was a soldier of the Japanese Imperial Army who held out long after the war was over. He was stationed on the island of Morotai in Indonesia. When the American forces attacked he managed to survive and evade capture. The Americans moved on and continued with their 'island hopping' campaign. Nakamura remained at his post, waiting for orders, for three decades. In the time he waited, he built a shack, tamed a wild boar, took a bird for a pet and sustained himself by farming. He had been declared officially dead in 1945.

An aircraft spotted Nakamura's settlement and offered a reward for his capture. Astonishingly the locals knew about him, and he even had a friend who ran errands, but because he refused to believe the war was over, he eventually gave up and left him to it. The guide explained the Indonesians would have to dress up and act like Japanese soldiers if Nakamura was to surrender. They did, and they arrested the man on 18 December 1974. At the time of his capture, he spoke no Japanese or Chinese because he was actually from the Amis people of Taiwan, an aboriginal tribe who were considered stateless in the 1970s.

Nakamura is the last known soldier of World War Two to surrender. Though a quick search on the internet gives the credit erroneously to a Japanese officer, Hiroo Onoda. Nakamura returned to Taiwan to find his wife remarried and children grown up in a world he did not recognize. He died five years later.

THE LAST TO SURRENDER?

A contender for the last to be liberated from the Reich at the end of the war is a little known small group of islands in the Channel Isles nicknamed 'The Minkies' (Minquiers in the original French). On 23 May, 1945, three weeks after the war had ended, a French fishing boat was at work off the island, and a fisherman noticed a German soldier on the beach. 'We've been forgotten by the British,' the Wehrmacht man told the boat's skipper, Lucien Marie. 'We want to surrender'.

The actual award for the very last to surrender, however, goes to the eleven men of top secret Operation Haudegen (swashbuckler), manning a meteorological station, used to determine weather patterns in Spitzbergen with its never-ending arctic summer. Due to the chaos at the end of the war, the men lost radio contact in May 1945 and were unable to get help, living off their two year supply of rations and fending off polar bears. It was not until 4 September, four months after VE Day, that a Norwegian seal hunting vessel came across them and they surrendered to the captain. The officer handed over his pistol and the captain replied, 'Can I keep this then?' Having been away from home so long, the men were in shock at the state of the nation, particularly Dresden, which had been devastated by

LEBENSBORN

For the Reich to flourish for a thousand years and for the Aryans to become the master race, they needed children, and lots of them. *Lebensborn* e.V (The Fount of Life Registered Association) was set up in December 1935 in Munich. The idea was to increase the Aryan birthrate by breeding racially pure 'specimens' irrespective of marriage or sentimental relationships.

Heinrich Himmler and various government departments believed that the only way to achieve a master-race of superhumans was by weeding out the physically and mentally weak. To this end, the notorious (and top-secret) T.4 programme was set up. The name came from its headquarters at 4, Tiergartenstrasse in Berlin. Run by Philip Bouhler and Dr Karl Brandt, it was state-orchestrated euthanasia. An estimated 50,000 people were murdered by gas or lethal injection between 1939 and 1941.

Among the Nazis policies was the banning of contraception and abortions (there were exceptions along T.4 lines) and financial incentives to mothers who had large families. Childless couples were fined. Mothers with four children would receive a bronze medal, six children would merit silver, and gold was awarded to those who had eight or more. Goebbels encouraged 'healthy eroticism' and had soft pornography produced to get the Aryans in the mood. It clearly worked for him – Magda Goebbels produced six children!

Although socially unacceptable at the time throughout the civilized world, the Nazis also quietly supported single mothers who could receive help from the SS via their *Lebensborn* project. Orphans would be raised and babies delivered in special homes, and given up for adoption if desired by the mother, providing the child was 'pure'.

The more depressing side of the desire to swell the German population, was the kidnapping of blonde-haired and blue-eyed children from occupied eastern countries, who would be stolen from their families then be raised in Germany. This Germanization was not proved at the Nuremberg trials, but it was probably true. The children would then be given new names and 're-educated'. Children who continually complained or cried for their families too much could find themselves sent off to a concentration camp.

Roughly 16,000 children were raised in *Lebensborn* homes; in later years they would be raised in orphanages or occasionally abused by unloving foster parents. They were often unfairly stigmatized as outcasts and Nazis and many suffered psychologically as a result. Children in the occupied countries who had German fathers were also treated badly, even when the relationship was voluntary.

Post war sensationalism peddled the myth that lebensborn included coerced sex with SS men, with drugged 'Aryan' girls producing babies almost on a conveyor-belt system.

THE LEGION OF ST GEORGE

The British Free Corps, also known as the Legion of St George, was the British arm of the Waffen-SS. It was the idea of John Amery, the son of a Conservative half-Jewish politician, who was Secretary of State for India.

His wife had been a prostitute but he was unable to provide her with the extravagant lifestyle she was accustomed to. They moved to France in 1936 following Amery's bankruptcy, and he spread the lie that he worked for General Franco's Intelligence Branch in the Spanish Civil War. Following the German occupation of France in 1940, Joseph Goebbels believed Amery could be a useful pawn for his propaganda and invited him to meet him in Berlin in 1942. In a similar role to 'Lord Haw-Haw' (William Joyce), Amery could become a broadcaster for the 'New British Broadcasting Station', encouraging the British to join the Nazis in their fight against communism.

Amery conceived the idea of a unit of British volunteers in the German army. He was given permission to travel the internment and POW camps and recruit 1,500 volunteers from them. His first speech was a disaster, with only one elderly academic offering to join up. By June 1943 he had recruited only 54 of his 1,500 quota, the strength never being more than 27 at any given time and some lasted only a few days. The volunteers were told they would never have to fight their countrymen and would be sent instead to fight the Red Army on the eastern front.

The lack of take up in the brigade was a disaster in the propaganda stakes. When the war finished the members of the British Free Corps were arrested, and most of the volunteers were treated reasonably mercifully. Some received jail sentences but it was generally accepted they were motivated to fight communism and not British forces. One member told MI5 that he had heard that Hitler's plan was to place Oswald Mosley as Prime Minister and Edward VIII (by then the Duke of Windsor, governing the Bahamas) as king in the event of a Nazi victory. As for John Amery himself, he was arrested and returned to Britain to be tried for treason. He was hanged by Albert Pierrepoint on 19 December 1945 in Wandsworth Prison. The executioner would later say Amery was 'the bravest man he ever hanged' and, at least according to one account, Amery said to him, 'Mr Pierrepoint, I've always wanted to meet you, but not, of course, under these circumstances.'

The British Free Corps and its lack of success was a victory for the British, whereas other countries had volunteered into German foreign legions in their hundreds and thousands. Their impact was minimal, but the sight of SS uniforms with the Union flag on the tunic sleeves has made rich pickings for writers of alternative history ever since.

THE LENINGRAD SYMPHONY

Dimitri Shostakovich was a composer from St Petersburg who wrote the music for one of the world's most surreal concerts. He had been evacuated from his home town of Leningrad and wrote *The Seventh Symphony*. The piece was performed in 1941 throughout Russia, Britain and America and would eventually be performed in Leningrad itself. The Nazis and the Finns had surrounded the city of Leningrad in the Winter War and laid siege to it for a year. The appalling conditions of Leningrad in those years made it a hell on earth. Crime rocketed and the people resorted to eating pets, rats and horses; there were even 2,000 arrests for cannibalism.

But the show must go on and the conductor Karl Eliasberg was ordered to perform Shostakovich's piece. A successful musical performance was seen as an act of defiance and a psychological victory for the Soviets. The performance would require 100 musicians but due to the state of the city and its inhabitants, only fifteen from the local orchestra turned up, with many dead or too ill to perform. Rehearsals were to be six days a week but were frequently interrupted by air raid sirens and attacks and the first rehearsal only went on for fifteen minutes as the starving orchestra did not have the energy to continue. Three would die during rehearsals. The Red Army sent in their own musicians to make up the numbers.

The performance was on 9 August 1942 in Leningrad's Grand Philharmonia Hall. The Russian army even bombed the Axis besiegers on that day in the hope of not having the concert interrupted. The performance went on, with many of the orchestra shivering, starving and exhausted. Loudspeakers and radios broadcast throughout the city and to the Axis soldiers surrounding it. One audience member of the packed hall would later comment on how ill and starving everyone was, but they were still dressed in bow-ties. 'The only thing we feared was that the Germans would start bombing us. I was thinking, "God, let us listen to it to the end."'

The performance did continue to the end, and was met with ecstatic applause. Shostakovich dedicated the *Seventh Symphony* as the *Leningrad Symphony*, in respect to the bravery of the people of the city, who would have to survive another year and a half before the siege was lifted in January 1944. The siege lasted for 842 days and it is estimated 800,000 people starved or froze to death. For those who clung to life, the classical performance echoing through the streets must have been an otherworldly spectacle.

LILI MARLENE

No self-respecting member of the Allies, whether military or civilian, during the Second World War would think of singing the *Horst Wessel* or the *War Song Against England*. Both were Nazi in origin and considered patriotic by Germans. *Lili Marlene* was different, however; it was sung by both sides. Originally called *Song of a Young Sentry*, written by Hans Leip and Norbert Schultz, it was recorded in a German studio by Lale Anderson and sold just 600 copies. It received an astonishing new lease of life however when it was one of the songs broadcast from Yugoslavia and reached the ears of Rommel's Afrika Korps. General Bernard Montgomery's Eighth Army picked it up too and both camps belted it out in the North African campaign.

Concerned about a lack of patriotism, Churchill's government got Tommy Connor (he of *The Biggest Aspidistra in the World*) to rewrite the lyrics. This version was recorded in London by seventeen-year-old Anne Shelton. Later in the war, the Anglo-German divide was neatly closed when Marlene Dietrich, a German who had fled the Nazis, made the song her own in the United States. It even became an Italian operatic number.

THE LITTLE DUTCH GIRLS

The Netherlands has a long feisty history in European politics. Fighting against the might of Spain for their beginnings in the sixteenth century, they emerged as a leading maritime nation a century later, going head to head with Britain for control of the northern fishing market. In the First World War, however, they remained neutral, appalled at the ease with which the Kaiser's army swept through 'neutral' Belgium just miles to the south.

On 10 May 1940, despite being officially neutral again, the Netherlands found themselves facing the German blitzkrieg, far more terrifying than the Kaiser's attack in 1914. This was *Case Yellow*, the code name for a simultaneous attack on the Netherlands, Belgium, Luxembourg and France. At last, the West could now believe that the 'phoney war' was over. Thirty divisions of German Army Group B under General Fedor von Bock swept the northern end of the Siegfried Line and made for the coast, Amsterdam and the Hague.

Five days later, it was all over. Holland has low-lying marshland that could slow an invasion, but had no mountain ranges or deep forests and it was no contest. Compared with other occupations by the Nazis, the German impact om the Netherlands was measured and mild, a 'velvet glove' approach all too rare in the 1940s.

The Oversteegen family knew about Nazi atrocities elsewhere. The war had been raging in the east for eight months by now and rumours had been coming out of Germany itself for years. Trijn, the mother, was a Communist who had already welcomed dissidents fleeing from the Reich, Jews and homosexuals among them. The Dutch Resistance approached her for support and her teenaged daughters, Freddie and Truus, readily agreed.

Often wearing their old school uniforms, the sisters flirted with local Wehrmacht units, young men who missed their girlfriends and wives and could be seduced fairly easily. On one occasion, Truus went for a walk in the woods with an SS officer and rather than the slap and tickle he expected, he met members of the Resistance, who shot him! The girls almost certainly killed men themselves, shooting soldiers as they cycled passed on their bikes. At other times, they sheltered Jewish children, not much younger than they were, keeping them away from the trains that were taking them for 'resettlement' in the east.

Children are often caught up in war situations and the danger was very real. One of their cell, Hannie Schaft, known to the Germans as 'the girl with the red hair' was caught and executed by Dutch Nazis three weeks before the war ended.

Both Oversteegen girls survived and were officially decorated by the Dutch government in 2014. Truus died two years later and Freddie in 2018. What they had done and what they had seen went to their graves with them.

LORD HAW-HAW

William Joyce, nicknamed Lord Haw-Haw for his posh accent, was one of the most memorable figures of the war. He was born in Brooklyn, New York, but his family returned to Ireland when he was a child. Later he lived in Britain, obtained a London university degree and applied for the Army, before eventually becoming involved in conservatism and fascism. He was attacked while stewarding a Conservative Party meeting in October 1924 by communists, leaving him with a deep scar across his face. Joyce contended that his attackers were Jews.

In 1932, he joined Oswald Mosley's British Union of Fascists, and became a popular and talented orator. He soon rose through the ranks eventually becoming Director of Propaganda and then deputy leader. Due to a difference in opinions, Mosley and Joyce fell out and he was eventually dismissed from the party. Hearing rumours that the British government intended to arrest him for his Nazi sympathies, Joyce fled to Germany with his wife in 1939, less than a month before the beginning of the war. This was the period when foreigners and anyone of dubious political affiliations could be rounded up under the paranoid government's Defence Regulation 18B and Joyce was taking no chances.

He soon found employment as a radio broadcaster with the Berlin *Rundfunkhaus* station. His English language broadcasts from the Reich became extremely popular in Britain. In a country smothered by censorship, Lord Haw-Haw's show was a rare window into the thoughts and opinion of the enemy. It may have been considered disloyal for Britons to listen to enemy propaganda but Joyce's message and his stage American-Irish-upper-class twang were so preposterous that his broadcasts were nearly as popular as Tommy Handley's *ITMA* comedy show.

Joyce continued his broadcasts throughout the war, receiving the War Merit Cross from Hitler. As the tide turned and defeat was imminent for the Nazis, Joyce can clearly be heard becoming agitated and distressed, frustrated with Britain for its 'war-mongering' and its blindness to the threat of the Soviet Union.

In the final days of the war, Joyce gave his final rambling, drunken and sometimes incomprehensible broadcast from Hamburg, a last desperate appeal from a man whose world was crumbling around him.

He was captured by the British at Flensburg near the Danish border and accidentally shot, perhaps appropriately, in the backside! He was tried for treason at the Old Bailey, despite the fact he was not a British citizen and was found guilty. His appeal was overturned. Joyce remained unwavering in his views until the end. He was hanged by the executioner Albert Pierrepoint on 3 January 1946 and is the last person to be executed for treason in Britain.

But Joyce was not the only traitorous broadcaster. American-born Mildred Gillars became 'Axis Sally', having moved to Germany in the 1920s. She told American GIs to 'go home and forget the war'. Arrested by the Allies in 1945, she served twelve years in a federal prison.

Less pernicious, perhaps, was Tokyo Rose, broadcasting to the GIs from 1943. She was probably Iva Toguri, an American citizen with Japanese parents. Convicted of treason after the war, she served eleven years in prison and was granted a pardon by President Gerald Ford in 1977.

THE LYKOV FAMILY

It's occasionally said that ignorance is bliss, and for one Russian family, in a war that claimed more than 20,000,000 of their countrymen, this must arguably be the case.

In 1936, under threat from communists, a couple, Karp and Akulina Lykov, who were 'Old Believers', fled with their two children. Two more were born to them while in self-imposed exile. The family of six lived apart from society in the vast wilderness of Tashtypsky district of Khakassia, Siberia.

The troubles of the war passed them by. The family seems to have had no outside contact until 1978, when a geologist's helicopter accidentally came across their dwelling. When outsiders finally spoke to the Lykov family, they were not even aware that the Second World War had happened. When offered the chance to reintegrate into society, they declined.

All of the family were dead by 1988 except the fourth child Agafia Lykova, who had no human contact except her family for her first 35 years. She was born in 1943 and continued to live alone and self-sufficiently until 2016 when she was airlifted to hospital. Agafia did not like the modern world -- the unbearable noise and air quality of the cities made her feel sick and busy roads were terrifying. She happily returned to the wild once her hospital visit was over.

Perhaps Bear Grylls and Cody Lundin could learn a thing or two from her?

MADAGASCAR PLAN

The Nazis were clearly obsessed as to what to do with all the Jewish people throughout Europe getting on with their lives and generally minding their own business. The 'final solution' to this 'problem' is horrific and well known, but there were other plans long before that. One of the oddest was the idea of deporting Europe's Jewish families to the African island of Madagascar.

Mass deportations were seriously considered, and conversations between Germans, Poles, French and Britons took place to discuss it. Based on detailed reports from the French Foreign Office, the island of Madagascar, a French colonial possession seemed a suitable option. The plan being for a million Jewish people a year to be transferred to the island over a four-year period, though it was argued the island could not support so many.

Finance for this project was to be found from the confiscated income and property of the Jewish people themselves. The Reich were prepared to allow the Jewish citizens of Madagascar to have their own administration and government (in the areas not needed for military purposes), although the island would be under the command of a police governor of the SS. Also, the Nazis believed the concentration of so many people in one place and at the mercy of Nazi Germany would ensure the good behaviour of the USA and its Jewish population.

An intercepted letter from a top Nazi Franz Rademacher discussing the plan contained the following:

'Use can be made for propaganda purposes of the generosity shown by Germany in permitting cultural, economic, administrative and legal self-administration to the Jews; it can be emphasized at the same time that our German sense of responsibility towards the world forbids us to make the gift of a sovereign state to a race which has had no independent state for thousands of years: this would still require the test of history.'

After the *Luftwaffe* failed to defeat the RAF or force a surrender in the Battle of Britain, the Reich shelved this idea. On 10 February 1942, the plan was officially abandoned and the 'evacuation to the east' (Holocaust) was their insane proposal. The Nazis can't take full credit for this idea of mass deportation, though. The concept of deportation of Europe's Jews to Madagascar was originally conceived by German scholar Paul de Legarde in 1885. In 1937, the Polish investigated the proposal themselves, though they concluded the island could only support a few hundred families at most.

Despite Nazi plans to stop a Jewish homeland that would 'require the test of history', the state of Israel was created in 1948, just three years after the war ended.

THE MAD COLONEL

A conflict like the Second World War throws up heroes and heroines of all shapes and sizes, but few stand taller than Lt Col Robert Blaire Mayne, DSO, known universally as 'Paddy'. It was only his select friends, however, who called him that to his face, because he was a huge, unpredictable Irishman and nobody could be sure exactly what he would do next. His favourite song was the German import *Lili Marlene*, and the First Special Air Service, of which he was colonel, often sang it into the small hours at their celebrated parties, in which 'conspicuous amounts' of liquor were consumed.

1SAS had its origins with the Long Range Desert group, a bunch of maverick commandos fighting in North Africa. Physically tough and highly-trained commandos, they and their naval equivalent – the Special Boat Services – had a reputation second to none for getting things done. They were all volunteers and the thought of being returned to their original units was the worst shame that could befall any of them.

His men worshipped Paddy Mayne, whether he was singing in the Mess, tackling them hard in a game of rugger or broadcasting over the camp radio in the days after D-Day when the SAS were scattered behind enemy lines. But he impressed them most when he led from the front, as he always did, facing every danger that the Wehrmacht could throw at them. Six foot three, a boxer and a former Irish rugby international, the colonel had made his name in North Africa before launching a series of spectacular raids on enemy airfields. He was determined, as many commanders were not, never to lose a man in the field. He slept in the open wherever he could and disliked the 'indoors' atmosphere of the officers' Mess. He had an air of carelessness about him and a fighter's instinct for danger. He missed nothing. A first class marksman, his eagle eyes were everywhere. He was known to be kind and generous over army infringements, but to him, the one unforgiveable sin was a man not wearing his beret straight. The sloppy wearer of the headgear at an angle was looking for trouble.

Perhaps Mayne's most dazzling exploit was while he was operating in conjunction with the Long Range Desert Group in North Africa. The unit launched a daring attack on the airfield of Sidi Haneish, thirty miles south of Mersa Matruh, a base for Stuka divebombers. The SAS, under David Stirling, went in, literally with all guns blazing, hitting the airfield at 1.30am. As luck would have it, a plane coming in at that moment lit up the whole strip and gave the SAS a spotlight for their targets. They drove their jeeps between the parked aircraft, shredding them with Vickers machinegun fire.

Paddy Mayne, having sprinted across open ground to plant a bomb under the wing of a Heinkel III and see it blow sky high, dashed into an outbuilding just as drunken Luftwaffe pilots were tumbling out of bed to see what the commotion was. Mayne opened up with his Bren gun and may have been responsible for more kills that day than any of the airborne aces of the war! Afterwards, with the airfield destroyed and daylight dawning, Medical officer Malcolm Playdell saw Mayne lolling in the back of a jeep reading a paperback. His comment on the raid? 'Oh, it was quite good craic!'

For several men of the SAS, the end of the war brought boredom and bitterness. Mayne himself drove his Riley sports car into a parked lorry after a few pints too many, in December 1955.

There is one curious story about him that has never been explained. For reasons unknown, he despised the broadcaster Richard Dimbleby who reported, for example, on the death camps discovered by the Allies in the autumn of 1944 and early 1945. He threatened to kill him on more than one occasion. Had he been serious and had he done so, how different the BBC of the post war world would have been!

THE MAD HATTER

Among the 'fellow travellers of the Right' who championed the cause of Fascism in the 1930s, James Larratt Battersby stands out. His family were successful hat makers at a time when stylish headgear was an essential fashion accessory for both sexes. The family produced 12,000 hats a week and employed over 1,000 people.

The Russian Revolution of 1917, based on the Communist doctrine of Karl Marx, had spread its ideas beyond the confines of the Soviet Union and Fascism had grown up as a rival orthodoxy. Whereas Britain was known for its tolerant, middle-of-the-road politics, countries like Germany, Italy, Spain and to a lesser extent, France, became caught up in the extremism of the age.

James Battersby joined the British Union of Fascists, the pro-Mussolini and pro-Hitler movement founded by Oswald Mosley, a prominent politician disillusioned by the spinelessness of the government of the day. Battersby ran the Stockport branch of the party, which became increasingly unpopular over its attitude towards Jews and, after September 1939, its support of the enemy. Along with several others, Battersby was interred at Camp 020, Latchmere House, under Regulation 18B which dealt with espionage and aliens.

He was eventually moved to the Isle of Man where he met Thomas Guillame St. Barbe Baker who believed that Hitler was the reincarnation of Jesus Christ. This was not too surprising – after all, millions of Germans saw him in the same light. In 1943 Battersby and Baker set up the legion of Christian Reformers Unity, a manifesto (along the lines of Hitler's *Mein Kampf*) which placed the Führer as God's champion against the devil.

After the war, as a shattered country tried to get back to normality, the deranged pair set up Kingdom House in seventeenth century premises at Peworth, Sussex, donated by another fellow traveller, the barrister W.G. Barlow. Here, a commune of Fascists held forth. They bought a bust of their dead Fuhrer from an auction and draped the building with swastikas. In 1952 Battersby did his best to interrupt the memorial service at the Cenotaph in Whitehall, ranting his Fascist nonsense before being arrested. The previous year he had published *The Holy Book and Testament of Adolf Hitler*, not exactly a runaway best seller.

In 1955 James Battersby killed himself by jumping from the Mersey ferry. His head was taken off by the paddles. In the suicide note he sent to a newspaper beforehand, he wrote 'My work here is complete. I follow the Fuhrer to glory and eternity. Through the sacrifice of the Aryan martyrs our world victory is assured. Heil Hitler.'

'MAD JACK' CHURCHILL

John Malcolm Thorpe Fleming Churchill was one of the most colourful and eccentric characters to emerge from the war. His nickname 'Mad Jack' was well earned. He graduated from the Royal Military College in Sandhurst in 1926 and served with the Manchester Regiment in Burma. After leaving the army ten years later, he worked as a newspaper editor; male model; actor and bagpiper in Raoul Walsh's *The Thief of Bagdad* and represented Britain in the World Archery Championships in Oslo in 1939.

With the outbreak of the war Churchill reenlisted and joined the British Expeditionary Force in France. His unit ambushed a German patrol near L'Épinette in the Pas de Calais, with Churchill using a bow and arrow to kill a soldier, the only known death by arrow in the entire war and the most recent confirmed archer kill in combat. Churchill insisted on carrying a broadsword and believed that any officer without one was 'improperly dressed', (this despite the fact that no English regiment *ever* carried a broadsword which was reserved for Scottish regiments).

After the evacuation of Dunkirk, Churchill signed up for the commandos in June 1940, a new unit developed by Winston Churchill (no known relation) to carry out raids against the Reich. During an amphibious assault on a German garrison in Vågsøy, Norway, Churchill, still a keen piper, began a solo performance of 'March of the Cameron Men' inside the first landing craft to disembark. Whilst in Italy, he took 42 Germans prisoner with an NCO and his broadsword. A raid that did not go to plan, due to the hesitancy of supporting partisans in Yugoslavia, saw the survivors of Churchill's unit all killed by mortar fire except him. He played on his bagpipes while waiting for his own death, which didn't come. As he was playing 'Will Ye No Come Back Again?', he was knocked unconscious by a nearby explosion. As a commando he should have been executed. Hitler's decree of 18 October 1942 ran;

'From now on, all enemies on so-called commando missions in Europe or Africa, challenged by German troops ... whether armed or unarmed, in battle or in flight, are to be slaughtered to the last man.'

The Wehrmacht captain who captured Churchill had either never read that or he was not prepared to follow that order. He refused to hand him over to the SS. 'You are a soldier, as I am. I refuse to allow these civilian butchers to deal with you.'

In September 1944 as the Allies pushed the Germans back across France, Churchill was captured and sent to Sachsenhausen, Berlin's own concentration camp. He escaped but was recaptured near Rostock. As the war came to a close, the SS guards abandoned the prisoners and Churchill walked 90 miles to Verona, where he met up with an American patrol. The close of the war was sad news for a man like Churchill, who commented 'If it wasn't for those damn Yanks, we could have kept the war going another ten years'.

THE MADONNA OF STALINGRAD

The Siege of Stalingrad, fought between August 1942 and February 1943, was a hellish battle of unbelievable proportions that would claim more soldiers' lives than the entire Western front. An estimated 1.7 million men were killed, wounded or captured. This battle was the eye of the storm and the German defeat there would mark the beginning of the end of the Reich.

Leutnant Kurt Reuber was a doctor in the *Wehrmacht*, stationed near the front lines of the battle to receive the wounded and dying. He was a talented artist and a Protestant pastor before the war. To cheer up the soldiers, he drew a sketch that would become known as 'the Stalingrad Madonna', a maternal image of Jesus being cradled by Mary. All who entered the trench where he worked would see it, and some – coming from any number of unimaginable horrors – would break down in tears at the sight of it. The dug-out was too cramped to work properly and he had to stand on a stool to look down on the charcoal work as he drew it.

In a letter home, Reuber explained that the image was meant to represent 'security' and 'mother love' for those who saw it and contained the text, 'light, life and love.'

A Christmas day celebration among the medical staff and the sick was cut short by nearby explosions, killing many in attendance. The charcoal Madonna was flown out by Dr William Grosse, Reuber's commanding officer, in the last plane to leave the area before General von Paulus' Sixth Army surrendered to the Soviets. Reuber was captured and died in a Russian POW camp in 1944; his letters and his pictures were returned to his family.

The Stalingrad Madonna remains a powerful image; that such a piece of art could be created in the hell on earth of Stalingrad did much to reconcile foes after the war. The picture now hangs proudly in the Kaiser Wilhelm Memorial Church in Berlin. Copies are also on display in cathedrals in Coventry and Volgograd.

THE MAGICIAN WHO WON THE WAR

Jasper Maskelyne was a British stage magician, whose grandfather had been the most famous illusionist on the Victorian stage. With the outbreak of war, Maskelyne joined the Royal Engineers where he convinced his superiors to let him put his skills to use. One account suggests he impressed officers by creating the illusion of a German warship in the Thames using mirrors and a model. He was transferred to the Camouflage Development and Training Centre at Farnham Castle in 1940 but found it dull. He entertained his comrades every evening but, as one remembered, was 'rather unsuccessful' at disguising 'concrete pill-boxes' which was what he was really there for. He went on to work with the secret service department MI9 in Cairo. However, by 1942 the British command appeared unimpressed, and Maskelyne was now being used as entertainment for the troops with magic and card tricks.

Opinion on his contribution to the war is divided. Some claim he created entire armies in the desert and could hide the Suez Canal. Others point out there is no record of this and the magician was more interested in tall tales and creating his own legend. He did design gadgets for captured POWs, such as a comb that could turn into a knife and a compass inside a jacket button.

Maskelyne's tragedy is that he spent so much time telling everybody how spectacular his 'magic' was that he probably came to believe it.

THE MAGINOT LINE

The First World War had devastated France. Four years of brutal, near-static fighting achieved little, except millions dead and millions more wounded physically and psychologically. The Great War, allegedly in the name of liberty, had resulted in little more than bankrupt nations, crumbling empires and fascist and communist dictators springing up everywhere across a ruined continent.

With a bitter Germany growing increasingly vocal and militaristic, the French were taking no chances. In the 1930s the French began to construct a series of fortifications along their border with Germany. Named after the Minister of War, Andre Maginot, this impressive chain of forts, including twenty-two huge fortresses and thirty-six smaller ones, was believed to be impenetrable. Any German attack would surely be deterred and, if not, the line could comfortably hold off any attack long enough for reinforcements to arrive.

The Maginot Line is in this book not because there is anything particularly weird about it - it was conceived and built with skill and imagination - but for the fact that it was a complete strategic failure. It led to a degree of confidence in French thinking, ignoring the competence of German military planning. After a year of the 'phoney war', when little happened in the West, the German *blitzkrieg* avoided the fortifications. Instead, the German forces bypassed them and advanced through Belgium. Since 1918, methods of waging war had changed with the advent of planes and tanks. The Maginot Line was a relic of the past. The British, French, Dutch and Belgians were caught on the back foot, and, with the exception of the British, all would be conquered. As for the British themselves, they were forced to scramble back to Britain via Dunkirk.

With the French armistice on 22 June 1940, the invincible fortresses became redundant. The soldiers defending it, who were willing to fight on, were ordered to march out and surrender, spending the rest of the war as forced labour or in POW camps.

In 1944, roles were reversed, with the Germans defending the line against the Americans – who took a page from the German military planner's war book, and largely by-passed it.

THE MAN WHO NEARLY SHOT HITLER

Henry Tandey was the most highly decorated British soldier of the First World War, receiving the Victoria Cross, the Distinguished Conduct Medal and the Military Medal and was mentioned five times in Despatches. A career soldier, he joined the Green Howards Regiment in 1910, fighting at the First Ypres, the Somme and Passchendaele. He is also remembered for one apparent moment that, if true, could have changed the course of history.

On 28 September 1918, the British took the village of Marcoing from the Germans. As the firefight raged, it is alleged that an injured German soldier entered Tandey's line of sight but he took pity on him and did not fire, saying, 'I took aim but couldn't shoot a wounded man. So I let him go.'

In 1938, during the failing peace talks between Britain and Germany over the Munich crisis, the Prime Minister, Neville Chamberlain, met Hitler in Bavaria. A photograph of Tandey carrying a wounded comrade emerged in the British newspapers, and was then painted by an Italian artist named Fortunino Matania. A copy of that picture, *Painting of Menin Crossroads*, was in Hitler's possession. 'That man came so near to killing me that I thought I should never see Germany again,' the Fuhrer explained to Chamberlain. He then asked to have his best wishes and gratitude passed on to the man who spared his life.

The truth of this story is difficult to separate from the legend and official records are not supportive. However, it *is* known that Hitler personally requested a copy of Matania's painting in 1937. Henry Tandey never denied the incident either and believed it to be true. In 1940, as Britain was on the run from Germany and defeat seemed imminent, Tandey, by then back in his native Leamington, said he regretted sparing him, 'If only I had known what he would turn out to be. When I saw all the people, woman and children he had killed and wounded I was sorry to God I let him go.'

THE MAN WHO NEVER WAS

Operation Barclay was the codename for a deception. The Allies had to convince the German High Command that their objective, early in 1943, was the invasion of Sardinia. In fact, it was Sicily. To pull this off, Operation Mincemeat was developed as an offshoot of Barclay and was the brainchild of Cand always close to the shore. Thanks to their ingenuity, the forty-five crewmen finally made it to Fremantle, Australia, after what must have been the longest and most bizarre eight days of their lives.harles Cholmondeley of the RAF and Ewen Montague of the Royal Naval Reserve. The idea, like something out of a spy novel, was to dump a body at sea so that it would be washed up on the coast of neutral Spain and the papers it was carrying (false information re the invasion) would find their way into German hands.

The whole thing seemed unbelievable. In fact, younger cinema-goers, seeing the movie version in 1956, assumed that it was fiction. The biggest problem was finding a suitable corpse. With the help of the legendary forensic scientist Bernard Spilsbury and an obliging coroner, Bentley Purchase, an apparent suicide was found that fitted the bill. Mentally ill Glyndwr Michael had appeared to have killed himself with rat poison, alternatively he may have mistaken it for a drink. The chemical reaction that resulted made it appear that the death was caused by pneumonia. Michael, who had no known relatives, became Acting Major William Martin of the Royal Marines. He was even given a girlfriend, 'Pam', who was actually Nancy Leslie, a typist with MI5. Her photo and love letters were found in the dead man's wallet when he was washed up from a fictitious plane crash on 30 April in Huelva, where he was buried with full military honours on 2 May.

Messages intercepted from the Ultra codebreakers at Bletchley Park proved that the Germans had fallen for Mincemeat hook, line and sinker and directed troops in the wrong direction as a result. On 9 July, the Allies invaded Sicily and it took three days for any serious opposition to arrive. 'Operation Mincemeat' was perhaps the most successful deception of the entire war and saved thousands of Allied lives.

THE MAN WHO SURVIVED

Tsutomu Yamaguchi is the only person acknowledged by the Japanese government to have survived the nightmare of the atomic blasts of both Hiroshima *and* Nagasaki. By the summer of 1945, the American president, Harry S. Truman, made the fateful decision to force a Japanese surrender quickly by using the atomic bomb that American scientists under Robert Oppenheimer had been working on. Having worked for Mitsubishi Heavy Industries for years, Yamaguchi was in Hiroshima on a three-month assignment. It was 8.15am on 6 August 1945 and he had just doubled back for the railway pass he had forgotten. The B-29 Superfortress *Enola Gay* flew overhead and dropped its deadly bombload three kilometres away. This was 'Little Boy' and its blast instantly killed around 80,000 people. Yamaguchi was left burned, temporarily blinded and deaf in one ear.

The next day Yamaguchi left the devastated city to return home to Nagasaki where he was reunited with his family. As he was explaining what had happened to Hiroshima to the company director on 9 August, a second bomb, 'Fat Man' was dropped at 11am from the B-29 *Bockscar*, bringing carnage yet again and ending tens of thousands of lives including radiation poisoning that began to spread among Allied POWs, and Korean forced labourers as well as Japanese in the town. This time, Yamaguchi was unhurt, but had a fever for a week. He became a campaigner for the abolition of atomic weapons and died in 2010 at the age of ninety-three.

THE MANNERHEIM RECORDING

The Hitler and Mannerheim recording was the secret tape of a 1942 conversation between the German leader and Carl Gustaf Mannerheim, Finland's commander-in-chief.

It was the 4 June, and Mannerheim's 75th birthday, so Hitler decided to pop by and pass on his best wishes. Finland at the time was a co-belligerent of the Nazis, although this alliance was based pragmatically on the survival of his nation. The Soviet Union had made their intentions clear, and the last-minute withdrawal of Allied support in the 1939 Winter War left Finland stuck between a rock and a hard place. Better to fight one megalomaniac than two at the same time. Mannerheim was involved in a delicate game and was embarrassed to learn that Hitler was coming to see him. Mannerheim was keen not to give the Fuehrer's arrival the appearance of an official, state visit, so they met in secret aboard Mannerheim's train for dinner.

Thor Damen was an engineer for the Yle broadcasting company and was permitted to record the beginning of their conversation; the official birthday congratulations and Mannerheim's official response. Unknown to Hitler however, the recording carried on in secret for a further eleven minutes. Upon realising Damen was still taping, the furious SS demanded he stop immediately. He ended the tape, but bizarrely, rather than destroying it, the SS allowed him to keep it as long as he promised to seal it up and never use it. Damen handed over the tape to his employer Yle, who kept the tape secret until 1957, when it was publicly announced and made available.

The recording gives an interesting insight into Hitler's candid thoughts. He is clearly sincerely shocked by the production capability and fighting power of the Red Army and dismayed by the Italians crumbling in the face of the Allies. He also discusses Romanian oil fields.

It was one of only a few surviving recordings where Hitler is not hysterically shouting, and the only one in which he speaks candidly and casually. There is no doubt that Hitler's power was in his voice and the skilled rhetoric that he knew stirred up his people. Here, in the tapes, he was more natural, less careful as to what he allowed let slip. Away, as he thought, from recordings, he was less cautious about what the public might learn.

What is weird here is not the secret recording, but the interest it has generated. It says much about the morbid fascination we have for Hitler and the myth he tried to create for himself that to hear him speaking normally is a revelation. Many thought it must be a hoax. Even Hitler's bodyguard, when hearing the tape, was not entirely convinced.

The train coach where this meeting took place can be visited to this day. You'll find it plonked next to a Shell garage off a main road near Sastamala where it's occasionally opened to the public.

MASS-OBSERVATION

The Mass-Observation project was a 1937 initiative set up by South African communist journalist, Charles Madge, and two of his English friends, Tom Harrisson and Humphrey Jennings. Their idea was to highlight the disparity between what the heavily censored newspapers were reporting and what people on the street actually thought. They published their manifesto for the concept as being *Anthropology at Home*.

Ordinary folk were asked a series of random (and frankly, quite odd) questions: about behaviour at war memorials, the behaviour and gestures of motorists towards each other, and people's behaviour in bathrooms. And they were asked to keep diaries of their thoughts and feelings on the 12th of each month. This led to negative reactions to the first report, published in 1937, since the opinions within included responses to the Coronation of King George VI and Queen Elizabeth after the Abdication that diverged from the intended propaganda. However, Mass-Observation was soon recognised as a valuable tool. In 1939, when Mass-Observation showed that the public was not responding well to a poster campaign, the Ministry of Information tweaked their propaganda accordingly.

Some people were (understandably) perplexed by the project, feeling it was an inappropriate and unnecessary intrusion into people's private lives and thoughts. Useful information included the average time to drink a pint -- about 7.3 minutes and that men drank fastest on a Friday, and slowest on a Tuesday. Another respondent moaned at the lack of charisma of Winston Churchill. 'He's no speaker, is he?' they complained.

'Liking' your partner was said to be the most important aspect of keeping a marriage going. The Lambeth Walk dance craze puzzled some participants, with one observer duly noting the men were holding the women inappropriately. Skippy, their pet rabbit went missing, wrote one, only to discover years later that Skippy had been served to them as dinner due to rationing. A father whose child was evacuated to the countryside, was upset by the 'fancy manners' his offspring had picked up.

After the war, a 1949 report from a gay man explains what a lovely time he had in Brighton, which even then was becoming a haven for homosexuals and those with alternative lifestyles. Others reported what a pain their neighbours were.

The interviews are a remarkable and charming glimpse into the past, and the sheer variety of the comments shared by the public is often amusing and poignant. For those of us in the modern age who are annoyed by the thousands of questionnaires, feedback forms and surveys that seem to appear out of nowhere, perhaps we can aim some of our grievances at Mass-Observation for starting them all.

The Mass-Observation archive can be accessed on the internet today. *Britain by Mass-Observation* (1939), published by Penguin, is another fascinating read.

MAX HEILIGER

Max Heiliger didn't exist. He was a fictional character invented by Walter Funk, president of the Reichsbank and Himmler's SS as a front for the possessions stolen from victims of Nazi genocide.   The name was a cynical and supposedly humorous play on the German word for Saint and was the code of the SS bank accounts used to launder anything from wedding rings, cash and gold fillings from the dead and imprisoned during the Holocaust. The items were also referred to as 'the property of resettled Jews' and filled several Berlin bank vaults by the end of 1942. The valuables and possessions of these 'resettled' people were then sold in pawn shops or melted down into gold bars. This internal embezzlement scheme helped self-fund the Holocaust.

Funk himself was found guilty on three counts at the Nuremburg trials and was sentenced to life imprisonment at Spandau. He was released in 1960 because of ill health.

MAXIMILIAN KOLBE

As in any war, individual acts of heroism stand out among the carnage and misery, but few can match the quiet intensity of the 'saint of Auschwitz', Maximilian Kolbe. He was a Catholic priest from Poland and as a child in 1906, he was visited by a vision of the Virgin Mary. He said –

'That night I asked the Mother of God what was to become of me. Then she came to me holding two crowns, one white, the other red. She asked me if I was willing to accept either of these crowns. The white one meant that I should persevere in purity, and the red that I should become a martyr. I said that I would accept them both.'

Kolbe would spend the rest of his life promoting the veneration of Mary.

Kolbe had a varied and interesting life with the Franciscan order, even founding a monastery in Japan which miraculously survived the atomic bomb blast on Nagasaki which struck the other side of the hill on which it was built. When Poland was occupied by the Nazis, the priest gave sanctuary to 2,000 Jews in the friary of Niepokalanów, realising perfectly well that his kindness could lead to his death. He continued to publish many written works on his views of fascism from the monastery, eventually being arrested for it and finally ending up in Auschwitz.

Kolbe's treatment there was appalling. He was often the victim of violence from the kapos, the brutal warders whose job it was to make inmates' lives a misery. When a small number of prisoners escaped, the Nazis decided to punish ten prisoners with starvation in an underground bunker as a deterrent to others. Ten men were randomly selected and one of them cried out, 'My wife! My children!' Kolbe offered to take his place.

Inside the underground bunker, Kolbe prayed for the nine souls with him. Without food and water, all of them would be dead with two weeks, except the priest. The guards were astonished to see that the man was still alive. How did they respond to this miracle, when a man shouldn't last more than three days? They gave him a lethal injection of carbolic acid. He went to the fires on 15 August 1941, the day of the assumption of the Virgin Mary.

The man that Kolbe swapped places with was a Polish army sergeant named Franciszek Gajowniczek. After the war he was reunited with his wife, though sadly his sons had already been killed by the Russians. Franciszek never forgot what the priest did for him and championed his saviour's message, saying to an American church through a translator, 'so long as he ... has breath in his lungs, he would consider it his duty to tell people about the heroic act of love by Maximilian Kolbe'. Franciszek died in 1995.

In 1982, Kolbe was declared a saint by Pope John Paul II who said he was 'the patron saint of our difficult century'.

MEIN KAMPF

What does every girl want on her wedding day? A copy of *Mein Kampf,* of course. 'My Struggle', was Hitler's famous autobiography written while in Landsberg Prison following the aborted Munich Putsch. It was considered a holy book to the most ardent Nazis. At every wedding throughout Germany, the happy couple would receive a leather bound copy of their leader's writings and every member of the armed forces had to own a copy too.

This wasn't quite as altruistic as it seems, as the local council was forced to buy their own copies using taxpayers' funds, landing Hitler a ten per cent royalty for each sale. By 1939, the book had been translated into eleven languages and sold 5.2 million copies and a special Anniversary Edition was produced, combining Volumes One and Two.

The icing on the cake was that once Hitler was in charge (becoming Chancellor in

1933), he decided he shouldn't have to pay any taxes and wrote off his own debts, including the slice of royalties that should have gone to his publisher.

Interestingly, despite the book's commercial success, Hitler seemed to regret writing it after he became chancellor. *Mein Kampf* was finally republished in Germany in 2016, the first time since the end of the war. His second book, largely on foreign policy, sank without trace, to the extent that it doesn't even have a title, being known simply as 'Hitler's second book'. Only two copies are known to exist and one of them was discovered in a German air raid shelter by an American officer. Even less readable than *Mein Kampf, der Zweites Buch* was badly translated into English in 1962 and an authoritative version as recently as 2003.

MEN IN HIGH CASTLES

The Man in the High Castle is an American television series whose dystopian plot is that the Germans and the Japanese won the Second World War and what happens in the United States as a result. There have been a number of movies and novels on this theme since the war, but there are two books that follow this line, written before the war began.

In 1924 an Austrian film company made *The City Without Jews* based on a book written two years earlier by Hugo Bettauer. At that time, the Nazi Party in Germany was new, tiny and on the lunatic fringe of politics. It barely existed at all in Austria. A year later, Arthur Landsberger's *Berlin without Jews* took up the theme. The plot line follows the fortunes of two families, the Jewish Oppenheims and the Lutheran Rudenbergs. A far right political party takes control of Germany and deports its Jews as the rest of the country looks on and does nothing.

What is weird about both these books – and films – is that they were eerily prophetic at a time when such a genre barely existed in fiction. But the endings in both are happier than in reality. In *Berlin Without Jews*, the country realizes that is a poorer place without them and invites them back. In *City Without Jews*, the whole thing turns out to be a bad dream!

The ghettoes and the death camps were not a bad dream, whatever Holocaust deniers claim today, but both books' authors faced nightmares of their own. Two months after Hitler became Chancellor of Germany, Arthur Landsberger killed himself. And Hugo Bettauer was murdered soon after the movie premiered, by Otto Rothstock, a hero of the Right who had recently been released from a psychiatric institution.

THE MEN WHO BROKE INTO AUSCHWITZ

When war broke out in September 1939, very few people had ever heard of Oswiecium, an obscure little village in Poland. By 1945, as Auschwitz-Birkenau, it was the most notorious of the death camps and remains today a grim testimony to the Holocaust and the evils of Nazi Germany. To anyone who knows it, it was hell on earth and the last place where anyone would go voluntarily. Or was it?

Witold Pilecki

When Poland fell in the September war, 1939, Witold Pilecki joined the resistance.

As veteran of the Polish-Soviet war of 1919-21, he was used to danger and hardship and did not take invasion lying down. Rumours began to spread early in 1940 of a camp being built on the site of an old army barracks which had been converted into a tobacco factory. It was surrounded by stagnant ponds, but the new buildings seemed to include bath-houses and corpse-cellars.

Hitler's plan was to obliterate Poland as a country and the Poles as a race and the Resistance watched every move by the army of occupation. The Wehrmacht had been followed quickly by the SS einsatzgruppen, death squads who rounded up Jews and troublemakers and hanged them from lamp-posts in towns across the country. They routinely rounded up 'undesirables' and herded them into the nearest camp. One of these men, who had loitered deliberately in order to be included, was Pilecki, using the name Tomasz Serafinski. 'Reality and logic,' he wrote, 'disappeared as soon as you went beyond the wires.' As a partisan, he kept his head down while secretly smuggling in food, medication and clothing. He also amassed astonishing information as to how Auschwitz was run.

Pilecki's first reports reached Britain early in 1941, but it was not until later that year that he wrote of a massive extension to the camp called Birkenau. Prisoners died at a frightening rate, overworked and starved in what was regarded as a particularly brutal labour camp. The capos, who carried out routine torture on the prisoners, were often Poles themselves and were worse, if anything, than the German guards.

Anyone who opposed the Nazi regime ended up at Auschwitz. Dissidents, like Pilecki himself, starved and stood for hours in the freezing weather of the parade ground, alongside Jews, homosexuals and gypsies – anyone who did not fit the image of the Aryan elite. Pilecki saw with his own eyes the murder of Maximilian Kolbe, a priest who offered himself in the place of fellow-Pole Francis Gajowniczek, on the grounds that the priest had no family and Gajowniczek was a married man.

While Auschwitz-Birkenau was morphing into a death-camp with genocide being carried out on an industrial scale, nothing was done in the West, despite Pilecki's reports. The decision must have been an agonizing one. Had the British and French been able to bomb the place (and France had fallen by this time) then the SS would have ensured that *everyone* died at Auschwitz. The destruction of railway lines would barely have slowed things down.

Pilecki stayed in the camp until 1943, until he was moved two miles away to work in the bakery. He cut telephone lines, disabled alarms, overpowered a guard and escaped using a cut key. He re-joined the Resistance and wrote *Witold's Report*, a harrowing account still available today.

But fate had not quite finished with Witold Pilecki. He offered his services to the Resistance in Warsaw that had been fighting a grim guerrilla war from the city's sewers for three years. Rumours abounded that Stalin's Red Army was on its way west and, motivated by this, the Poles launched an offensive in April 1943. The SS had vowed to liquidate the ghetto in three days; in fact, it took them twenty-eight. Among the prisoners, fewer than a hundred of them, was Pilecki, who was now interned at another infamous death camp, Treblinka. The camp was liberated by the Americans in April 1945 and Pilecki joined the Polish army as an intelligence officer.

Poland had been a political football for years and with the rise of the 'iron curtain', the country had simply swapped one jack-booted enemy for another. Stalin, although it took the West far too long to realize it, was as much as a murderous psychopath as Hitler. In 1947, Pilecki was caught spying on the Russians, working, in the left-wing propaganda of the time, for 'foreign imperialists'. He was tortured, made the victim of one of Stalin's show trials and executed in 1948. His burial place remains unknown.

Until 1989 when the Berlin Wall fell and everybody could see through the lies and hypocrisy of the communists, Pilecki was forgotten or regarded as a traitor. His reputation has now been fully restored, but no one can quite understand how a man, who could easily have avoided Auschwitz, went there of his own accord.

Denis Avey

Even more bizarre is the story of Denis Avey. Pilecki was a local man, on the spot in terms of Auschwitz, but Avey, as a British army officer, was not. In April 2011, his best-selling book *The Man Who Broke Into Auschwitz* caused a sensation, but there were doubts about the whole thing and the doubts have not gone away.

Avey was taken prisoner and sent to a sub-camp for British POWs called E715. He deliberately swapped places with an inmate of the main camp to find out what went on there. The details that he gave ring true, but those details have been available in the public domain now for years and anyone can access them. Yad Vashem, the World Holocaust Remembrance Centre, have been unable to give Avey the accolade as 'righteous among the nations', granted to outstanding people who helped the Jews during the Holocaust, because they have been unable to find anyone who can effectively corroborate his story.

Another British prisoner of E715, Brian Bishop, said, 'I can't understand how he did it. To do something like that you need to have several people helping on both sides – our side and the Jewish side.' Another POW, Ron Jones, found it hard to believe that a large, well-fed Englishman could blend in unnoticed with starving inmates. Sam Pivnik, sent to Auschwitz from a local ghetto in August 1943 as a 16-year-old, said, 'Avey's story seems to me highly unlikely. Swapping places with an Auschwitz prisoner isn't just risking his own life, but those of everyone else in his block and he was taking a huge risk that he wouldn't be informed on. It isn't a chance that I would have taken.

Prisoners in Auschwitz were so desperate you could not take the risk of trusting them.'

The key to it all was probably a Jewish prisoner called Ernst Lobethal whom Avey befriended at E715. The BBC tracked the man down in the United States long after the war but how much he knew of the details of Avey and his venture into the main camp is not clear.

The same problem that we faced for Pilecki goes doubly for Avey. What would prompt a man to go deliberately from the frying pan into the fire and, in Avey's case, why did he take so long to tell the world about it?

MESCHUGGISMUS (THE CULT OF INSANITY)

In Nazi Germany, because the Führer saw himself as an art guru (he painted very average landscapes and sold them as post cards), anything new and avant garde was denounced as degenerate art. Anyone who liked modern styles – expressionists, impressionists, surrealists, etc. – were lumped into what the Nazi speechmakers called meschuggismus, the cult of insanity.

In fact, the whole Nazi regime was an example of an insane cult. Below are some examples.

<u>Adolf Legalite (Adolf the legal one)</u>
After the failed putsch of the beer-hall in Munich in 1923, Hitler claimed that everything he did afterwards would be within the bounds of the law and he repeated the claim constantly. In fact, if we listed the *illegal* actions carried out by the Fuhrer, it would fill this book.

<u>Ahnenpass (Ancestry passport)</u>
Because the Nazis were obsessed with race, cards were issued to every German which proved their Aryan ancestry. Like all official documents however, these could be faked and big money could be made out of falsifying such cards.

<u>Angstbrosche (brooch of fear)</u>
Members of the Nazi party wore circular, enamel, lapel badges with the swastika in the centre. Their opponents, a brave and dwindling bunch as time went on, called it the brooch of fear.

<u>Anti-Semit</u>
Long before it was decided that smoking was dangerous, a popular brand of roll-your-own cigarettes in 1920s Germany, was smoked by Nazis. It was called, appropriately, Anti-Semit in line with their opposition to Jews.

<u>Beefsteak Nazis</u>
The original twenty five points of the Nazi Party contained far left ideas. After all, the official name of the group was The National Socialist Workers Party. Although all this was played down later, the concept never went away entirely. 'Beefsteak Nazis' were those whose allegiances were doubtful – brown (the colour of the SA's shirts) on the outside, but red (the Communist colour) on the inside.

'Call me Meier!'

Hermann Goering was absolutely confident that his Luftwaffe (air force) was so superior that no bombs would ever fall on Germany. On 9 August 1939, less than a month before war began, he said 'Not a single bomb will fall on the Ruhr [Germany's Industrial heartland]. If an enemy plane reaches the Ruhr, my name is not Hermann Goering. You can call me Meier!'

Meier was a typical Jewish surname. In the years ahead, how the Reichmarschal must have regretted this boast!

Deutsche Blick (the German glance)

After 1933, it became the custom for Nazis – and eventually all Germans – to greet each other with the straight arm salute and the words, 'Heil Hitler'. In reality, many people avoided this as being too ludicrous. They swivelled their heads from side to side to make sure no-one was looking (the German glance) then greeted each other normally.

Feindhörer (listens to enemy broadcasts)

A key weapon of the Second World War was the radio. It kept morale high and was used by Allies and Axis powers to spread information or disinformation, depending on the situation. Large numbers of Britons, for example, listened to the broadcasts of William Joyce, Lord Haw-Haw, claiming that Britain was finished as a world power. Likewise, agents like Sefton Delmer, who spoke fluent German, let the Nazis know that their regime was doomed. In Nazi-controlled areas, those who listened to such broadcasts, as opposed to Josef Goebbell's official radio outlets, were regarded as enemies of the people. Children were encouraged to shop their offending parents to the authorities.

Góldfasan (the golden pheasants)

The Nazis liked dressing up. Only Mussolini's fascists looked sillier than men like Herman Goering, in his white uniform loaded with medals and gold braid (the sort of thing the British called 'scrambled egg'). The pheasant was used as a stupid, gaudy bird in contrast to the all-powerful eagle which was a German totem, itself pinched from the Romans.

'Heil Hitler!'

The phrase became a legal requirement in Nazi Germany. Every adult was expected to use it as a greeting, extolling the Nazi cult of leadership to a ridiculous level. For children, every school day began with the words and they were expected to use it up to 150 times a day as part of the indoctrination programme.

Honorary Aryans

The problem with a regime that is based on racism is that alliance with other races is difficult. In two glaring examples, however, Hitler ignored the racial inconvenience and got on with it. In 1939 he signed an agreement with Josef Stalin, the Russian leader, to the effect that Germany and the Soviet Union would carve up Poland between them.

The famous cartoon by the British cartoonist David Low, shows Hitler and Stalin greeting each over the corpse of Poland. The Fuhrer is saying 'The scum of the earth, I believe.' Eastern Europeans were the Slavs, a people way down the social scale in Nazi philosophy; likewise, the Japanese. Long before the attack on Pearl Harbor, which effectively made Hitler and Emperor Hirohito allies, a German-Japanese agreement had been signed in November 1936. The common enemy of both countries were the Communists and on that basis the Japanese were made honorary Aryans as a token of Nazi esteem. The term was, of course, a token of Nazi hypocrisy.

Kampfbund Des Gewerblichen Mittelstandes (Militant Association of Retailers).

We still complain about supermarkets and chain stores squeezing out the high street retailes today, but in Nazi Germany, this took on a more sinister term. It is believed that such stores were run by Jews and therefore should be closed down. Many of them were.

'Kinder, Kirche, Küche' (children, church, kitchen)

Women were nowhere in Nazi ideology. Hitler planned, among many other architectural ideas, to build a vast shrine to Nazism in Berlin, with the names of thousands of prominent Nazis chiselled on the marble; not one woman was mentioned. Instead, women's place was in the home and the phrase 'kinder, kirche, kuche' summed it all up. Female emancipation was a product of degenerate thinking, and the various female organisations in Germany, like the League of German Maidens, were merely pale copies of the male originals. Women were engaged to marry Aryans to breed Aryan children. They even received gold, silver and bronze decorations for doing so. Leni Riefenstahl, the director who made the Nazi PR film, *Triumph of the Will,* was almost unique as a woman carrying out the roles of a man.

Lebensborn (The Fountain of Life)

Heinrich Himmler's drive to create an Aryan master-race that would dominate world affairs for a thousand years led to the Lebensborn programme whereby perfect Aryan specimens, with fair hair and blue eyes, would be made pregnant by SS superstuds. Marriage was not necessary and romantic relationships unimportant. Once pregnant, girls were sent to a special maternity centre where every care was taken of them and their infants. In addition, Aryan children from outside Germany were kidnapped to add to the breeding stock, indoctrinated as good Nazis and adopted by 'racially trustworthy' parents. Thousands of children became victims.

Marzgefallene (those who joined in March)

When Hitler came to power in March 1933 there was a stampede to join the Nazi party. Diehard Nazis who had been there since the early '20s regarded such people with contempt.

Max Heiliger Deposit Account

The mass deportation of Jews and other people deemed undesirable by the Third Reich, meant that, apart from the appalling treatment and loss of life, a vast fortune of belongings of all kind was looted from emptied ghettoes or which ended up on the railway platforms of camps like Auschwitz. The valuables here, including gold fillings from people who had 'gone to the chimneys' were collected in an SS bank account, with the full connivance of the Reichsbank president, Walter Funk, under the fictitious name of the Max Heiliger Deposit. Although some of this treasure was returned after the war, much of it was never recovered, its original owners long since dead.

Pour Le Semit (To the Semite)
The most distinguished military decoration for Germans in the First World War was the Maltese Cross with the French label Pour Le Merite, known as the Blue Max. Pour le Semite was the ironic term used by Nazis for the yellow star of David that Jews were forced to wear in public.

Schleiferi (grinding)
From time to time in the British and American press today, there are shocking stories of horseplay among students and cadets that has got out of hand. The Americans call this 'hazing' and it has a centuries old pedigree. In Nazi Germany, the Hitler Jugend (Hitler Youth) went through this ritual as a matter of routine. The purpose was to make Aryan soldiers out of them and harsh physical punishment was de rigeur. Many boys broke down under this cruel regime, but most put up with it, believing in the justification behind it.

Sitzkreig (The Sitting War)
Britain called it the 'phoney war'. France knew it as 'drôle de guerre' (the funny war), but in Germany the period from September 1939 to May 1940 was the 'sitting war' or 'armchair war'. This is understandable for the British and French because in that time period there was no military activity in the west. In the east, however, on Germany's doorstep, the Wehrmacht was busy invading Poland. Nobody was sitting down through that.

Totenbergen (Castles of the Dead)
Among the vast architectural schemes that Hitler planned for what he believed would be a successful European war, the castles of the dead would have been astounding. They would have been huge variations of the cenotaph in London's Whitehall, one on the Atlantic coast facing west as a token of Germany's achievement in liberating Europe from British influence and the other on the Eastern front where 'the chaotic forces of the East' (Russian) had been overwhelmed. Neither castle got beyond the blueprint stage.

MICKEY MOUSE
With the war raging, and the imminent threat of biological and chemical weapons, gas masks became the must-have essential. Countries were seeking ways to allay the fears of their citizens, particularly children. After the 1940 attack on Pearl Harbor, America was taking no chances and distributed gas masks to its citizens, but it was important to prevent panic and keep the public's fear under control. One of the ways this was

achieved was by using Mickey Mouse gas masks.

Walt Disney's Mickey Mouse was well known, first being introduced in 1928 in the famous *Steamboat Willie*. A thousand were made, the masks fitted with the smiling face of the comic mouse and were specially designed to fit those aged between 18 months and four years old, costing $1.25.

Thankfully, the need for gas masks never arose – perhaps the world was still horrified by the use of mustard gas in the First World War. Interestingly, even in his final desperate months, and tormented by his growing delusions, Hitler refused to entertain the use of biological weapons.

Few Mickey Mouse gas-masks have survived into the present day, and their creation, though understandable and well-meaning, has not aged well – looking to a modern eye like the stuff of horror movies and nightmares. That being said, the desire for some sense of normalcy, and for children to know the world had not gone completely mad, was important. Of Walt Disney's most memorable films, *Pinnochio, Fantasia, Dumbo* and *Bambi* were all released during the war years.

THE MIDWIFE OF AUSCHWITZ

Stanisława Leszczyńska was born to a devout Catholic family in Lodz, Poland in 1896. She spent her childhood in the Brazilian city of Rio de Janeiro, married in 1916 and returned to Poland – enrolling in the midwifery school and raising a family.

With World War Two marching on apace, Leszczyńska and her family did their bit to try to help the Jews of Lodz ghetto, smuggling in food and false papers. The local neighbourhood police caught her, and in an act of infamy, handed her to the Gestapo. Naturally, the entire family had to be punished. Two of her sons were shipped off to Mauthausen-Gusen, her husband and one son managed to escape capture, while Stanisława and her daughter Sylwia, a medical student, were taken to Auschwitz on 17th April 1943.

The Leszczyński women were assigned to the Auschwitz infirmary, where they became familiar with Dr. Josef Mengele. What happened to them and what they witnessed is the stuff of nightmares, but we shouldn't shy away from it. We owe it to them to know their stories.

Unbelievably, Auschwitz had a 'maternity ward' – which is odd enough. Pregnant women arriving at the site were normally sent straight to the gas chambers; if they didn't know they were pregnant until later – a bullet would do. So with this in mind, the existence of the ward seems bizarre.

The horrible reality of the place began to sink in for the Leszczyński women. The so-called nurses already there took no part in the births, their job was to immediately snatch the newborns from their mothers and drown them in buckets or barrels. When Stanislawa discovered what was expected of her, she refused.

Whilst the other 'nurses' went about their business, the new Leszczyński additions helped care for the mothers and, in the midst of squalid and appalling conditions, and without any equipment, gave it their best shot. With no option, they welcomed the little arrivals - although it was greeting them at the doorway to hell. Stanisława prayed for each and every tiny soul she delivered and baptized those who were Christian. She became affectionately known as 'the Mother'.

Her kindness cost her, she was physically, mentally and emotionally exhausted and the work was back-breaking. Her refusal to kill the babies constantly got her in trouble, even being scolded by Mengele. *What was the point of helping them? They were going to die as soon as they were born anyway. There was nothing to be done.* That may be, but *she* wasn't drowning babies in buckets: that was someone else's choice; that was on someone else's conscience. Surprisingly, despite her refusal to do Mengele's bidding, no punishment came, and Stanisława continued her work.

Some babies who were 'Aryan' enough were snatched from their mothers to be adopted as part of the SS' *Lebensborn* project and sent to new homes. Despairing mothers would often kill their young rather than let them fall into the hands of the enemy. Mysteriously, a handful were allowed to keep their babies, but why, and for how long, and what happened to them, is unknown.

The statistics are grim and upsetting, but we owe it to the victims not to ignore them. It is estimated of 3,000 babies born in Auschwitz, 1,500 were drowned, 1,000 died of cold or starvation and 500 were taken by the SS to be raised in Nazi Germany.

The work must have felt utterly, cruelly futile. If one, just one, newborn could survive being born in Auschwitz and escape hell with their mother, it would be miracle. But Stanisława was a realist: miracles didn't happen in Auschwitz. It was better to forget hope and carry on with the work.

Stanisława and her daughter survived the war, remaining at the camp until its liberation on 26 January 1945. She returned home and was reunited with her other children, though was heartbroken to discover her husband was dead, having fought and died in the Warsaw uprising. She continued her work as a midwife and only spoke of her ordeal when retiring in 1957. An account of her experiences, *The Report of a Midwife from Auschwitz*, is freely available. She passed on in 1974.

As for the maternity ward: it was not the case that one baby escaped with its mother... *thirty* did. Maria Saloman, one of those mothers would later say, 'To this day I do not know at what price [she delivered my baby]. My Liz owes her life to Stanisława Leszczyńska. I cannot think of her without tears coming to my eyes.'

Hospitals, organisations, a street in Lodz and a road in Auschwitz are all named in her honour. A campaign from admirers to have the midwife of Auschwitz canonized and declared a saint continues to this day.

MOLOTOV COCKTAILS

A Molotov cocktail is another name for a petrol bomb or 'poor man's grenade', a relatively simple incendiary weapon which came to popularity during the Spanish Civil War as an anti-tank device. It was widely used during the war and even issued to the British Home Guard under the auspices of General William Ironside, if only because the 'cocktails' could easily be made by civilians at home. The name itself was given by the Finns, who fought against the Soviet Union during the Winter War of 1939-40. Vyacheslav Mikhailovich Molotov was the Soviet foreign minister and announced on radio that the aerial bombardment against Finland was in fact the dropping of food and humanitarian aid to the starving population.

The humour of this was not lost on the Finns, who referred to these bombs as 'Molotov bread baskets'. From there the petrol bombs used to repel the Soviets were eventually referred to as 'Molotov cocktails', a drink to accompany and wash down Molotov's bread!

THE MONKEYS OF GIBRALTAR

The Mediterranean island of Gibraltar, off the coast of Spain has been part of the British Empire since the 1713 Treaty of Utrecht. During the war its strategic location, essentially controlling, as it did, the entrance to the Mediterranean Sea, made it a vital point for domination.

The civilian population were evacuated, and it became a target of bitter contention. Germany's Operation Felix, the invasion of Gibraltar, was stopped because Fascist dictator Francisco Franco, playing a delicate balancing act of neutrality, would not allow foreign troops to travel through Spain.

But was there another, more indirect way, by which the island could fall? Gibraltar is shared with a second population: Barbary macaque monkeys, the only wild monkeys of Europe. A legend states that as long as the monkeys live on the island, Britain's rule of it will never falter. In 1942, news reached Churchill that the monkey population was falling at an 'alarming rate'. Critically, only seven known macaques were known to have survived. Churchill went into action, ordering that reinforcements be brought in from the woodlands of Morocco and Algeria to replenish their strength.

The British Army cared for the monkeys. They even employed a guardian holding the post of 'Keeper of the Apes' (even though they were monkeys). Their job was to keep track of the animals, listing their dates of birth and controlling their diets. Births were announced in the local newspaper, *The Gibraltar Chronicle*.

Though the legend was safe, and the monkeys were brought back to strength, human/macaque relationships were not always friendly. In 1944, British troops executed Tony, the ape colony leader. Tony had become a nuisance and violent, entering people's homes and attacking other monkeys. He was succeeded by six-year-old Pat. Today, there are estimated to be 160 - 300 of the monkeys living on the island.

The sovereignty of Gibraltar has remained contentious, with Spain continuing to stake a claim. However, referendums conducted in 1967 and 2002 found that the population rejected leaving Britain.

THE MOUSE THAT INVADED

We have all seen the photographs – the grainy black and white memorials to the men who were part of D-Day, the culmination of Operation Overlord when the Allies set foot on European soil for the first time in three years. The terrifying guns of USS Nevada blasting out against Utah Beach on the coast of Normandy. The scenes in the 'ducks', the amphibian vehicles grinding through the shallows towards 'bloody' Omaha, where 200 Americans would die in minutes. The British commandos, in their khaki and their red berets wading ashore on Sword Beach, keeping their rifles above the water line.

To those of us of a younger generation, we have all seen *The Longest Day* and *Saving Private Ryan*, two incomparable war movies that have recaptured that dazzling and horrific episode in history.

What we probably have not seen is the photograph of one of the most unlikely 'combatants' with the Allied Invasion. 156,000 soldiers hit those beaches on 6 June 1944, the day of deliverance, and in somebody's pocket, on one of the landing crafts, was Eustace, a piebald mouse who was a regimental pet. It is not known what deeds of valour he witnessed or exactly what part he played, but we know, from the photograph, that he was there. And we know he survived to get back home again.

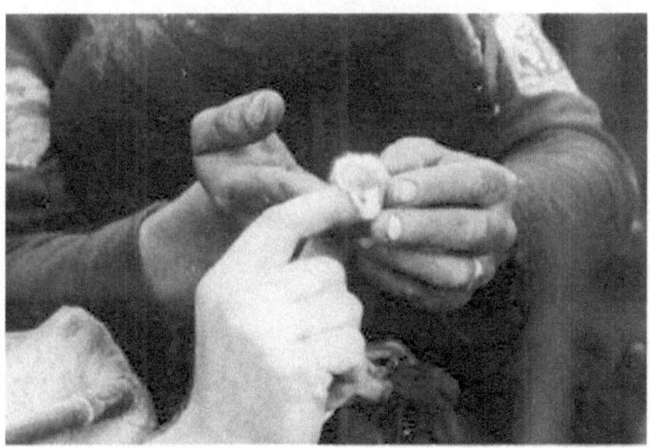

MR CHAD

There are a few theories as to the rise of the 'Mr Chad' graffiti. One of the most commonly accepted views is that it was conflated with the 'Kilroy was here' graffiti introduced by the American GIs and possibly used by them before America's entry into the war in December 1941. A 1946 *New York Times* article wrote 'During the war [James Kilroy] was employed at the Bethlehem Steel Company's Quincy shipyard, inspecting tanks, double bottoms and other parts of warships under construction. To satisfy superiors that he was performing his duties, Mr. Kilroy scribbled in yellow crayon "Kilroy was here" on inspected work. Soon the phrase began to appear in various unrelated places, and Mr. Kilroy believes the 14,000 shipyard workers who entered the armed services were responsible for its subsequent world-wide use.' As a humorous tribute, American servicemen then began writing 'Kilroy was here' wherever they could.

Meanwhile in Britain, another piece of graffiti was emerging. A long nosed man named Mr Chad began peering over a wall with the phrase 'Wot? No [blank]', the blank representing something the country was short of due to rationing, such as 'Wot? No Bananas?', 'Wot? No Petrol?' and 'Wot? No Spam?'. The origins of Mr Chad are not certain either, but one theory is that a lecturer discussing the effect of a capacitor in a circuit drew a diagram on a board, which looked similar to a face, with one student then writing 'Wot? No Electrons?' underneath it – as the electrons would have been discharged.

The figure may also have been invented by the Australians, perhaps as early as the First World War. There he was called Foo and appeared first on the side of railway carriages used by the Australian army.

Mr Chad and 'Kilroy was here' became fused and he started to pop up throughout the world, from British pubs and the Houses of Parliament where someone had drawn 'Wot? No Tories?' in 1945 after Clement Atlee's Labour victory over Winston Churchill. Mr Chad followed the soldiers into battle too, appearing everywhere from Japanese pillboxes to Nazi strongholds to gents' lavatories. In the last instance, one common variant on the theme runs –

'Clap my hands and jump for joy'
I was here before Kilroy.'

to which another wag added –

'Sorry to spoil your little joke;
I was here, but my pencil broke.
Kilroy.'

MR. DOKTOR

Henryk Goldszmit, better remembered by his pen name Janusz Korczak, is one of the gentler heroes of the war. His kindness and compassion was an astonishing example of selflessness.

Born in 1878, he was a Polish Jew who in later life became a children's author and teacher, affectionately known by the children close to him as Pan Doktor (Mr. Doctor).

He despised corporal punishment and all violence towards children and would go on to become director of the *Dom Sierot* Jewish orphanage in Warsaw.

In the aftermath of the German invasion of Poland, the orphanage was forced to relocate to the overcrowded and squalid ghetto in 1940. Despite opportunities to escape and save himself, Korczak chose to go with the children.

In August 1942, with the Nazi's 'final solution' in full force, the occupiers came to collect the 192 orphans. They were to be taken to Treblinka extermination camp, where they would be murdered. The children couldn't be helped, but the Polish resistance offered to save Korczak. Once again, he would not abandon the children. He refused to be liberated and went with his charges to Treblinka.

The tragic scene of Korczak, his assistants, and the column of little ones leaving the orphanage must have been haunting. The children, from little tots to teenagers, were dressed in their best clothes, each with their favourite book or toy and holding hands with each other.

Once more Korczak had a third opportunity to save himself; it is alleged that an SS officer recognised the man as the author of his favourite children's book. The SS officer, depending on the source, either offered to help him escape, or to send him to Theresienstadt, where he at least had a chance of surviving. Once more Korczak said no, if his children were 'unworthy of life' and the powers-that-be determined they must be murdered; then he would die as one of them. With immeasurable inner strength and courage, he had made his choice.

And so the little column marched off, like some nightmarish distortion of the Pied Piper of Hamelin. Wladyslaw Szpilman, whose memoirs became the famous book *The Pianist*, gave a distressing report of what he saw that day:

'He told the orphans they were going out into the country, so they ought to be cheerful. At last they would be able to exchange the horrible suffocating city walls for meadows of flowers, streams where they could bathe, woods full of berries and mushrooms. He told them to wear their best clothes, and so they came out into the yard, two by two, nicely dressed and in a happy mood. The little column was led by an SS man.'

Korczak was with them at the end, Mr. Doktor did not leave his children for one moment. They were not left alone. As the metal door slammed shut, and the poison gas choked them, they all went to the meadows of flowers together.

Two of Korczak's children's books have been translated in English, *King Matt the First* in 1986 and *Kaytek the Wizard* in 2012. Statues of Janusz Korczak and his children can be found in Warsaw and Jerusalem.

MRS O'GRADY

The British government was convinced, especially in the early stages of the war, that there was a Fifth Column operating in the country. A network of spies, they feared, was providing the Germans with vital information to ensure the overthrow of the last European country not to have fallen to the Nazis. This delusion can be called weird in itself but there was one piece of evidence that seemed to prove that the paranoia was not misplaced.

Dorothy O'Grady lived at Sandown in the Isle of Wight where she ran a boarding house. The island was a sensitive area that was within the defence perimeter of the naval base at Portsmouth. She spent a lot of time pestering soldiers who patrolled the barbed-wire beaches of the Island, made positive comments about Hitler and wore little swastika flags sewn into the lining of her coat. Her husband, meanwhile, was away on active service. In August 1940, she was charged with being in a prohibited area and skipped bail. Detailed maps and sketches of the coast were found in her home and in December, she was sentenced to death under the Treachery Act for sabotaging telephone wires in an attempt to impede army movements. There were rumours that she was part of a nest of British Union of Fascists centred on Southsea, but that was never proved.

What is more weird here? A British housewife acting as a saboteur for the Nazis or a British government that was planning to hang her for it? In the event, it was decided that she was clearly deranged, a mentally disturbed masochist according to the prison psychologist at Holloway, and her sentence was commuted to fourteen years in prison.

In later interviews, she claimed that the whole thing was 'a huge joke'.

THE MYTHS AND MIRACLES OF DUNKIRK

When is a victory not a victory? When it is left in the hands of Winston Churchill's government and a compliant media at a desperate time in British history.

In simple terms, the British Expeditionary Force, commanded by Lord Gort, was driven back to the French coast, wrong-footed by the speed of the German advance under Gerd von Rundstedt. They ended up on the coast of Normandy around the previously anonymous little town of Dunkerque. This was in May 1940. Churchill had recently taken over from Neville Chamberlain as prime minister and *somehow* the thousands of men on the French beaches had to be rescued. Enter myth, propaganda and situations that still, eighty years on, have yet to be explained.

In nine days between 26 May and 3 June, almost 338,000 Allied troops, including Frenchmen, were evacuated, giving rise to the Dunkirk spirit, fortress Britain and even a victory against impossible odds. The BBC claimed that the BEF had 'come back to glory'. The *Daily Telegraph*'s banner headline read 'Defeat Turned to Victory'. Let us look at the reality.

The Thin Red Line

One of the myths of Dunkirk is that the BEF was outnumbered. It wasn't. The Allies had a million more men than the Axis powers and five extra divisions.

Gas! Gas!

The rumour spread that the Germans were using gas, like the phosphorus of the First World War, in defiance of the Geneva Convention. They weren't.

The real situation was that the British Army was not ready, in terms of weapons, equipment and training. As Field Marshal Bernard Montgomery wrote after the war, 'In September 1939, the British Army was totally unfit to fight a first class war on the continent of Europe' – and little had changed by May 1940.

The Impossibility of a German Victory

British troops believed wholeheartedly in the smug, over-positive view of the media, which extolled their preparedness, guts and knowhow. The lightning advance of von Rundstedt's panzers exposed the inadequacy of the French and British armies. France fell in six weeks, largely due to its own incompetence.

The British Soldier is Second to None

There are many examples of this being true, but in the spring of 1940, the second line troops were badly trained and led. Not one of the Territorial brigades withstood the German assault. The retreating mob seen by Lt Hadley, an infantry officer, says it all – 'a disorderly mob of soldiers, grimy, bloodstained and badly scared ... very much like the popular conception of the Italian army'.

26 May was declared a national day of prayed and the Archbishop of Canterbury spoke over the wireless to bewildered households all over the country. Everyone hoped for a miracle. In fact, the first of the Dunkirk miracles had already happened. Two days earlier, Hitler halted the German advance, for reasons still debated by military historians. Were the Wehrmacht exhausted, needing time to regroup? Did Hitler want to appease the British in order to secure a peace-deal? Or was he, as many contended at the time, simply mad?

The weather turned against the Germans too. Poor visibility made Luftwaffe attacks on Dunkirk impossible – although, of course, the same was true of the RAF, who were accused of abandoning the army. It was even claimed that smoke from German artillery drifted westwards and covered the men being evacuated from the beaches.

The 850 'little ships', many owned and piloted by civilians along the south coast, provided a hitherto unprecedented armada to get desperate men off the sands. It was an extraordinary event, but these boats only got 26,000 (8 per cent of the total) out of France; the rest was down to the Royal Navy. The boats did indeed provide ammunition and vital supplies and the heroism of those civilians should not be underestimated. Whether this constitutes a 'miracle' is another question.

Lastly, there was the millpond surface of the English Channel, famous for its usual choppiness, which allowed both the little ships and the navy to operate effectively.

The loss of equipment was a major blow and recriminations followed for years that the RAF had not done their bit and, from the French, that Britain had abandoned is ally. In fact, 47,000 French troops were evacuated, ready to fight another day.

Dunkirk was a defeat, pure and simple. But would it have been even worse without the 'miracles' in the paragraphs above?

NAZI CHIC

There is a sub-culture in East Asia which, if not massively offensive to Westerners, is at least very peculiar. Cosplay, when participants dress up in costumes to imitate film heroes or characters from books, is popular in the West, however, in East Asia a minority of youngsters dress up as SS and Nazi officers.

Examples of this 'Nazi chic' include, in 2016, a Taiwanese school holding a mock Nazi parade, students saluting each other with 'sieg heils' and carrying Swastika flags. Elsewhere, there have been Nazi themed bars, such as the *Soldaten Kaffee* in Bandung, Indonesia, which was finally shut down in 2017 after protests. Even the most forbearing were appalled by *Jail* in Taipei, Taiwan – a concentration camp themed restaurant, complete with toilets labeled as 'gas chambers', a mural of pathetic inmates behind barbed wire, and photographs of actual historical atrocities on the wall. A small fried chicken takeaway, called *Hitler*, was threatened with a lawsuit by KFC for copying the image design of Colonel Sanders for the dictator.

Sony Music apologized for Japanese girl band Keyakizaka46 dressing up in outfits similar to the SS. South Korean pop group Pritz apologized too for a similar gaffe, as did Indonesian pop star Ahmad Dhani.

The occasional foible happens in the West too. In 1999, James Brown, the editor of men's magazine *GQ* was fired when Field Marshall Erwin Rommel was listed as one of the best dressed men of the 20th century.

One expert, Elliot Brennan, of the Institute for Security and Development Policy, investigated this phenomenon. He stated that it is difficult for Asian peoples to relate to the Western view of Nazism. Hitler and the European war happened far away, and the same taboos do not exist for them. This is more due to ignorance than anything malevolent. It was a demonstration, in much the same way that rebellious Western teenagers would wear Che Guevera or Mao ZeDong clothing, or display Soviet paraphernalia in an attempt to shock their elders and those of a conservative disposition. The same cannot be done in Asia, as these symbols are in fact the symbols of 'the man' – meaning that, oddly, Nazi chic is considered an anti-establishment equivalent.

Perhaps Nazi chic can best be summarized as simple ignorance of the historical underpinnings. In the same way that we in the West may be ignorant of the taboos of the Asian war, in which higher estimates propose that as many as 20 million Chinese were slaughtered by the Japanese, something which sullies diplomatic relations to this day. Likewise, Asians are less aware of the impact of the Nazi atrocities in Europe.

Things are, however, moving in the right direction. Most reasonable people would agree that the right to shock and offend, express themselves and show individuality is important. On the other hand, mutualism, respect and sensitivity to each other is equally important. If we can avoid the banal hysteria that threatens to derail and debase both sides of the argument; education and healthy dialogue will surely only help these contrasting views reconcile sooner rather than later.

NAZI SEX DOLLS

The Second World War is one of the biggest hotbeds of history for rumours, hoaxes and wild claims. Although it has been widely discounted, one of Hitler's most innovative plans led to the invention of the blow up doll, which would be distributed to the Wehrmacht.

The story goes that the High Command were concerned about the rise of syphilis among the men who were frequenting brothels in Paris. Hitler approved the creation of the sex dolls to be sent to the men, which could be carried in their backpacks and inflated in time of need, to stop them visiting prostitutes. The idea was called the Borghild Project and was the brainchild of the Racial Hygeine and Demographic Biology Research Unit.

Amusingly, after thorough testing, reports suggest when the first fifty were ready to go out that soldiers refused to carry them for fear of embarrassment if they were captured by the enemy. For those who believe the tale, the bombing of Dresden wiped the sex doll factory and its evidence from the face of the earth. Experts have dismissed this story, but it has never quite gone away and some claim that the blonde, blue-eyed polymer versions were modified for children and became Barbie years later!

THE NEGRO SOLDIER

The first African-American soldiers were recruited in North Carolina during the American Civil War and two cavalry regiments – the 9th and 10th – continued to serve the US government against the plains Indians in the 1870s and '80s. Units like this had white officers and the attitudes of many white Americans remained hostile to the idea of the free negro long after the Civil War was over.

The Negro Soldier was an American propaganda movie produced by Frank Capra for the US War Department. Capra had produced a series called *Why We Fight*, designed to encourage public favour for the war. This 1944 feature was created in the hope that more black men would sign up. While the film itself is perhaps not very offensive, the subliminal message is manipulative. *The Negro Soldier* emboldens black men to fight and die against racist Germany and promotes the positive contribution black people have made to America, showing recruits enjoying their training.

Black soldiers in the Second World War were treated harshly by their white comrades and even the uniform didn't stop abuse. The units were heavily segregated and when the GIs arrived in Britain and later France, the locals couldn't fathom why the white Americans were so hostile to the blacks. Fights often broke out between black and white army units, often over the fact that black soldiers were dancing with white girls (something that many states did not allow). It is a measure of how ludicrously politically correct we have all become that today, even the title *Negro Soldier* would cause offence to some.

THE NIGHT WITCHES

Walpurgisnacht is celebrated in Germany on the eve of St Walpurga's day, 1 May. It is the equivalent of the British and American Halloween, a time when the witches ride, swarming through the air on horse and broomstick, accompanied by shrieking devils. They head for the mountains like the Brocken or the Blockburg, dancing like maniacs in an orgy with the devil.

But the *Nachthexen* (night witches) of the Second World War were not the lurid imaginings of Renaissance Europe or occult writers from Aleister Crowley to Stephen King. They were real. They were Russian. And they were deadly.

I have in front of me a photograph of these women, relaxing at a forward airbase somewhere on the Eastern Front in 1944. Some are making tea, probably to be drunk the Russian way, sucking it through a sugar cube. They are all in their twenties, in the shapeless Cossack-style uniforms worn by their men. They are smoking and chatting, comfortable in their fur-lined flying boots. Only one of them has seen the camera and she is checking her hair and smiling.

Traditionally, women had no place in war. They waved a tearful goodbye to their menfolk all over the world before 1914-18, urging those men to do their bit for king and country and even giving them the white feather of cowardice if they did not sign up. All that changed during the First World War, with women taking over male roles on the land and in the factories. A handful had been nurses long before Florence Nightingale made the job respectable in the Crimea (1854-6) but now those numbers swelled. War became up-close and personal in 1914-18 and remained so between 1939 and '45. The Second World War in particular was the 'people's war' and the Home Front was as real and dangerous a place as distant battlefields used to be.

The Russian experience was different. Even before the Revolution of 1917, women were allowed to raise their own fighting battalions. Determined feminists like Elena Tsebrzhinskaya, dressed as men to be allowed to serve as nurses at the Front. In the Revolution itself, shaven-headed 'death battalions' fought both for and against the Bolsheviks, trying to create order in a broken, chaotic society or establish a brave new world, depending on whose side they were on.

Russia was no more ready for the Second World War than Britain or France.

The hopeful dreams of 1917 had morphed into the nightmare of Josef Stalin, the Union of Soviet Socialist Republics and blind obedience to the state. First happy to ally with Hitler to partition Poland and add to his already vast empire, the 'Red Tsar', Stalin', had to switch allegiance abruptly in June 1941 when the Third Reich launched Operation Barbarossa and invaded the Soviet Union. Russia had been a backward power for two hundred years; modernity and technology had passed her by and the intransigent, blinkered Communist state did little to remedy that. The Russian strategy in wartime, apart from allowing the appalling winter weather – 'generals Janvier and Fevrier' – to wipe out invasions, was throw thousands of men to their deaths. Stalin was doing this with a vengeance after 1941.

Among his cannon fodder was a group that turned out to be rather elite – the all-female 588th Night Bomber regiment. But if the unit was elite, the aircraft were not. The Polikarpov Po-2 was an outdated biplane, literally made of plywood and they were no match for the state-of-the-art Messerschmitts of the Luftwaffe. There were no cockpits and the fuselage was so cold in the Russian winter that touching them would rip skin from fingers. They had no radios and their slow speed meant that as daytime fighters, they were useless.

After dark, however, it was a different story. The Po-2 was too small to be picked up on enemy radar and, like the flimsy aircraft of the First World War could land and take off virtually anywhere. They carried two bombs at a time (their maximum weight load) and each plane made eight to eighteen sorties a night. Over their targets, the pilots switched off their engines and let the aircraft glide, with a swishing sound like a witch's broom.

So successful was the 588th that the Germans gave them the name Nachthexen, believing that they were desperate homicidal criminals sent on forlorn-hope missions. They were also rumoured to have been injected with a new chemical to enable them to see in the dark. The unit became the most decorated female outfit of the war but were not allowed to take part in Stalin's lavish victory parade and were disbanded six months later. For them, the patriotic war was over.

THE NIIHAU INCIDENT

The Niihau incident is one of those rare events that somehow doesn't quite ring true, it feels more like a boy's own comic adventure, but it did happen and the facts speak for themselves.

It was the 7 December 1941 and Shigenori Nishikaichi, a Japanese pilot of a Mitsubishi Zero fighter had just taken part in the Pearl Harbor attacks. Returning from the bombing run, Nishikaichi's squadron was attacked by American Curtiss P-36A fighters. The Zeroes made quick work of these and won the dog fight, but the pilot's plane had been hit, his engine was failing, and he fell behind his comrades.

During the pilots' briefing that morning, the men had been told that, if any of their aircraft were damaged, they should attempt to land on the uninhabited island of Niihau, the westernmost island of Hawaii, and await rescue. Nishikaichi found the island and began to descend. As he did, he discovered something wasn't right -- he saw buildings. Braced for a rough landing, he came down, hit a wire fence and crashed.

Niihau was in fact inhabited. It was owned by the Robinson family, who bought it from King Kamehameha V in 1864. The island was off limits to outsiders, and only the native Hawaiians and a handful of others lived there; the Robinson's themselves living on the larger island of Kauai.

A local, Howard Kaleohano, came across the wreck and the dazed and confused pilot. He took his papers and sidearm, and then helped Nishikaichi. The pilot was even fed breakfast. Blissfully unaware of the attack on Pearl Harbor, they were curious as to what a Japanese pilot was doing so far from home.

Japanese-born Ishimatsu Shintani also lived on the island as a beekeeper. He was asked to translate. Shintani, who only wanted a quiet life, begrudgingly accepted. Upon speaking to the pilot, it is said that he turned pale and walked off in disgust.

There were two other Japanese on the island who could help, Yoshio and Irene Harada, and it was their turn to speak to Nishikaichi. The pilot informed the Haradas of the attack on Pearl Harbor, and that Japan and the United States were now at war. The Haradas didn't pass this on.

Oblivious to the day's attack, the Hawaiians had a party for their guest, complete with guitar songs – but the party was about to turn sour. The island had a battery operated radio, and this radio announced the attack. The Haradas had a hard choice: loyalty to Japan, or loyalty to America. The locals couldn't tell the Robinsons on Kauai, what was to be done?

Nishikaichi confided in the three Japanese locals. Whatever was said, soon Shintani went to ask Kaleohano for the pilot's papers to be returned, but Kaleohano refused. Events soon spiralled out of control. Sources diverge slightly, but the main events are clear.

It appears Yoshio Harada stole a shotgun and attacked Kaleohano's house to get the papers back by force. Kaleohano managed to escape and hid the papers at his mother-in-law's. Despite an emergency naval ban that had come into effect, Kaleohano and five others rowed to Kauai to warn them of the two-man invasion. Meanwhile Nishikaichi and Harada had taken one of the machine guns from the crashed plane and were shooting into the air, demanding the return of the papers.

Eventually the Japanese took a married couple, Benehakaka 'Ben' Kanahele and

Kealoha 'Ella' Kanahele captive. However the captors were weak and tired. Ben and Ella pounced on them. In the ensuing fight, Harada shot Ben three times, but Ben had enough strength to throw the pilot through the air, his wife smashed the pilot's head in with a rock and Ben slit his throat. Harada, seeing this, turned the gun on himself and pulled the trigger.

Next morning, by the time Howard Kaleohano, the five Hawaiians, Robinson and the army authorities arrived, the invasion was over. Shintani was interned, finally receiving citizenship in 1960. Irene Harada was jailed until 1944. Ben Kanahele recovered from his wounds and received the Medal of Merit and the Purple Heart, his wife received nothing. Nishikaichi's Zero is on display to this day at Pacific Aviation Museum Pearl Harbor.

The fact that the Haradas, who previously had been considered to be good neighbours, could have changed their allegiance so quickly shocked the US authorities. This incident must have contributed to Executive Order 9066, where some 120,000 Japanese-Americans were taken from the West Coast and interred for the remainder of the war.

THE NIGHT AND FOG DECREE

President Franklin D Roosevelt rightly called 7 December 1941, when the Japanese attacked Pearl Harbor, 'a date that will live in infamy'. But it is infamous for another reason too. That was when Hitler decided on the *Nacht und Nebel erlass*, the Night and Fog decree, which was designed to obliterate enemies of the Reich. From that day on, anyone who was declared a dissident, in Germany or German-occupied territory, was to simply disappear. 'The prisoners,' ran the decree, 'will vanish without a trace. No information may be given as to their whereabouts or fate.'

What is weird about this is not the decree itself but that a government should give such a melodramatic name to it. It comes from Hitler's obsession with Teutonic mythology and from the *Ring* cycle of his favourite composer, Richard Wagner. 'Night and fog,' wrote Wagner, 'make you no one.'

NIMROD

Edward Elgar was a British composer, famous for his *Pomp and Circumstance*

Marches. To this day, *Land of Hope and Glory* is belted out annually by a packed hall during the prestigious last night of the Proms musical event.

He is equally remembered for his *Enigma Variations,* composed of fourteen variations of an original theme. Variation 9, called *Nimrod,* is now inextricably linked with the war in Britain; always played at remembrance services, and is synonymous with the Cenotaph memorial service on Remembrance Sunday. Hazy memories claim that this music was played at Winston Churchill's funeral and, although it would certainly have been fitting, in fact it was not. Churchill's funeral was codenamed Operation Hope Not, something which would have fitted his sense of humour to a tee.

Elgar enjoyed cryptology and would often write to his friends in riddles and puzzles, probably to their occasional chagrin. His greatest puzzle, which has never been solved, is the mystery behind the *Enigma Variations* itself. This piece, written between 1898-1899, has intrigued music lovers ever since. The puzzle first came to public attention during the programme notes from its first performance. It was tantalizingly noted:

'The Enigma I will not explain – its "dark saying" must be left unguessed, and I warn you that the connexion between the Variations and the Theme is often of the slightest texture; further, through and over the whole set another and larger theme "goes", but is not played... So the principal Theme never appears, even as in some late dramas – e.g. Maeterlinck's *L'Intruse* and *Les sept Princesses* – the chief character is never on the stage.'

So what was the mystery behind the Enigma? It has certainly captivated musicologists, historians and armchair detectives ever since. The proposed solutions are as varied as they are countless, and there are far too many to list. They range from hints at the overlaying theme, musical notes translating to letters in the alphabet, secret codes or identifying a hidden overarching theme. Some of the suggestions are so mind-bogglingly complex, they themselves would take teams of professionals to unravel. Simpler answers include playing *Twinkle, Twinkle, Little Star* over the piece in minor key, or Martin Luther's *A Mighty Fortress,* though a Catholic composer using a protestant anthem seems unlikely. Bob Padgett, perhaps the world's most fervent Enigma codebreaker, has taken on this unlocking of this riddle – even turning to Christianity, the bible and God for an answer.

Elgar vaguely teased a solution a few times but not agreeing with any of the answers put forward to him – he took his secret to the grave in 1934. So what was it? It's unlikely we will ever know. Perhaps it was something so infuriatingly simple as to pass us all by, or so convoluted as to be indecipherable by anyone.

Elgar's work, particularly *Nimrod,* received an astonishing new lease of life when it was used as the inspiration for the soundtrack of Christopher Nolan's powerful 2017 film *Dunkirk.* The composer Hans Zimmer was touched by *Nimrod,* and his own equally moving version, *Variation 15,* plays out as the story ends.

Thanks in part to *Dunkirk* and its fifteenth variation, Elgar's *Nimrod* is back with a vengeance. Peculiarly, this majestic piece of music has found a solid home in advertising, it's appeared everywhere from commercials for beer, banks, pastries, cars, shops, dog food and even Marmite!

NO SMOKING!

One of the more surprising ideas to come out of the Reich was the most advanced anti-tobacco campaign of the age. Previously, those who were anti-smoking were dismissed as the lunatic fringe or equated with the same puritan ethic that disapproved of any enjoyment. The most famous anti-smoker in history was James I, king of England, who wrote an attack on 'the noxious weed'. But then, he also believed completely in the power of witches!

In post war Germany, the infant Nazi Party had their own roll-ups, called, appropriately, Anti-Semit, but by 1939, a study from the German scientist Franz Muller revealed the link between smoking and cancer and the dangers of passive smoking. For the Nazis, hell bent on physical perfection and 'racial hygiene' this was unacceptable. Hitler went from being a heavy smoker (up to forty a day) to finding the habit decadent and the American Indian's revenge for the white man having given him hard liquor!

In 1941, the heroically named 'Struggle Against Tobacco' was formed, led by an SS officer. The Reich became pioneers in health and wellbeing, information leaflets were distributed, encouraging people to give up. Counselling and medication was offered to addicts and smoking was banned in places like schools and cinemas. It annoyed Hitler that Herman Goering, Martin Bormann (the Nazi Party leader) and his own Mistress, Eva Braun, were unrepentant smokers.

Smokers in Germany were liberated in 1945. The campaign fell apart with the end of the Nazi government and smoking levels began to rise again. The research of the Reich was either unknown or ignored by the victorious Allies and the British scientist, Richard Doll, was knighted in the 1970s for being the first to show the links between smoking and cancer.

THE NOBEL PEACE PRIZE

Another story blown out of proportion is Hitler's nomination for the 1939 Nobel Peace Prize, a prestigious international award for champions of peace and brotherhood. Hitler *was* nominated for this prize by the Swedish politician Erik Brandt, but there is much more to it than that. Laying aside the bizarre situation that the creator of the Peace prize (actually one of the fraternity), Alfred Nobel, was the inventor of dynamite and that he was called 'the merchant of death', some very odd people have been nominated for the award and same very deserving ones have been overlooked.

At the time of the Munich Crisis (1938) the British Prime Minister, Neville Chamberlain, was nominated, but his name was quickly withdrawn when the Norwegian government pointed out that in his capitulation to Hitler, Chamberlain was 'the front runner for handing over a small country to destruction, possible annihilation'. Three days later, Brandt proposed Hitler –

'By his glowing love for peace, earlier documented in his famous book *Mein Kampf* – next to the Bible perhaps the best and most popular piece of literature in the world ... Adolf Hitler is by all means the authentic God-given fighter for peace and millions of people all over the world put their hopes in him as the Prince of Peace on earth.

After intense public outrage, Brandt withdrew his nomination and claimed it was an ironic joke. Historians debate whether it was in fact a joke taken out of context or as a way for him to play down the unexpected hostility he received. Brandt's actions would suggest the former, since he later protested Sweden's refusal to take more Jewish refugees and spoke out against their treatment at the hands of the Nazis. So over the top was his endorsement of Hitler that he cannot possibly have been serious. On the other hand, there were more sensible ways to demonstrate opposition to the Nobel Commission's decision-making.

An important and overlooked part of this incident is that Hitler was outraged by the prize. In 1935, the German pacifist Carl von Ossietsky was awarded it. He was languishing in a concentration camp, convicted as a traitor for his whistle-blowing and exposing German rearmament and died in 1938. Hitler was incensed that a treacherous criminal and enemy of the Fatherland could receive such a prestigious award. He forbade any German from receiving the prize and the press were banned from even mentioning it. In this context, Brandt's nomination as an irony makes perfect sense.

Either way, the Nobel Peace Prize has no control over who is nominated for the award and Hitler was never shortlisted for it.

AN OFFICER AND A GENTLEMAN

If your name is Digby Tatham-Warter, what else could you become but an army officer? Digby was born in 1917 and his father was in the trenches of the Western Front that year; he died as a result of gas poisoning when Digby was eleven. At the age of twenty, Digby graduated from the Royal Military College at Sandhurst and, as a commissioned officer, was sent out to India.

The brightest jewel in the Imperial Crown was fading by then and the ever-growing number of those clamouring for India's independence, wanted the British out. Even so, true to the long history of British rule in the sub-continent, Tatham-Warter enjoyed tiger-hunting, and pig-sticking, both of which would fill today's 'woke brigade' with horror. He thought nothing of 'borrowing' an American Dakota bomber and flying the officers of his company to London's Ritz hotel for a party.

It is highly likely that Tatham-Warter was a throw back. He never got on with radio signals as a means of communication and relied on bugle calls instead, once essential on the battlefields of Europe. Passwords were not for him either, especially as the high command were constantly changing them, so he took to carrying an umbrella with him all the time, if only to prove to Allied support troops that he was an Englishman!

Arnhem has gone down in military history as a 'bridge too far' when, in September 1944, the Allies were brought to an abrupt halt by unexpectedly fierce German resistance in the Low Countries. Parachuted into Holland on the night of the 17th, Digby snuck his men, commando-style, through back gardens rather than main roads, taking 150 prisoners en route. They reached the bridge at Arnhem at 8pm and ran into enemy fire. True to form, their radio packed up and Tatham-Warter put his bugler to good use. The German counter-attack, which included panzers, did not faze the commander at all. Wearing an actual bowler hat, as opposed to the 'battle bowler', he led a bayonet charge, waving his umbrella at astonished soldiers of the Wehrmacht, who had never seen anything like it. One soldier probably never saw much again as Tatham-Warter jabbed his umbrella through the eye-slit of an armoured car and took the driver's eye out!

The umbrella was doubly useful that day. Tatham-Warter's chaplain was pinned down by enemy fire trying to reach the wounded. The commander opened the umbrella, which of course was no defence against bullets at all, and got the man to safety. Lieutenant Pat Barnett, who witnessed all this, asked him why the !*!* he carried the umbrella. 'Oh my goodness, Pat,' Tatham-Warter said, 'what if it rains?'

The fight was hopelessly one-sided and eventually Tatham-Warter and Barnett were captured. The last bugle call sounded, blasting out *God Save the King*.

For a man who had fought at Arnhem, a German field hospital was not a problem. He and Barnett escaped and made it to Dutch civilians who disguised them as a painter and decorator. Digby Tatham-Warter became Peter Jensen, the deaf-mute son of a lawyer, in that speaking Walloon was not one of the officer's accomplishments. So cunning was the disguise that even when German soldiers were billeted with the Jensens, they never suspected a thing. In the end, together with 150 other escapees, Tatham-Warter cycled his way across Holland to take part in Operation Pegasus.

Had the battle of Arnhem been the success the Allies hoped for, the war might have been shortened by six months. No blame can be attached to the men who fought there. And as for Digby Tatham-Warter, they just do not make men like him any more!

THE ONE-EYED GHOST

Of all the countries of the British empire to do their bit for King and Country, Canada was a front runner. 'Nobody' a Wehrmacht general said ruefully in 1942 'fights like the Canadians'. And the war-time career of one Canadian, Leo Major, is proof-positive of this.

He enlisted in Le Régiment de la Chaudière, based in Quebec in 1940 and took part in Operation Overlord, landing on the Normandy beaches on 6 June 1944. In a gun-fight with four German soldiers, and a half-track, he was partially blinded in his left eye by a phosphorous grenade. He made the point that sniper like him only needed one good eye and he fought the rest of the war with an iconic eye patch over the useless one.

In the heavy fighting around the River Scheldt in October, Major captured 93 Germans single-handedly. His plan had been to capture only two, but his rate of fire was such that dozens of the enemy threw down their rifles. In an appalling act of self-destruction, the Waffen-SS, always the most fanatical element of the German army, opened fire on Major's prisoners, killing seven of them. When his Bren Carrier struck a land mine, Major was thrown into the air, breaking both ankles as he fell. As with the eye wound, he refused to be evacuated home and waited at a base hospital while his leg-bones knitted.

Major's finest moment, and one still shrouded in mystery, was the action at Zwolle in the Netherlands, in April 1945. The Medieval town was heavily fortified and Major and Corporal Wilfrid Arsenault volunteered to undertake a reconnaissance mission. They were caught and Arsenault was killed. Major went on a one-man mission to take Zwolle. Carrying two Sten guns and a handful of grenades, he made as much noise as possible in the early hours. The garrison were largely asleep and the sentries were not ready for what they assumed was a large liberation force. They ran and Zwolle was indeed liberated.

While all this sounds like a Boys' Own adventure, it is difficult to explain Zwolle's fall any other way. Major got lucky, that was certain, but he also had extraordinary courage. 'The one-eyed ghost' went on to fight with his accustomed bravery in the Korean War too and became the only Canadian to receive a DCM in two different conflicts.

OPERATION CLAYMORE

Operation Claymore, named after the Scottish sword, was a daring raid on the Norwegian Lofoten Islands. On 4th March 1941 British commandos, supported by other units, were ordered to destroy a number of important factories used by the Reich. The mission was a success: eleven (or eighteen) factories, five ships and 20,000 tons of shipping were destroyed. In addition, around 800,000 gallons of oil went up in smoke and hundreds of Germans were taken prisoner.

The raid was so unexpected that many locals assumed it was a training exercise. Not a single Allied soldier died in the raid: only one received a mild injury (an accidental, self-inflicted wound). Fortunately the defenders were caught unawares, and 228 soldiers surrendered with little resistance, though this lack of action was disappointing to many of the more gung-ho commandos.

With the humour typical of the British at the time, one officer sent a telegram from the local post office to an *A Hitler*, 'Herr Hitler. Reference your last speech: you said whenever British troops land on the continent of Europe, Germany will face them. Well, where are they?' Some commandos made a day of it, even taking a bus ride to a local seaplane base!

Three hundred and fourteen Norwegians volunteered to join the Allies as part of the Free Norwegian Forces and returned with the commandos to Britain. Some British officials did not see the strategic value in commando raids such as this, but they incensed Hitler, who became convinced Britain was going to launch a full scale attack on Norway. This led to him taking men from theatres elsewhere to defend the long Norwegian coast. Crucially, the commandos also came across codebooks and parts of an Enigma machine, which could be carefully studied at Bletchley Park and helped Alan Turing and his team understand the workings of the complex Enigma machines.

Winston Churchill passed on his personal thanks, 'To all concerned, my congratulations on the very satisfactory operation.'

OPERATION MISTLETOE

In the black art of espionage, all rules of conventional warfare were off. Knowing your enemy was key to success in any military operation and it was known, or at least generally believed, that many leading Nazis were obsessed with astrology and omens. There is a very long history of all this from the British point of view; John Dee, Elizabeth I's magus, not only advised the monarch about the right and wrong time to make vital decisions, he also worked with Francis Walsingham, the queen's spymaster, to undermine Catholics and *the* threat to Britain in the sixteenth century, Philip II's Spain.

In fact, it was German Intelligence who began the use of astrology in the Second World War. Before America's entry to the war in December 1941, German agents operated freely in the United States, prophesying Reich victories and the collapse of the Reich's enemies. Given the whirlwind success of blitzkrieg in the war's opening months, this was neither difficult nor supernatural, but gullible people bought it all nonetheless.

British Intelligence, the SIS, countered this by focussing on the natural interest in the occult which they believed was paramount in the minds of Hitler, his deputy Rudolf Hess, Heinrich Himmler, head of the SS, Alfred Rosenberg, the Nazi ideologist and an arguable 2,000 others! Cecil Williamson took all this a stage further. Calling himself a neopagan warlock, he founded the Witchcraft Research Centre and a museum of witchcraft which has moved around Britain in the years since its creation. Now at Boscastle in Cornwall, it had earlier existed at Bourton-on-the-Water in the Cotswolds.

Williamson's idea was to set up a centre for astrological espionage at Ashdown Forest in Sussex, one of the 'haunted' places of Britain associated with pre-Christian ritual and ceremony. Forty Canadian soldiers, with a radio transmitter code-named Aspidistra, took part in elaborate rituals to predict the future for the Third Reich. This was Operation Mistletoe.

The whole thing could be shelved under the heading of 'nonsense', the sixty per cent of espionage undertakings that the Macmillan theory says do not work. *Except* that a night chosen of great astrological significance was 10 May 1941, when six planets were aligned in Taurus and conjoined to a full moon. That was the night of the worst London blitz of the entire war. It was also the night when a lone Be 110 was spotted flying over Scotland. Its pilot bailed out and the plane crashed. He gave his name to the arresting authorities as Hauptmann Alfred Horn. In fact, he was Rudolf Hess, Hitler's *stellvertreter* (deputy), nominally the second most important man in the Third Reich, and a great believer in horoscopes. Had a secret agent reported the Ashdown Forest shenanigans to him and had he timed his flight to coincide with the planets' movements?

What is indisputable is that as soon as Hess's flight became public knowledge, Hitler launched the Aktion Hess, a rounding up of hundreds of German fortune-tellers, astrologers and cranks. Perhaps the Fuhrer realised that the stars were never on his side, after all.

OPERATION STARFISH

The bombing of Coventry in November 1940 was so devastating that a new word – 'coventrate' – entered the language. In a bizarre attempt to lessen the impact on real cities in the Blitz, Colonel John Turner, newly retired from the Air Ministry, came up with the idea of decoy sites, given the codename 'Q'. They had been devised as early as the outbreak of war, with the example of the Spanish city of Guernica, blitzed during the Civil War, in mind. Daytime sites – 'K' - made aircraft, aircraft hangars and entire airfields out in the countryside. The 'Q' sites proper were the night-time equivalent, with lights mounted on poles to replicate an airstrip.

By the end of 1940, the idea had extended to 'S.F.', 'Special Fire'. Decoys were set up – controlled fires in concrete pill boxes dotted around the country. In a decade when pilots relied on the visual as much as their instrument panels for finding targets, this made some sense. 'S.F.' became known as Starfish to those in the know, but it is debatable how effective the idea was. One book on the subject suggests that 968 tons of German bombs missed their real target as a result, and there were 237 Starfish sites by the end of the war. On the other hand, it meant that random bombing now took place over the countryside, putting otherwise safe villages at risk.

PARACHUTING NUNS

They first came out of a deadly sky in May 1940. The Dutch Foreign Minister, Eelco van Kleffens, reported that parachutists had landed in Holland wearing priests' cassocks, nurses' uniforms or nuns' habits. He wrote it all down solemnly in *The Rape of the Netherlands* which appeared later that year.

Stories of nuns shaving and German troops caught putting the habits on under hedgerows and behind haystacks began to emerge from the British army pulling back to Dunkirk. Neither the otherwise paranoid Ministry of Information nor the more sensible Mass Observation Unit took these stories seriously. An MOI report from 24 May reads, 'the usual crop of rumours about "hairy-handed nuns" and parachutists', adding one about a gang of blind refugees armed with machine guns.

Harold Nicholson, Parliamentary Secretary to the MOI said in one of his brilliant radio broadcasts for the BBC, that 'Mr Chatterbug' (the epitome of loud-mouthed hysteria which could unsettle a nation) was sitting in a train when a nun in his carriage dropped her Bible. As she picked it up, Mr C. very clearly saw a muscular male wrist and the tattooed name of Adolf Hitler.

The disturbing thing about these silly rumours was that men who should have known better, like Winston Churchill, believed at least some of them. As First Lord of the Admiralty early in 1940, he accepted that there was an active Fifth Column of at least 20,000 people operating all over Britain. It may be that the government actually welcomed such rumours because it took the attention of the public away from military cock-ups, of which there were many.

PARACHUTING SHEEP

Benito Mussolini saw himself as a latter-day emperor, commanding invincible armies and recreating the 'grandeur that was Rome'. One of the few geographical areas still available for such conquest was Africa, specifically Ethiopia, so the Italians were caught up in the unforgiving Danakil Desert, known for its oppressive heat, during the second Italo-Ethopian War from 1935-36. The area is volcanic and was described by the prestigious *National Geographic* magazine at the time as 'the cruellest place on earth'. It has been claimed that the Italian army were fussy eaters, but it's more likely the technology for pre-packaged rations had not yet been fully developed so feeding the Italian army and stopping rations from spoiling, became an issue. Either way, the army needed to move fast and be fed.

The solution to this? Planes could fly in much-needed water, but how about fresh meat? That answer, too, was simple – parachute sheep straight to the soldiers. Seventy-two sheep and two bulls did their bit for the war effort and served in Mussolini's flying column. How delicious they were or whether they survived the landing is not known. This was not, in fact, the first time that flying livestock had been seen. In the 1780s, the ballooning Montgolfier brothers tested primitive parachutes by dropping sheep from farm rooftops.

PAVLOV'S HOUSE

The Battle of Stalingrad was the bloodiest battle in human history. Added to the ideological importance of a city named after the Soviet leader - the showdown here was violent and unforgiving, either the Soviet defence would crumble or the Axis forces would perish. Neither dictator would consider backing down, and there were no other options. Stalin's order No. 227 stated 'not one step back'.

Germany, Italy, Hungary and Romania lost the equivalent of 100 divisions between them. 'It is hell.' said one soldier, 'No, this is ten times worse than hell.' he was corrected.

Nothing encapsulates this battle better than 'Pavlov's House', named after Sergeant Yakov Pavlov. The house was strategically important. It overlooked the Volga embankment and gave a clear line of sight in three directions. Layers of barbed-wire were installed and mines laid, machine guns were placed in every available window, doors were barricaded – the defenders were planning for a long fight, and they were not disappointed. Ongoing fighting and the sounds of war made sleep almost non-existent. It's even claimed that the piles of German dead were so high, the Soviets were forced to sneak out to knock down the walls of corpses.

The fighting from July 1942 was savage: bitter house-to-house fighting, with men constantly in danger among the ruined buildings. Each scuffle was a fight to the death.

Remarkably, the Soviets held out, despite constant attacks, for two months. On 25 November 1942, Pavlov and his men were finally relieved by reinforcements. They became national heroes.

The Battle for Stalingrad raged on for months, officially ending on 2 February 1943, at the cost of over a million lives. Stalingrad was the first time Hitler openly admitted he had suffered a defeat.

The Soviets joked that the fight for Pavlov's house was costlier to the Germans than the entire invasion of Paris.

The last survivor of Pavlov's defenders, Kamoljon Turgunov, died on 16th March 2015. The remains of the bricks of the house have been used to build a memorial.

THE PEOPLE'S COURT

The *Volksgerichtshof* ('People's Court') was created by Hitler in 1934. The legal system of Germany, even under his rule, didn't suit him. He was infuriated that all but one of the defendants at the Reichstag fire trial of 1933 were acquitted. The People's Court is listed here because it was so farcical, that it made even the most corrupt show trials and kangaroo courts look legitimate in comparison.

The president of the People's Court was Roland Friesler, a particularly cruel and sadistic man. Under his dominion the farcical courts lost any semblance of justice and legal procedure. Friesler was a master of surreal theatrics that turned the courtrooms into pantomimes. Here oratorical skills and a cunning tongue were more important than facts and context. Defendants were sent to their deaths, sometimes on less than two pages of text. The death sentence was liberally imposed on 'antisocial parasites'. Being defeatist or being found to be involved in a 'work slowdown' could also send you to the gallows. Brother and sister Sophie and Hans Scholl of the White Rose movement, an anti-Nazi academic leaflet campaign, were beheaded by guillotine.

The defendants' lawyers, were, of course, part of the system. Their roles seem to have been reduced to little more than 'explaining the process' (whatever that means in regards to the People's Court). Sophie Scholl's defence lawyer even lambasted his client, telling her she would pay for her crimes! The defendants would then be hauled in front of the judge, who generally insulted them, while the defence lawyers remained silent. A person could be in and out, and sentenced to death, in fifteen minutes.

The most famous trial was that of the conspirators of the 20 July plot to assassinate Hitler. Friesler talked over any attempts made by the defendants to speak. He called Colonel-General Erich Hoepner a 'schweinhund'. To Field Marshal Erwin von Witzleban, who was given oversized clothing and denied a belt to hold them up, he shrieked, 'You dirty old man, why do you keep fiddling with your trousers?'. The shambolic farce of this 'courtroom' must have left all who were thrown in front of it with a depressing realisation of their fate. Attempts to take part were pointless and would only have appeared to legitimize the trial. Most must have simply wanted it over and done with as quickly as possible. In all, Friesler decreed 5,000 death sentences in his three year period.

Many of the 20 July plotters met a grisly end, being hanged by rope so thin it was known as piano wire. Various estimates suggest it took between 45 seconds to 10 hours (!) to die. This was all filmed and sent to Hitler for his viewing pleasure. Many, such as the stoic Admiral Wilhelm Canaris of the *Abwehr*, were given the added humiliation of being naked when they were executed.

A surviving movie reel shows one of Friesler's trials. As a defendant explains his motives, and his disgust at Nazi murders, the judge bellows like a demented villain, reminiscent of Oliver Twist's Mr. Bumble: 'Murder?' he shouts, 'You miserable scum!'

There are many different theories as to the end of the People's Court. It was either bombed by the USAAF 8th Air Force on 3 February 1945 – crushing Friesler under a collapsed pillar, while he was still holding his files; or he made it out onto the street before bleeding to death on the pavement; or it was bombed by the British – killing Friesler but sparing two women in the dock. Either way, one lucky escape, was the 20 July conspirator Fabian von Schlabrendorff. His trial was meant to be held later that day, but the bombing of the courtroom destroyed his file. He survived the war and lived on to 1980. When Friesler's body was brought to the hospital, it is claimed that a worker said 'It is God's verdict.' Friesler was buried ignominiously with an anonymous gravestone in his wife's family plot in the Waldfriedhof Dahlem cemetery.

Apart from the Chief Prosecutor, Ernst Lauz, who was imprisoned for four years, no one was punished for involvement in the People's Court. The perverse excuse for this was that, under the laws of the Reich, their actions were completely legal. Yet so too were the gas chamber killings of the SS concentration camp guards, the murders of the Einsatzgruppen, and the other despicable acts of elements of the regime. Those people were punished for their atrocious crimes. But the 570 judges and prosecutors involved in the People's Court went free, and they would continue in the lucrative world of the law for the remainder of their cosy careers.

PETS' WAR

Inevitably, in a country that set up the Royal Society for the Prevention of Cruelty to Animals as early as 1824, there was concern for family pets during the Blitz. The RSPCA recommended a hood, placed over the dog's cotton-wool-filled ears and tied under its chin to minimise the noise of explosions. Wisely, the officials warned that 'few cats will tolerate anything of the kind'. Since the cotton-wool pads were to be placed under the ear flaps and not in the ears themselves, only certain breeds would feel the benefit. German Shepherds, for example, would not be able to use these hoods!

Pet food was at a premium, just as human food was and again, the RSPCA suggested mashing up and boiling stale bread (toasted), cabbage, cauliflower, brussels sprouts and turnips. A similar stodge was recommended for caged birds.

In the meantime, some hopefuls called upon Parliament to provide a small milk ration for cats.

THE PHANTOM FORTRESS

It was 23 November 1944, when an Allied airfield in Belgium had an unexpected visitor. A solitary B-17, one of the bombers nicknamed a 'Flying Fortress' for their toughness and weight of armaments, was heading their way a bit too fast for the liking of the ground crew. It must be an emergency landing. Not that there was anything odd about that, it happened all the time.

The B-17 came in on a wing and a prayer, it was a clumsy landing, but it landed in one piece. The ground crew waited for the pilot and crew to disembark, but for twenty minutes it just sat there with the propellers whirring and the engine running. Eventually, the observers decided to investigate.

The plane, unbelievably, was empty. Like a flying version of the Mary Celeste, the ghost ship that haunted sailors' nightmares, there was simply no one on board. The plane had all the signs of life, including half-eaten chocolate bars, the log book's cryptic final entry simply read 'bad flak'.

An investigation by the 8th Air Force revealed that the plane had taken part in a bombing run of German oil refineries. The crew were tracked down elsewhere and were all alive and well.

It turned out that during the run, the B-17 was hit by enemy fire, an engine was damaged and the bomb bay was hit, although miraculously it didn't detonate the payload. The plane was damaged, an engine was down, and with fears that the bombs could go off any moment, the crew made the justified decision to parachute out. The last crewman putting the plane into autopilot before he jumped out. The pilot Harold R. DeBolt would say, 'I'll be damned if I know why the bombs didn't explode'.

What happened next is murky and hotly debated, but it seems that with the perfect combination of the right speed, the failed engine making the plane lose altitude and a huge pinch of luck the plane appeared to those on the ground to be making a half-decent landing.

Many accounts of pilotless planes flying on were accounted for during the war, though this is the only known successful landing. There is a lot to this account that raises the eyebrows of historians. Nevertheless, the phantom fortress and its spooky landing still intrigues servicemen, military buffs and paranormal enthusiasts alike!

THE PHOTOGRAPH ALBUMS OF AUSCHWITZ

The Auschwitz Album' is a one-of-a-kind collection of photographs taken from inside the infamous concentration camp. The album contains 193 images, evidencing the horror of Auschwitz-Birkenau.

The upsetting images storyboard the nightmarish experience of a newly arrived group of Hungarian Jews in 1944. We follow the victims through their journey, from the unloading of the trains and the 'selection' process of those who were deemed unfit for work being sent to their immediate deaths, where they have to seemingly wait their turn on the grass outside a crematorium. An area mockingly named as *Kanada*, (Canada) 'the land of plenty', where the stolen belongings of the victims were sorted is also pictured.

The evidence seems to suggest the photographs were overtly taken by the SS themselves, but if this is the case – why? The Nazis were careful to keep the death camps a secret from the outside world and it is unclear what official purpose the images would serve.

The Auschwitz Album is not in this book because it is weird in itself, or even that the motives or identities of the photographer(s) have never been revealed. It is here because of its astonishing survival through the decades, particularly when we consider the zealousness of the SS in destroying all evidence of their crimes.

Even more remarkable than its survival, is the unbelievable way it was discovered. A survivor of Auschwitz, Lilly Zelmanovic, was recovering in the now liberated Dora concentration camp after the liberation of the Allies and was resting in an old SS barracks. In the barracks, she happened to come across the album in a nearby cupboard, not only containing pictures of herself and her family but many of her neighbours. This is even more surprising when you consider that Dora is over 400 miles away from Auschwitz!

Other than a handful of surreptitious and blurry photographs taken by brave sonderkommandos, this album is the only photographic evidence we have of the inner workings of Auschwitz. The contents of the album were later used in war-crime trials. Lilly Zelmanovic donated the album, minus pictures she donated to friends and other survivors earlier, to Yad Vashem in 1980 and it was published later that year. Despite speculation, the identity and motive of the original photographer(s) will likely never be certain.

Contrasted with the wholesale slaughter of the *Auschwitz* Album is the *Höcker Album*, named after Obersturmfuhrer Karl Höcker, who is assumed to have been its original owner. The 116 pictures in this album, without context, seem harmless enough, but knowing that the smiling faces within belong to the wardens of Auschwitz make it all the more sinister.

Höcker and his colleagues, along with the Helferinnen (women helpers) are pictured joking and laughing, enjoying a getaway to the lakeside resort of Solahutte, 30 kilometres from the main camp. An accordion player leads a sing-along with 70 SS men. Höcker sits among the Helferinnen enjoying blueberries and sunbathing in deck chairs. All this in late 1944, a particularly busy and brutal time for the death camp, the crematoria at some points being unable to keep up with the queue of new corpses.

The Hocker album is unique and priceless, identifying key architects of the Holocaust. Particularly important were the images containing Dr. Josef Mengele, the eight pictures of him within are the only photographic evidence we have that he served at Auschwitz.

This album was found in circumstances equally as extraordinary as those of the Auschwitz Album. An American intelligence officer was billeted to a Frankfurt apartment after the war. Within this apartment, he casually happened across the photo book. He donated it to the United States Holocaust Memorial Museum in 2007, under the condition his identity would be kept confidential.

Höcker was put on trial in Frankfurt in 1965 and sentenced to seven years in prison. He was released after five. He was sentenced to a further four years imprisonment in 1989 and died in 2000, aged 88.

PIGEON GUIDED MISSILES

Pigeons had been used for years as carriers of messages in warfare, most notably from one trench to another in the First World War, but the Second World War saw an entirely new role for them. 'Project Pigeon' was the idea of American psychologist and Harvard professor Burrhus Skinner. He believed that the accuracy of missiles could be increased by training pigeon pilots to sit in them as they were fired and guide them from within. Skinner designed a missile that had three windows to look through in the nose cone where the pigeons, in a sock to limit their movement, were placed. The 'pilots' were specially trained and conditioned to peck at the windows when they saw their target and to keep it in the centre of their vision. If the missile began to go off course the pigeons would tap the window which would alert the sensors of the missile when a window had been pecked and the tailfins would then change direction accordingly and guide the explosive and its passenger to the target of choice.

Despite the absurdity of this, the project appears to have been a great success – with the kamikaze pigeons working better than expected. The only reason for its cancellation was that the military commanders wanted to direct their resources into other projects. Skinner complained, 'no one would take us seriously'.

THE PIGEON MYSTERY

Anyone today who has open fires is familiar with the problem. Unless the cowling on chimney tops is secure, birds of every feather will fly downwards, looking for...whatever birds look for. David Martin had this problem at his home in Bletchingley, Surrey, in 2012 when he cleared out his chimney. The bones of a pigeon came down with the soot and he thought little of it until he noticed a small red capsule attached to a leg bone. He was able to unscrew it and found inside a coded message on paper.

The message was written by Sergeant W. Stott, to a recipient known only as 'XO2'. Intrigued, Martin sent copies of the message to GCHQ, the high security in Cheltenham and to the museum at Bletchley Park, the famous code-breaking centre that unravelled the Enigma mystery.

Coded messages had long been used by soldiers and agents in war and peace time, around the world, but there were problems in deciphering this one. The cracking of codes depended on two parties, the sender and receiver, having the same explanatory code-books. These were changed regularly to prevent vital information (like Enigma) falling into enemy hands. As GCHQ admitted, without the original code books they were stymied. Despite the assertion by some people that they have cracked the code, we are no further forward. There is speculation that the message was sent either to Bomber Command or to Field Marshal Montgomery's headquarters at Reigate, not far from David Martin's home.

The pigeon took its secret to a smoky grave.

PINK POWER

The unusual story of pink spitfires led some to believe it must be a hoax, or the result of too many pink gins. Why on earth would the RAF paint their most prized aircraft in such a garish colour?

And yet the RAF did use pink spitfires, and they were surprisingly effective.

In simple terms, the colour theory for traditional spitfires was that when seen from above, their mottled camouflage greens and browns would blend in with the ground below, and when seen from below, their pale blue/grey undersides would blend in with the sky. At the time of sunrise and sunset however, pink is an excellent choice. The colour was used by the RAF's photographic reconnaissance unit, whose pilots would fly behind enemy lines and photograph targets.

It wasn't just spitfires that were pink, ships appeared to disappear on the horizon when painted a similar cover, giving the Royal Navy a natural advantage. First used in World War I, the colour became known as Mountbatten Pink after Lord Mountbatten, and was used by several warships, despite protestations from more traditional sailors. Experts disagree on how successful the grey-mauve colour actually was.

THE PINK TRIANGLES

Homosexuals were one of the myriad groups persecuted by the Nazis in Germany. By 1945, 100,000 had been arrested, 50,000 were in prison, and up to 15,000 were in concentration camps – the pink triangle on their clothes marking out their 'crime' for all to see. This figure of course doesn't include homosexuals who had found themselves in trouble for other reasons such as being social democrats, Jews or 'asocials'.

The treatment of gay men was appalling. In the curious homo-erotic world of Nazism, they were considered the lowest of the low. Many within the Nazi ranks were homosexual, or had homosexual tendencies, but those who were 'hard' could hide it, those who were 'soft' (read effeminate) weren't so lucky. Homosexuality and sexual promiscuity were commonly used for ad hominem attacks on the opponents of the Nazis, designed to wreck their reputations and social standing, even when utterly without foundation.

Homosexuals could sometimes 'redeem' themselves with acts of manliness or accepting 'cures'. These 'cures' included taking hormone supplements and undergoing experiments on their testicles. Gay men would often be forced to perform sex acts on female inmates, lesbians would have to do the same with men in camp brothels. The cruel dog-eat-dog world of concentration camps saw them abused and attacked by fellow inmates.

Unlike other categories of prisoners, who could look forward to freedom and liberation with the arrival of the Allies, homosexuals had no such guarantee. Depressingly, many of them found they were left in, or sent back to, prison to complete their sentences, because homosexuality was a crime in the eyes of the liberators as well. One instance showed the West German government had kept survivors on a sex offenders' list long after the war.

Gay people received some respite in the 1970s when 'sodomy laws' were repealed. The German government apologized in 2002. Testimony of these 'forgotten victims' who died before the world was ready to accept them is, as a result, tragically sparse.

PRIVATE SNAFU

Private Snafu was a bungling cartoon character who served in the United States army. His name comes from a slang acronym used by the armed forces to describe the general chaos and make-it-up-as-you-go-along attitude of war. To more respectable audiences S.N.A.F.U was bowdlerised as 'Situation Normal, All *Fouled* Up'.

Private Snafu served in cartoons from 1943 to 1945 and was voiced by Mel Blanc, the legendary voice over actor who also gave us Bugs Bunny, Daffy Duck, Porky Pig, Speedy Gonzales and countless others. The cartoons were written by a team including Theodor Geisel, better known by his pen-name Dr. Seuss.

Not all soldiers serving in the armed forces were literate. Many received inadequate education. Private Snafu was on hand to help, his light-hearted cartoons show him demonstrating how to behave. Therefore, by getting things wrong, the audience could understand the need for military protocol and correct behaviour.

The cartoons were intended solely for a military audience, and a whole range of paranoid security measures were put in place to keep Private Snafu a secret from the enemy and civilians. Workers on the animation were only given ten celluloids at a time, to stop them working out in advance the plot of the cartoon!

Private Snafu may not have made it into this book if it wasn't for his episode 'Going Home'. In this 1944 cartoon, Snafu is returning to the United States on leave. While home he wanders around town, carelessly blabbing military secrets to civilians. In the next scene he is in a cinema with a young lady, and this is where things get interesting.

In the cartoon clip, the cinema screen shows a secret weapon that is being developed by the Americans. This 'bazooka bomb' has, at a push, some similarities to the atom bomb, which in the real world was being developed as part of the top-secret Manhattan Project. The bomb then obliterates a Japanese island to which the narrator jokes, 'What hit you, Tojo? Wouldn't you like to know.'

It's been alleged that this cartoon disturbed the powers that be so much they had the cartoon pulled and it was never shown. This seems somewhat over the top, given Private Snafu's track record it is unlikely he had prophesied nuclear warfare. What *is* unusual though is it is not clear exactly why this particular episode was never released and there are several theories on this.

Could the cartoon have been a bit too close for comfort to the top-secret atomic bomb? Given the behavior and paranoia of all governments across the world at the time it is not outside the realms of possibility.

Snafu finally revealed himself to the civilian world in a 1999 VHS collection. He is now in the public domain and his cartoons can be viewed freely on the internet.

PROPER PROPAGANDA

Propaganda during the Second World War was an unavoidable aspect of daily life. It must be a situation that is hard to relate to for those of us in the West born too late or too young to remember the war or the decades afterwards. The idea that you must always be alert to the ominous drone of the air-raid sirens as you went about your business, or that your home could be destroyed in an aerial bombardment at any moment is very hard to comprehend. But those who lived through the war knew it was perfectly possible that the Wehrmacht could soon be marching through the streets, with all the chaos, fear, death and destruction that that would imply.

Against this backdrop we can understand why propaganda was so vital to all sides of the conflict. For those interested in the psychology of the past, propaganda posters are a great glimpse into the (understandable) paranoia, hysteria and concerns of those who created them, and the message they thought it was necessary to promote to everyone else.

All of these posters served some sort of purpose, and modern cynicism means it is often hard not to scoff at some of them, because to us they are now often unintentionally humorous or offensive. Those in government at the time knew that war had evolved. The Great War had changed much, and this latest conflict with Germany would create a huge strain, both in terms of morale and in the nation's resources, and it was vital to have and maintain full support for the war at home.

While propaganda was nothing new, it came into its own during the Second World War. British posters were, in the main, created by the controversial Ministry of Information, a government department that was dissolved soon after the war and probably one of George Orwell's inspirations for 'Big Brother'. Many contemporary members of parliament were very disturbed by the agenda of this department and protested that there was a very real danger that Britain could ironically sleep-walk into becoming the fascist, brain-washed state with which they were at war.

The messages behind most of these posters is overt and obvious. The well-known, but never actually distributed, 'Keep Calm and Carry On' posters are still recognisable to us today, over 70 years later. Other messages may verge on the bizarre to those who never knew the horrors of the conflict first-hand. One poster shows a soldier and his partner on a sofa with the message 'Keep mum (stay silent), she might not be so dumb', implying that his girlfriend may, at best, be a loudmouth who will report his military operations to everyone in town and, at worst, be a Gestapo agent who had been planted into his home. This isn't to mock the sentiment, but simply to point out how difficult it is for a modern mind to understand.

Other posters urging mothers to evacuate their children away from towns as refugees to find safety in the countryside, or even abroad to the security of Canada or other parts of the empire are quite shocking. Still more so are those which implied that people taking a day off work due to sickness could be shirking, or that those who lost a tool at work were aiding Hitler, are quite unsettling even now.

American propaganda was often racist, showing rat-like Japanese. One dramatic poster, featuring two creepy children in their gas masks and proclaiming 'Dear God, keep them safe!' is still striking.

On the Axis side, they were oddly obsessed with reminding Allied soldiers, particularly Americans, that their women were back at home, probably sleeping with someone else and that 'the negroes' were now running the country.

Soviet sources claim they recovered Nazi prototypes for German TV shows which would be played on huge screens in public areas. Overseen by engineer Walter Brutsch, show ideas allegedly included 'Family Chronicles: An Evening with Hans and Gelli', a reality TV type show, where Hans and Gelli would demonstrate the Aryan ideals of home life. Executions would also be filmed and shown to the public.

RECON FLIGHT 300

December 1942, and the war was reaching its zenith. No one could confidently predict how it would all pan out: who would win, who would be crushed. The Allies were growing in strength, but Germany and Japan were still enormously powerful and dangerous. It was now that the war presented one of its most chilling, and still unexplained, mysteries.

Three hundred miles north of Bergen, Norway, the RAF reconnaissance flight 300 was taking photographs of key locations deep within the Scandinavian country. Upon returning to Britain and having the film developed, shocked analysts caught a glimpse of something unnatural. When they magnified the shot, something ... appeared. The aircrew had inadvertently taken a picture, and provided real evidence of, a Norwegian mountain troll.

Or so the story goes.

There is no need to look deeply into this. It is plainly a hoax. The actual photograph could be from the time, but it is clearly doctored. The picture, which was probably altered with Photoshop or a similar digital editor, shows what appears to be the outline of a gigantic troll moving through the fog, towering over a forest below.

This prank is worth noting, though, because it is so modern and demonstrates perfectly the nonsense (before, during and after events) that serious academics, historians (and writer-researchers!) often find themselves having to sift through to find the elusive nuggets of truth. The 'culprit' behind this jape is unknown - the evidence appears to point in the direction of a talented freelance illustrator, photo-manipulator and artist.

Even if we consider this story and photograph with a completely open mind and give them the benefit of the doubt, there are so many questions that the whole matter quickly becomes laughable. For example: who and what was 'Recon Flight 300', and what was their actual military objective? Why, in other words, were they overflying and photographing a section of forest? If they *didn't* see the troll, why take a picture of the woods? If they *did* see the troll, why didn't they at least report it, and take many more pictures to verify their sighting? Finally, how could such a gigantic creature feed, eat, shelter and breed – while its Norwegian neighbours remained blissfully unaware of its gargantuan presence?

My own personal opinion, though not corroborated in any way, is that this picture was a tie-in to generate buzz for the mockumentary film *Trollhunter*, directed by André Øvredal and released in 2010.

THE RED BOOK

The gung-ho war movies of the 1950s portray a stoic British nation, usually embodied by lantern-jawed actors like Jack Hawkins and Anthony Steele, united in a patriotic cause against the tyranny of Nazi Germany. Actually, it was not quite like that. As in *The Gauleiter of the Bahamas*, there were elements of the aristocracy in particular who were not only pro-peace (the Hitler appeasers like Neville Chamberlain) but anti-Bolshevik, anti-Semitic and pro-Nazi.

Nowhere was this more obvious than in the creation of the Right Club in 1939, shortly before the outbreak of war. Their names – 135 men and 100 women – were listed in a lockable, leather-bound ledger called the Red Book. Had the Germans successfully invaded in the summer of 1940, which was the plan, these 'fellow travellers of the Right' would have been heroes.

The leader of the club was Archibald Maude Ramsay, an MP and minor Scots aristocrat who left the group because Oswald Mosley, also an MP, effectively took it over. Together with the Link, another pro-German group, there were several thousand people in pre and early war Britain who were rightly regarded with suspicion by MI5 and Churchill's government. Some of them left the groups when war was declared, but others stayed on, making broadcasts on behalf of the 'New British Broadcasting Service' from Germany that was busy counting 'the lies' of the Jewish-owned BBC proper!

Ramsay gave the Red Book to the American embassy in London. The United States did not join the war until December 1941 and Ramsay no doubt hoped that the list, effectively on American neutral soil, would be safe from the British authorities. The Scotsman had sensitive documents from Churchill to Chamberlain at this crucial – and confused – time in British politics, and he believed that publication of these papers would dissuade the States, under President F.D. Roosevelt from joining the war.

In the event, MI5 moved faster. The Red Book fell into their hands and lots of the list were arrested as would-be enemy agents under the new Defence Regulation 18B. Ramsey himself, Oswald Mosley and his wife, Diane Mitford and Sir Barry Domville, once director of naval intelligence, all found themselves behind bars.

RESCUE DOGS

For those of us who have never experienced it, we can only imagine the claustrophobic nightmare of being the victim of a bombing raid, trapped under piles of brick and dust, choking, perhaps being slowly crushed, in the dark, with limbs injured, and in a great deal of pain. This was the fate of untold civilians throughout the war who were victims of the Blitz and similar air attacks.

Imagine then, being met by a wet nose and a pair of furry paws. For 100 lucky victims of the London Blitz, this was Rip the dog. Rip himself had been a victim, being found as a stray after a 1940 attack on Poplar. He happened across an air raid warden, E. King, King threw the dog some scraps in the hope the dog would go away, but he didn't, and an unlikely friendship was formed.

Rip was a natural for search and rescue operations and helped those scrabbling through the rubble for survivors. He was said to be unbothered by dangers such as fire and smoke and the horrible drone of the air raid sirens. What is so remarkable about Rip, is unlike later dogs, he had no training and did his work on his own volition. The success of Rip gave the authorities thought for the use of dogs in future search and rescue operations.

Rip was awarded the Dickin Medal and wore it the rest of his life. In 2009, the medal was auctioned and sold for £24,250.

There were countless other canine heroes, and recipients of the Dickin Medal, such as Jet the German Shepherd from Liverpool who saved around 150 people. Jet would howl every night, but he finally stopped at the same time as the air raid attacks ceased.

Crumstone Irma worked with her owner, Margaret Griffin, and another dog, Psyche, both Irma and Psyche were German Shepherds. Irma was able to give different sounding barks depending on whether those under the ruins were dead or alive. Two young girls had been trapped under a building for two days, Irma barked 'alive!' – she wouldn't give up. The rescuers around her thought, 'Poor Irma, she must have got it wrong. No one's coming out of that ruin alive.' But she got it right. To the amazement of the rescue workers, the girls were pulled out and survived.

Thorn, another German Shepherd, once detected the scent of a family trapped under a burning house – how a dog could pick up the scent among the smoke and flames baffled the rescue workers – but Thorn was right, and another family was rescued.

It is interesting to note that 'Alsatian' and 'German Shepherd' are terms for the same breed. The name was changed during the First World War. Fearing that people who kept a 'German' shepherd would be displaying an unwholesome affinity with the Hun enemy, it was decided to refer to the breed as Alsatian, after the Alsace region of France. The Americans changed the name to 'Shepherd Dog' in 1917. In the United Kingdom, the Kennel Club returned the breed to German Shepherd once more in 1977 - but 'Alsatian' continues to linger on as the colloquial name for the breed to the present day.

THE RIDDLE OF RUDOLF HESS

Perhaps the single most weird incident of the Second World War happened on the night of the 10/11 May 1941 when Rudolf Hess, Hitler's deputy in the Third Reich, took off from Augsburg airfield in a Messerschmitt Bf110 and crash-landed hours later at Eaglesham, Scotland. Hess himself bailed out and was captured within minutes, spending the rest of his long life in various prisons. His purpose, most researchers believe, is that he was attempting to broker a peace deal with British dissidents anxious to remove the war-mongering Churchill and bring the war to an end. The controversy rages over who exactly Hess thought he was going to meet – such people could have been hanged for treason – and whether the whole thing was an example of Hess's own delusions or whether he was lured across by British Intelligence.

Two particularly odd incidents stand out in this bizarre story. The first is that it had been predicted in fiction. In 1940, Peter Fleming, brother of Ian who would go on to create James Bond in the Cold War era, wrote a novel called *Flying Visit* in which Hitler himself parachutes into England. Was this purely coincidence or had Rudolf

Hess seen a copy (his English was pretty good) and had it given him the germ of an idea?

The first that Churchill knew of Hess's arrival was when he was briefed by telephone at Ditchley Hall, his 'safe house' near Blenheim. Having been informed that an airman looking remarkably like Rudolf Hass had arrived, he went to see a private screening of a Marx Brothers comedy at the house. The obvious explanation is that Churchill already knew about the Hess flight, because it was, indeed, engineered by British Intelligence with the Prime Minister's blessing. If he did *not* know, going to watch the Marx Brothers at so crucial a time would have given both Churchill's allies and his enemies pause for thought over the man's sanity!

ROBINSON CRUSOE

The Warsaw Uprising was a brave action in August 1944 by the Polish to throw the Germans out of the city that they had occupied for five long and cruel years. The uprising was planned to coincide with the Red Army advance, and the Polish resistance fighters hoped to aid the Soviet attack to join in the liberation of their city, but the Soviet advance halted. It is suspected that Stalin had decided to leave the Polish, his former enemy, to their fate.

Unsurprisingly, without outside help, the German military overcame the resistance and destroyed over a quarter of the buildings in the city, in some areas going from house to house with flamethrowers. Including the buildings destroyed beforehand, Warsaw saw some 85% of all its buildings demolished during the war.

The Polish fought bravely, holding out for 63 days, but with little support, they could do no more.

There were some groups of survivors from the uprising, and remarkably there were still Jews among them. Some took their chances and ran, while others decided their best hope was to stay and hide in the ruins until it was all over. Surely the Soviets would be there any day.

These survivors became known as the Robinson Crusoes of Warsaw, named after the eponymous hero from the famous 1719 book by Daniel Defoe, which followed the life of a castaway on a desert island who survived many adventures before finally returning to civilization. One survivor of Warsaw, David Fogelman, wrote 'We lived like Robinson Crusoes, with the one difference he was free.' Fogelman's fate is unknown.

The number of different groups of Crusoes, ranging from individuals to dozens, is believed to be as high as two thousand. Most were eventually caught and killed, and the stories of the survivors alone are known to us. That some groups survived so long is astonishing.

Warsaw was the bare husk of a city. Himmler had decreed 'the city must completely disappear from the face of the earth'. The Crusoes endured in maddening isolation, hiding like rats and scavenging, if strong enough, by night. Water was precious, and a good day was had by finding a toilet cistern or an old boiler. Finding a few scraps of food made for an excellent day. Survival was not easy. Many were finished off by the cold, as lighting a fire involved the risk of exposing their position to the enemy. The undying myth of drinking your own urine also took many lives.

There are many notable cases of Crusoes. One, or perhaps a collective, called himself Ares, after the Greek god of war and became a local legend. He would ambush enemy soldiers and graffiti his name among the ruins as a warning. On one victim he left a note, 'Ares is a ghost, not matter – your search for him is useless.' One story states Ares was dying of poisoning, after eating food that had been deliberately contaminated and left as a trap, not before firing off a few shots with his pistol into the enemy ranks and taking his own life. Another legend states that Ares arranged dead combatants sat in a circle and listening to a gramophone. When the enemy went to investigate, he ambushed them with grenades.

The most famous Crusoe was Wladyslaw Spilzman. He wrote his harrowing story in 1946, in a book called *The Pianist,* which was adapted to become Roman Polanski's 2002 film of the same name. He was spared, and aided, by the chivalrous German captain Wilm Hosenfeld – who was made Righteous Among the Nations by Israel's Yad Vashem. Five years after the war Spilzman learned of Hosenfeld's identity and tried to help him, but he without success. The captain died two years later in a Soviet POW camp.

The Soviets – who had previously invaded Poland with the Nazis - left the Polish to it for three agonizing months. Even refusing permission for the planes of the Western Allies carrying aid to land. The Polish government-in-exile implored the Allies to assist, but they would not move without Stalin's agreement. Churchill asked Roosevelt and Stalin to take part, but they didn't. He eventually authorized clandestine RAF supply drops by night from Italian airfields, 223 sorties were made, but it was simply too little to be of much assistance. The Germans eventually abandoned the city in 1945.

ROUND CORNERS – *KRUMMLAUF*

Much of the hand-to-hand fighting in the Second World War, by commandos as well as regular assault troops, took place in cities, towns and villages where buildings provided both cover and death-traps, depending on their situation. The obvious problem of physics is that a soldier cannot see what is hidden around a corner! One solution was a Krummlauf (bent barrel), an attachment for the Sturmgewehr 44 assault rifle used by the Germans. There were many variations from a 30 degree bend all the way up to 90 degrees. The concept of the Krummlauf was to allow soldiers to continue firing without breaking cover; a complex scope allowed them to do this. The bent rifles weren't particularly effective, having a short life span and questionable accuracy.

The Russians issued a variant to their tank crews in the war's later stages but today, Krummlaufs are displayed in museums as technological oddities.

THE SAILOR BOY

The First World War has a number of stories about patriotic lads volunteering for the services, lying about their age and stuffing their boots with paper to increase their height. Many of these are apocryphal, but one, from the Second World War, is completely genuine.

Calvin Graham is the youngest person ever to serve in the United States military. He was just twelve years old when he signed up. After boot camp in San Diego, he joined the Navy and served on a battleship, the USS *South Dakota,* based at Pearl Harbor, now rebuilt after the Japanese attack ten months earlier. In October 1942, he saw action against the Japanese at Santa Cruz and Guadalcanal and was wounded by shrapnel, receiving the Bronze Star with combat 'V' and Purple Heart medals.

Graham was absent without leave from the Navy when he returned home to Texas for his grandmother's funeral, at which point his mother told the military that her son was only twelve. He spent three months in prison because he had absented himself without permission and was dismissed from the Navy without his medals or benefits on 1 April 1943.

Graham would join the Marines in 1948 but again was dismissed after an injury three years later. He was finally given an honourable discharge in 1978. His story was immortalized in the 1988 film *Too Young the Hero* starring Ricky Schroeder, after which he received full disability benefits. Graham's Purple Heart medal was finally reinstated in 1994, two years after he had died.

SALON KITTY

Salon Kitty was a brothel located at 11, Giesebrechtstrasse in Charlottenburg, an upmarket area of Berlin, run by the glamorous Katharina Zammit who called herself Kitty Schmidt and provided expensive services for diplomats, top civil servants and senior politicians. Madame Kitty was also sending money to Britain via those fleeing the Nazis and tried to escape herself in June 1939. She was captured and forced by Walter Schellenburg, the operational director of the SD, the Reich's secret service, to cooperate or be sent to a concentration camp. Having been coerced, Salon Kitty was now a Nazi brothel.

The notion of using Salon Kitty for spying and intelligence came from Reinhard Heydrich, the 'blond beast' who was Heinrich Himmler's Number Two in the SS. A secret code word was given to those in the know – 'I come from Rothenburg' – which would allow them access to the exclusive club. This code word only failed once, when an actual man from Rothenburg knocked. Unbeknownst to the visitors, the girls were Nazi sex spies and within the basement of the brothel, SS officers were secretly listening in to the conversations between the girls and their customers, the idea being that the relaxed and private setting would give away the true feelings of the men there. The clients were well cared for and filled with wine and the specially trained girls would ask leading questions to ascertain the loyalties and secrets of those they were entertaining.

The information gleaned was perhaps not as useful as was hoped. Galeazzo Ciano, Mussolini's son-in-law, moaned about Hitler but generally it just ended up revealing the sexual preferences of Nazis, including Sepp Dietrich, Commander of the elite *Liebstandarte Adolf Hitler* unit, who wanted twenty girls for an orgy. Joseph Goebbels enjoyed 'lesbian displays'. Heydrich took it upon himself to 'inspect' the girls from time to time, the microphones being switched off for these visits. It is estimated that 25,000 recordings were made, most of which fell into Soviet hands when Berlin fell in 1945.

In July 1942, the salon took a direct hit during an air raid and although the business was relocated, the SD decided that it had more urgent problems than snooping on its own people. Madame Kitty continued to run the brothel after the close of the war and took her business's secret Nazi past to her grave.

SANTA'S WARS

In the irreligious twenty-first century, the most persistent surviving myth relating to St Nicholas (Santa Claus) is that he lives in Lapland, working hard all year round with his faithful team of elves to make the toys he then delivers to all good children at Christmas time.

The Lapps, who call themselves Samelat, can be found across the modern state frontiers of Norway, Sweden, Finland and Russia, with a sizeable colony in Alaska. They are a shamanic people, like the Inuit, worshipping the bear, not a white-bearded old man driving reindeer, although the Scandinavian Lapps are reindeer-nomads. With the coming of Christianity, most of them became Lutheran.

The Second World War, for most of us in the West, is seen as a continuous struggle from 1939 to '45 but in Finland, it forms three distinct campaigns. The first was the Winter War (30 November 1939-13 March 1940) when, in accordance with the Ribbentrop-Molotov agreement, the Soviet Union invaded. Britain and France were sympathetic to the Lapps. Although the Russo-German accord was secret, no free people were happy with unjustified invasion. The problem was that the west had its hands full against the speed and power of the German blitzkrieg and could not help the Finns out. In fact, the Finnish army, used to their vicious winters and equipped for them, fought the Russians to a standstill. Stalin, of course, had a dozen excuses: the winter was worse than usual (it wasn't); the Mannerheim Line was stronger than the Maginot (it wasn't); and the Americans had sent a thousand pilots to bolster up the fledgling Finnish air force (they hadn't).

The second campaign was the Continuation War (25 June 1941-19 September 1944). With no help from the west (despite America's involvement by this time) the Finns chose the lesser of two evils and joined the Axis to regain the territory taken from them by the Russians. Somehow, the fighting spirit of the Winter War had gone. The Finns got no further than Leningrad and stayed there for years.

The third campaign was the Lapland War (15 September 1944-27 April 1945). The Soviet Union gave Finland an ultimatum – kick the Germans out of their territories or face the consequences. This was a grim task, as the Wehrmacht retreated westward carrying out a scorched earth policy and leaving nothing but devastation in their wake.

Finland's political position in the Second World War was unique. It changed sides twice and was the only democracy allied with the Axis powers. It was also the only country east of Germany that did not become a Russian puppet behind the Iron Curtain from 1946. And Helsinki, the capital, was the only capital in Europe, other than London and Moscow, that did not fall to the enemy.

One of the Lapland towns that was obliterated in the German retreat was Rovaniemi. It was rebuilt by architect alvar Aalto in a reindeer-shaped street grid and Eleanor Roosevelt, widow of the American president, made a surprise visit there in 1950 to launch Roosevelt Cottage, a UNICEF project. Originally a Luftwaffe airfield, the local airport was renamed Santa's official Airport and Santa's Village stands over an old Wehrmacht barracks, visited by thousands of tourists every year. Seven hundred thousand letters from children around the world reach Rovaniemi every year.

Let's hope that Father Christmas will never see another war in his homeland!

THE SAUSAGE WAR

Before the war, Stalin and Hitler carved up Eastern Europe between them in secret talks. In these discussions, Stalin was given Finland – which he wanted back after they broke away from Russia following the Russian civil war.

Despite a ten-year non-aggression pact signed in 1932, on 30th November 1939 the Soviets bombed Helsinki, and the Winter War began. The British and French were outraged, and the Soviets were expelled from the League of Nations. But Britain and France had to tread carefully. They were already at war with Nazi Germany and taking on the Soviet Union too would have been suicidal. Most assumed Finland would crumble after a few weeks. There was nothing to be done to save the Finns from the Soviet onslaught.

Despite being overwhelmingly outnumbered, the Finns put up a brave fight, their knowledge of the land and the harsh winter of 1939 caused chaos for the Red Army. The Finns were like ghosts, suddenly appearing, fighting with determination and skill and then melting away into the snow after each fight – but one alleged battle was not quite so mysterious and romantic.

On 10 December it is claimed the Soviets launched a surprise attack on the Finns near the village of Illomantsi. The Finns weren't prepared and fled. But the battle took an unusual turn. The Finnish cooks had just finished preparing a batch of delicious sausages in their cooking tents, and the smell was too much for the attackers. The starving Russians stopped and began tucking in to the sausages. The pause gave the Finns long enough to regroup, reform, and counter-attack. Their ferocity and the unpreparedness of the Russian soldiers meant that only a few of the Soviets survived. It is claimed that many of the Red Army died with sausages still in their hands and their mouths. This incident would become known as 'the sausage war'.

Is the sausage war true? We have only the word of the victorious Finns, but it was not a surprising event. Throughout history, starving soldiers have been known to set aside their weapons when finding food and drink. It has been reported that Ludendorff's swift advance in 1918 was halted not by Allied counter-attacks, but by the discovery by German soldiers of stockpiles of food and wine. Exhausted and starving, the soldiers fell on the supplies and the German attack was halted. Still, the Sausage War does show the disorganization of the Soviet army, mostly caused by Stalin's paranoid purges of his military elite at the time.

The Finns held out long enough to force the Soviets to reach a cease-fire. Later, the Finns were caught between a rock and a hard place. Finally, they felt forced to ally themselves with Nazi Germany, from motives of self-survival against the threat once more from Russia, though they did not join the Axis.

In the west the Allies understood Finland's unique position. The British formally declared war – probably to assuage Stalin – but America didn't bother. It is thought that the Finns' courage had an even more world-changing consequence: the poor performance of the Soviets was noted in Germany. Perhaps it stirred stronger ambitions in Hitler: perhaps the effectiveness of the Finns in the Winter War convinced him that an attack on Russia could succeed. Perhaps his eye turned, earlier than he originally planned, to the east.

The Soviet Union continued to deny the existence of the Molotov-Ribbentrop Pact long after the war, dismissing it as Western propaganda, until finally doing the honourable thing in 1989.

SAVITRI DEVI

Maximiani Portas was a French-Greek-Italian mystic who went by the pseudonym Savitri Devi. She is considered by some to be the founder of 'esoteric Hitlerism', the belief in the divinity of the Fuehrer.

After the First World War, Devi believed that Greece and Germany had been humiliated and unjustly punished as whipping boys for the bloody aftermath of the conflict, despising the harshness of the Treaty of Versailles. She blamed Judeo-Christianity for eradicating any memory of a heroic Aryan past, and believed, like many others at the time, that the Aryans descended from India.

Travelling to India, the sight of a white woman travelling fourth class by train raised the eyebrows of many and the British began to keep her under surveillance. She learned Indian languages, married a Brahmin, and went to work on her writings of a mystical Aryan utopia. Devi was an ardent admirer of Hitler, believing him to be an Avatar – an incarnation of the Hindu god Vishnu – as stated in her book *The Lightning and the Sun*. She travelled the country giving lectures and quoting liberally from *Mein Kampf*. During the war, she even spied for the Axis, and passed on vital information to the Japanese forces.

In 1948, three years after the war, Savitri Devi travelled to Germany and began distributing leaflets boasting 'One day we shall rise and triumph again! Hope and wait! Heil Hitler!' This message was divinely inspired, she would write. Arrested and charged, she was sentenced to two years in prison, where she befriended Nazi and SS inmates, including a 'beautiful-looking' female warden from Belsen. After eight months she was released and deported. She then went on a 'pilgrimage' of Nazi sites. Rumours spread that Francoise Dior, niece of Christian Dior the fashion designer was her lesbian lover. She befriended the unrepentant Nazi, Hans-Ulrich Rudel, and wrote *The Lightning and the Sun* at his home.

Her later years saw her return to India with a collection of cats – and a cobra. She did not have the same disdain for animals that she exhibited towards humans. She travelled to England in 1982, dying the same year. Her ashes were laid to rest with full honours next to George Lincoln Rockwell, head of the American Nazi Party in Arlington, Virginia – now the site of a coffee shop.

What is weird here is how an animal-loving French-Greek-Italian mystic, the wife of a Hindu Brahmin, who befriended a swathe of neo-Nazis, could reconcile Hindu mythology with National Socialism, and how her occultist theories and cosmic inventions would be taken so seriously by some of her readers.

THE SCHICKLGRUBER LIBEL

A common story is that Adolf Hitler was in fact Adolf Schicklgruber, but changed his surname to Hitler. This isn't quite true and the story has its roots with the propaganda and psychological warfare that raged on both sides of the conflict. The supposed scandal of Hitler's unconventional family life and upbringing and the comedy of the name Schicklgruber was dug up by the Allies and they felt it was too good to miss, sharing the tale in newspapers and on the radio. The Schicklgruber story is usually attributed to Hans Habe, an Austrian journalist who escaped Nazi persecution and became an American citizen in 1941. He worked at the Psychological Warfare Unit of Military Intelligence at Camp Ritchie in Maryland. He joined the 1st Mobile Radio Broadcasting Company, accompanying the American army to North Africa and Italy.

There is much dispute of the parentage of Hitler's father Aloïs. It seems he was either the illegitimate child of Johann Heidler and Maria Anna Schicklgruber, or Heidler took on Maria's family, or he may have been the lovechild of Johann Nepomuk. In any case, eventually Heidler and Maria were married but Aloïs was not legitimized. Upon Johann's death Aloïs was finally legitimized by his uncle and took the name Heidler from 1877 onwards. Surnames and spellings took many variations at this point so Heidler could be Hytler or Hitler or other variants. Aloïs had six children with his wife, Klara, (who, if he was Nepomuk's son, was his half-niece), the granddaughter of Johann Nepomuk. Hitler was the surname spelling that was always used, in Aloïs' family from 1877 when the official name was registered at the government offices in Mistelbach, Austria.

THE SCHOOLGIRL AND THE SPITFIRE

The Second World War has been called the 'Wizard's War' – never before had so much ingenious technology been used to defeat an enemy.

Captain Fred Hill was a 'boffin', a scientific officer working for the British Air

Ministry, itself a novel organization in terms of the history of warfare. His particular area of expertise was the development of Supermarine Spitfires and Hawker Hurricanes, the fighter aircraft that have an iconic status today. Each plane was equipped with four cannon (the obsolete term for guns was still officially in use) and Hill doubted whether that would be enough in aerial duels with the enemy.

In the 1930s, everybody was working in the dark. The threat was from aggressive, ambitious Nazi Germany but the official government line from prime ministers Stanley Baldwin and Neville Chamberlain, was one of appeasement - work with Herr Hitler and all would be well. Behind the scenes, however, more pragmatic minds had to prepare for any eventuality. The Luftwaffe was an unknown force. In theory, the Treaty of Versailles had severely limited the size of Germany's armed forces - the air force could only fly gliders, for example. In practice, Herman Goering's Luftwaffe were building aircraft secretly in Soviet Russian territory - Dorniers, Heinkels and Messerschmitts.

The military dictum was that 'the bomber will always get through' because bombing was a new and terrifying concept. Only German bombing of Guernica in the Spanish Civil War stood to bear witness to just how terrifying. Captain Hill wanted to balance the odds. Convinced that four guns per fighter would be inadequate, he spent night after night at his kitchen table, working with his 13-year-old daughter, Hazel, to calculate trajectories, rates of fire and gun-weight. Hazel was what today we would call dyslexic, but her grasp of numbers was astonishing and if Dad could not work it out, Hazel could. Hill presented his findings to the Air Ministry, proving that the eight-gun nay-sayers were wrong; eight guns would not slow a fighter plane appreciably and the fire-power advantage was incalculable. The Ministry was impressed - eight guns it was.

The result was the unprecedented Battle of Britain, with dog-fights snarling over the skies of southern England. The Luftwaffe was outfought because it was outgunned - thanks to Captain Hill and his girl. In 2020 the remarkable story was told in a BBC documentary *The Schoolgirl Who Helped To Win a War*.

SEALAND V REGINA

The history of the Principality of Sealand is one of the most fascinating and charming curiosities of the modern age. It is a contender for the smallest country on Earth, has its own royal family, is not recognized by anyone internationally, and it encompasses solely one small metal and concrete platform just off Felixstowe, with no permanent population except a handful of security guards.

As part of Britain's defences during the Second World War, a chain of sea forts fitted with anti-aircraft guns were built in the North Sea to protect the country's vulnerable eastern flank. However, several of these forts were constructed in international waters and were outside British territorial waters and therefore jurisdiction, not that it would have mattered during the crisis and urgent need of war. Churchill would not have been concerned so long as Britain had her defences.

One of these sea forts called 'Knock John', abandoned at the war's end, lay invitingly in the North Sea. The charismatic Major Roy Bates of the British Army sensed an opportunity that was too good to be missed. Major Bates travelled to the sea-fort and set up a pirate radio station. The British government weren't impressed and took legal action. Bates took on the might of the Crown in a legal battle, which he naturally had no chance of winning. The courts declared Knock John was within British territory. But why let the Crown pick the battlefield? Another fort, 'Roughs Tower', was seven nautical miles out and, in the eyes of their own law, beyond their three-mile grasp.

In September 1967 the Bates family, supported by a small contingent of friends and well-wishers, took over Roughs Tower, declared their independence and claimed sovereignty with the birth of the Principality of Sealand. His wife became Princess Joan.

The British establishment was infuriated. Some tried to claim, somewhat melodramatically, that they feared Sealand could be a 'Cuba off the east coast of England.' They blew up all the remaining sea forts and used helicopters to intimidate the Sealanders by hovering close above their platform. A demolition crew was to be sent to threaten the nascent nation with imminent destruction. Prince Michael, the son of Roy, fired off a few warning shots, the queen's men fled and the first battle of Sealand was a glorious victory. As British citizens, the police charged the Bates' men with fire-arms offences, the prosecution desperately trawling through 17th century laws to find an actual crime for which they could be convicted. Yet the judge agreed with the Bates – Sealand lay outside the rule of British law, and the English court had no authority in international waters. The case was thrown out.

Prince Roy had won. By 1975 Sealand had its own flag, constitution, national anthem, currency and passports. The rest of Sealand's colourful history is astonishing, there have been military coups and armed takeovers, diplomatic standoffs and there was even a government-in-exile!

Thanks to an overreach of British coastal WW2 defences, Britain has a nuisance neighbour which survives to this day. The current reigning monarch of Sealand is Prince Michael, son of Major Roy Bates. Prince Michael's 2015 book *Principality of Sealand: Holding the Fort* gives a fascinating account of the adventures of the Bates family. Prince Michael has three children himself, and the Royal line is well and truly secure.

I myself (RD) was so charmed by the story of Sealand that I have since become ennobled. My new title is Lord of Sealand (available from their official website with a certificate). The cash-for-honours fiasco, which shamed Britain, could be coming my way!

THE SECOND BOOK

Hitler's 'great opus', part autobiography, part mission statement, was *Mein Kampf* (My Struggle) written in Landsberg prison in 1924. After a failed coup in Munich, the Nazi party was broken up and everybody assumed that the world would hear no more about it. For Hitler however, it was only just beginning. With help from the university-educated Rudolff Hess (in gaol with him) and Hess's mentor, Professor Karl Haushofer, her wrote a pseudo-philosophical rant, mostly about the purity of the Aryan race, which became the bible of Nazism. When Hitler came to power in 1933, *Mein Kampf* was a must-have. Every German household was expected to buy one, making the Fuhrer a millionaire in his own right. Lavish leather-bound copies were given to Aryan newly-weds as wedding presents and the book was translated into dozens of languages to be sold world-wide.

But Hitler wrote a sequel. Or did he? The *Zweites Buch* (Second Book) was written supposedly in 1928, by which time the Nazis had re-emerged as a growing political force in Weimar Germany and the terrifying SS had been set up. Put together with *Mein Kampf*, the second book was a diatribe against the Jews, but it is also a blueprint for what would happen if the Nazis assumed power. Germany would ally with Italy, as the Fascist 'fellow travellers' and with Britain, because of the Saxon racial links and the fact that Britain had no political ambition in Europe, content with its vast colonial empire. France was the enemy in the west (as it had been long before 1871 when the German state was first set up) and once she was defeated, Hitler's new Reich would head a crusade against Poland and the Soviet Union.

The second book's take on America is fascinating, and accords with the confusion and lack of clarity of most of Hitler's prognostications. Perhaps because there were so many Jews in the United States and because the country had joined the Allies in the First World War, America was seen as an ongoing threat. On the other hand, the equally powerful German lobby in the White House corridors of power, as well as the country's toxic attitude to blacks and Native Americans made the culture of the United States something to be admired.

The type-written drafts of the *Zweite Buch* were locked in a safe in the offices of Eher Verlag, who had published *Mein Kampf*. In 1928 sales of the first book were dwindling. It was arguably the catastrophic financial chaos of the Wall Street crash the following year that made Nazism topical again. Perhaps this was why the publishers quietly forgot about it. Found, along with much else pertaining to the Hitler years, by the US Army in 1945, it was finally published by Gerhard Weinberg in 1958 and then with notations two years later by Deutsche Verlagsanstalt of Stuttgart. An English edition did not appear until 2003.

The question remains; how much of the second book is actually Hitler? Bearing in mind the input of Hess and Haushofer in *Mein Kampf*, it is likely that there was similar co-operation for the sequel. That said, had the book been published before 1933, it might have made the appeasers of crypto-Nazism in Europe, rather more realistic in their dealings with Hitler.

THE SEPTEMBER CAVALRY

The First World War was the first of the truly modern wars and the last to see horsed cavalry used in the conventional way, charging over open country. The long-range artillery made such tactics obsolete and the solution to the problem was the British invention of 1916, the tank. Horses were still used widely during the Second World War however and armies were not as mechanised as if often thought.

The rumour ran that when the Germans invaded Poland in *Fall Weiss* on 1 September 1939, the Polish military were so weak and disorganized that they charged on horseback towards Panzer tanks, being completely annihilated for their stupidity. This didn't happen. The Polish horsemen *did* charge infantry, but had to withdraw due to machine gun fire. Once the tanks and war correspondents arrived, they used their artistic licence to give us the myth that still survives to this day. The story was spread by Axis and Soviet media, keen to show how militarily inferior the Polish command were.

In Napoleon's day, the Polish Lancers of the Vistula were a feared force on the battlefield. Not only could Hitler boast that his panzers had destroyed this reputation for ever; he could also use the ineptitude of the September cavalry as an example of the racial inferiority of the Poles themselves.

THE SEVEN DWARFS OF AUSCHWITZ

The Ovitz family, were entertainers known as the Lilliput Troupe. The Hungarian family included seven dwarfs who, because they were Jewish, eventually ended up on 19th May 1944 at Auschwitz. They are not in this book because there is anything remotely weird about them, but for the extraordinary way in which they were treated, and how they survived against the odds. An SS officer, noticing them disembark from their train barked orders to 'wake the Doctor', referring to Josef Mengele, known as the Angel of Death. The family waited nervously amidst the chaos of the train station as the rest of the crowd was moved on around them.

It was well known among his men that 'peculiar' people, such as twins, and hermaphrodites obsessed Mengele and the seven dwarfs were of equal fascination. The youngest of the family, Perla, asked a Jewish Sonderkommando where they were, and where the streams of people were going. 'This is no bakery – this is Auschwitz and you'll end up in the ovens too' he candidly replied.

The family intrigued Mengele, and they did not have to go through the process of shaving their heads and losing their clothes that the other victims did. Though receiving slightly more humane conditions, the dwarfs and their siblings were subjected to endless tests and cruel torture. If the females weren't wearing a full face of makeup, Mengele would notice and comment on this. Offset with Mengele's insincere charm was his power over life and death and the horrific way he would treat people with whom he had grown bored.

The Lilliput Troupe were performers, playing music and singing songs across Romania, Hungary and Czechoslovakia. They were forced to 'perform' at Auschwitz too, by standing on a stage naked, in front of an SS crowd, being prodded and leered over as specimens. Some of the things the family experienced and witnessed were so disturbing, they are perhaps inappropriate to mention in detail in a book like this. Some of these events were filmed, though the film reels are not believed to have survived.

They endured long enough to be liberated by the Red Army on 27 January 1945. They returned home to find it had been looted and, with nothing left to stay for, they moved several times before settling in Israel.

The last surviving dwarf Perla died in 2001 at the age of 80. Of Mengele she said 'If the judges had asked me if he should be hanged, I'd have told them to let him go. I was saved by the grace of the devil — God will give Mengele his due.'

Mengele, who spent his remaining years on the run in fear of discovery, fleeing across South America, was discovered drowned in 1979. To this day, Mengele's bones are at the Sao Paulo Institute for Forensic Medicine, occasionally being hauled out for medical students to study.

The 2014 book *Giants: The Dwarfs of Auschwitz* by Yehuda Koren and Eilat Negev explains their astonishing story further.

THE SHIP THAT BECAME AN ISLAND

HNLMS *Abraham Crijnssen,* named after a seventeenth century admiral, was a Dutch minesweeper that survived the disastrous Battle of the Java Sea against the Imperial Japanese Navy in 1942.

In common with most European countries, the Netherlands had colonies in what were still called the East Indies and that brought them into direct confrontation with Japan. With the Allied fleet in tatters, the Dutch warships were ordered to flee to Australia. The *Crijnssen* was supposed to evacuate with three other ships but it soon became separated. It could only reach speeds of 15 knots and was only lightly armed so the odds of making it were well and truly against the crew.

A plan was hatched; disguise the ship as an island. The crew disembarked and began cutting down trees and branches and used them to cover the surface of the vessel; uncovered areas were painted over to look like rocks. The plan wasn't fool proof, as the Japanese forces would certainly be curious about a moving island in the ocean, so the *Crijnssen* only moved during the cover of darkness and always close to the shore. Thanks to their ingenuity, the forty-five crewmen finally made it to Fremantle, Australia, after what must have been the longest and most bizarre eight days of their lives.

THE SHRUNKEN HEADS OF BUCHENWALD

The long list of horrors that came to light after the war across Nazi-occupied Europe shocked the world. Since then, the crimes committed have lost little power to appall those who were born long after the atrocities. Some of them were so savage, pointless and inhuman, that it is tempting to believe that they are mere fictions, and never happened. Take, for example, two shrunken heads, alongside human skin, taken from the SS-Pathology department at Buchenwald concentration camp.

The testimony of Kurt Sitte, a Czechoslovakian doctor of Physics who had been a political prisoner in Buchenwald from 1939, sheds some light on this. Sitte revealed that the two heads belonged to prisoners who had escaped but were recaptured. They were subsequently beheaded on the orders of SS Doctor Mueller.

Some asserted that the heads were souvenirs or curios from South America, but science doesn't agree. There is no evidence to support this claim.

One of the heads was produced as evidence by Thomas Dodd at the Nuremberg trials. The sheer barbaric lunacy of it almost made Dodd apologise for presenting it as an exhibit, but explained he felt compelled to let the court see it for themselves.

The shrunken head shocked the court. Many simply couldn't, or wouldn't, believe it was real. Evidentially it served little purpose, other than to demonstrate the kind of experiments conducted by Mueller and others. There it was, a hideous trophy displayed for all to see. A civilized Western nation, a Christian state, had experimented and shrunk a man's head. It was worthy of the most lurid fiction, or a gruesome Boy's Own adventure.

Francois de Menthon, the chief French prosecutor at the trials said, 'the work of twenty centuries of civilization, which believed itself eternal, [could be] destroyed by the return of ancient barbarism in a new guise.'

Buchenwald was unique in that it didn't carry the (false) motto of other camps, *Arbeit macht frei* ('work sets you free' – it didn't). Buchenwald instead went for *Jedem das seine* 'to each his own', a quote from Martin Luther. This sign, oddly, faced inwards for those inside the camp to see. It can also be translated as 'everyone gets what they deserve'. Perhaps those words came to mind for those who ended up in the dock at the subsequent war crime trials.

SIGNALLING TO THE LUFTWAFFE

The Second World War saw the plane come of age as a weapon of war. Although well established by the end of the First World War, the technology of the 1930s meant that bombers and fighters had more accuracy and longer ranges than their prototypes of 1914-18. The Blitz in particular, which followed the Battle of Britain, brought the air war to ordinary people.

Given the supposed existence of a Fifth Column in various European countries, especially in the early stages of the war, it was natural for myths to grow that ingenious methods were being devised to guide the Luftwaffe bombers to their targets. Pro-Nazi Poles were believed to have painted roofs and chimneys white, created obvious patterns with hay bales in fields and hidden radio transmitters in trees and graveyards. However much this was part of paranoia, its results were horrific. Thirty-four people were shot in the town of Thorn for signalling to aircraft with flags and mirrors.

In Britain, two cases reached the courts – and therefore the press. Since most people believe what they read in the papers must be true, the legend became fact. In Kensington, a German Swiss was arrested for dodgy use of a cigar – 'He was puffing hard,' claimed a witness, 'to make a big light and pointing it at the sky.' The Welsh had got there first; only a day into the war, when everybody expected instant annihilation; a man was prosecuted for striking a match on the platform at Bridgend station.

SILBERVOGEL

Silbervogel (silver bird) was one of the proposals put forward for Hitler's ambitious Amerika Bomber project, with which he hoped to attack the US mainland. There was no real chance, even in 1942, of the Kriegsmarine ever being able to supply and protect aircraft carriers near enough the United States to pose any substantial threat to the US mainland. So could a bomber travel the 5800km journey itself?

Behind the complex concept was an equally complex design, formulated by Eugene Sanger and Irene Brant. The idea was, in simple terms, that the Silbervogel would be launched like a rocket from Europe and ascend to the fringes of space. Once there, it would travel across the Atlantic in a series of sub-orbital 'hops', before dropping its payload and returning home.

The Luftwaffe were impressed – but it was horribly impractical and expensive, and the limited resources of Nazi boffins were needed elsewhere.

After the war, with President Truman and Premier Stalin at loggerheads, the Soviets tried to persuade Eugene Sanger, who was now living in France, into working for them. When their charm offensive failed, it is alleged they tried to kidnap him, which fortunately failed.

The United States were also impressed, and though the Silbervogel was a failure in its time and place, it is believed by some that the theories involved would go on to inform the scientists working on the NASA space shuttle design.

SIWASH

Siwash, from New Zealand, was a duck that served with the First Battalion of the Tenth Marine Regiment in the Pacific theatre. The legend says Sergeant Frank Fagin, a US marine, won the duck in a raffle (or a poker tournament) in 1943. Siwash would become the unofficial mascot of 2nd Marine Division. The duck also enjoyed beer, as long as it was warm, which appealed to the troops.

When the marines went into battle at Tarawa in 1943, Siwash valiantly fought alongside them. Earning a citation:

'For courageous action and wounds received on Tarawa, in the Gilbert Islands, November 1943. With utter disregard for his own personal safety, Siwash, upon reaching the beach, without hesitation engaged the enemy in fierce combat, namely, one rooster of Japanese ancestry, and though wounded on the head by repeated pecks, he soon routed the opposition. He refused medical aid until all wounded members of his section had been taken care of.'

Siwash, now a sergeant, also saw action at the battles of Saipan and Tinian. After the war, Siwash, according to the source, either took on the role of a Marine recruiter for the Korean War or retired at Lincoln Park Zoo in Chicago. Siwash died of liver problems in 1954.

But Siwash had managed to keep one secret from, but a select few, of its comrades during the entire war, *he* was actually a *she*, Siwash was a girl, one of only a very few cases - or perhaps the only one - of a recruit successfully hiding their gender to fight on the front!

SLINKY

Every post war generation has been enthralled by it, the sight of a tightly coiled metal spring tumbling down flights of stairs and falling from high places. It fascinated toddlers who could watch Slinkies doing their stuff for hours. And it fascinated them all over again at secondary school when their Physics teachers explained the science behind it.

What is not generally known is that Slinky was a child of the Second World War. In 1943, mechanical engineer Richard James was investigating ways to keep sensitive ship equipment safe at sea. He accidentally knocked some samples of a shelf, watching then expanding gracefully rather than falling and breaking. James could also see, after the war, the beauty of a Slinky as a child's toy – he thought of the name as a commercial selling-point but he and his wife Betty were disappointed to find that nobody wanted to know.

All that changed in late 1945 when Gimbels Department Store in London let James run a demonstration on the shop's stairs. Shoppers were fascinated – the stock of 400 sold out in minutes. Two hundred and fifty million Slinkies later, they still have a place in our hearts, appealing to kids big and small.

SMOKY THE DOG

Smoky the dog entered the war in mysterious circumstances. The Yorkshire Terrier was discovered by an American patrol in March 1944 in New Guinea, hiding in a foxhole. She was sold to Cpl. Bill Wynne for two Australian pounds, and backpacked with him through the unforgiving jungle. The dog did not appear to understand English or Japanese, so her reasons for being at the front are unclear.

Smoky survived 150 air raids and Wynne believe she saved his life by warning him of incoming artillery strikes, ducking in time to dodge a barrage that killed eight of his comrades.

During the bombardment of the Lingayen Gulf airfield on Luzon, her heroics came into their own. She aided the troops by running a telegraph wire for the Signal Corps through a 70ft long pipe. It is believed her courageous run saved 250 men what would have been the equivalent of a dangerous three-day task. It was Smoky's finest hour.

Smoky's positive impact on hospitalized soldiers was noted, and the idea of therapy dogs was catching on. By 1947, 700 dogs were working in hospitals. Cute pictures of Smoky sitting in a GI's helmet and proudly standing over a trophy still survive.

Smoky became a national hero and after the war continued to entertain America by performing tricks such as riding a scooter, spelling her name and tight-rope walking. She performed 42 times on television.

Smoky died peacefully in her sleep in 1957 at the age of 14. A bronze statue erected in 2005 at Cleveland, Ohio, celebrates her remarkable life.

SONDERKOMMANDO ELBE

The beginning of the war demonstrated to the world the seemingly invulnerability of the Luftwaffe. No country on the continent had survived the onslaught of the German Blitzkrieg. Hermann Goering was so confident of his air arm that he left the destruction of the trapped pocket of men at Dunkirk to his airmen. Then they were to be entrusted with bringing Churchill to heel during the Battle of Britain. With the British gone, a jubilant Hitler boasted they would never return to the continent.

The war in 1945 was a completely different story. The Allies had air supremacy, and in some areas the Luftwaffe had ceased to exist. Sonderkommando Elbe was a last desperate gamble. Simply put, it was a unit designed to collide with enemy aircraft and knock them out of the sky. The plan was that the attackers would eject just as they were about to crash into their target, using their propellers like a circular saw. The optimal targets were the vulnerable points, the cockpit, the empennage and an area near the fuel system.

The stripped down planes only flew one mission on 7 April 1945. Their attack was arguably effective, with eight of fifteen Allied bombers being destroyed. However, it was never going to make a difference, and squandered those pilots and planes the crumbling Reich had left. Unlike the fanatical kamikaze 'divine wind' pilots of Imperial Japan, it was hoped, albeit unlikely, that the German pilots would try to survive their missions.

THE SPANDAU SEVEN

After the war and the subsequent Nuremberg trials, many of the Nazi leadership were executed for war crimes. A group of seven were instead jailed at Spandau prison in West Berlin. The group, known as the Spandau Seven, were Baldur von Schirach, Hitler Youth leader; Erich Raeder, Grand Admiral; Konstantin von Neurath, diplomat; Karl Dönitz, Admiral; Albert Speer, minister for war production; Walther Funk, minister for economic affairs and the enigmatic Rudolf Hess, former deputy of the Reich.

It was a complicated arrangement. The Americans, British, French and Soviets would each run the prison for three months of the year before handing over to the next. The prison was well guarded, with at least sixty soldiers, because it was feared that any remnants of the Nazi cause, if they existed, could try to rescue their leaders. The daily routine for the seven was strict and orderly, and communication with the outside world was, officially, forbidden. The 600 common criminals of Spandau were moved out of the 134 cells they shared to make way for the VIPs.

The Spandau Seven are not in this book because there was anything weird here - other than the idea of a prison run for just seven men – but for the childlike, petty rivalries that these former heads of the Reich indulged in.

Admirals Raeder and Dönitz made one team, although Raeder still had a private grudge from 1943 when Dönitz replaced him as head of the navy. Speer was an outcast, shunned by the others for disloyalty and his brown-nosing of the Allies. Hess was a loner, who cared as little for the other six as they cared for him. Shirach and Funk became best friends, and the social butterfly Nuerath fluttered effortlessly between the factions.

Speer kept himself busy, secretly writing two books and going on walking holidays in his imagination, using the prison garden for measurement. Raeder placed himself as head of the library, with Dönitz his assistant, and thus was 1943 avenged.

The most mysterious of the inmates was Rudolf Hess. His time in Spandau is as obscure as the reasons for his bizarre one-man flight to Scotland on 10th May 1941. Hess has given historians headaches ever since. He kept to himself, and even in the petty world of Spandau politics he wasn't popular. Constantly fearful of being poisoned, he was often bed-ridden, complaining of agony, real or faked, which saw him avoid having to work.

By 1966 all of the prisoners had been released except Rudolf Hess who, bizarrely, had the entire prison to himself for a further twenty-one years, until his death in 1987. The 93 year old apparently hanged himself with an extension cord in a summer house. However, the circumstances surrounding Hess's death are contentious. According to the British, attempts to let him go free were blocked by the Soviets. Hess's son believes the British murdered him in order to prevent him revealing embarrassing wartime secrets. Other historians state his suicide note was actually written in the 60s. Why Hess was the only one of the seven to actually serve a whole life sentence remains an intriguing question.

The prison was demolished in 1987 following Hess' death to stop it becoming a neo-Nazi shrine. A car park and shopping centre were built in its place. The Berlin Wall would come down four years later. The pop band *Spandau Ballet* take their name from the prison: 'ballet' being a grim reference to the frantic death throes of those hanged at the gallows.

THE SPEAR OF DESTINY

'One of the soldiers,' St John's gospel tells us, 'pierced His side with a lance and immediately there came out blood and water.' The crucifixion of Christ is described in the New Testament but only John has the story of the spear. The blood of the wound symbolized Christ's humanity and the water represented divinity, according to the first church council at Nicea convened by the emperor Constantine in 325AD. It is the rather spurious Gospel of Nicodemus that gives the soldier a name – Longinus – and a later tradition still calls him a centurion, the officer in charge of at least eighty men in a Roman legion.

The lance, which would probably have been a hasta, a thrusting spear as opposed to a thrown javelin, a pilum, became one of many famous religious relics in the Middle Ages. The true cross, the crown of thorns and the lance were venerated throughout Medieval Christendom, but it is noticeable that there were several of them. At least four examples of the lance, or portions of it, existed simultaneously in the fourteenth century. It is the one in Vienna that brings us forward to the Second World War and Adolf Hitler.

The notion that Hitler and more specifically Heinrich Himmler, head of the SS, was involved in the black arts was not generally held during the war, although Lewis Spence's *The Occult Causes of the Present War* (1943) claimed that there was a Satanic element in Nazism. Hitler himself is on record as saying that any attempt to recreate Wotan (the Norse god Odin) was dead in the water because Christianity had such a hold on Europe. Spence was a conspiracy theorist before the term existed, maintaining that Hitler was 'the creature of shadowy people', whatever that meant.

Since the war, a plethora of books has been written which attempt to link the Nazi's Ultima Thule society via Karl Haushofer, the geopolitician, Himmler's SS HQ in the castle of Wewelsburg and his supposed attempts to establish an archaeological basis for the existence of a pure-bred Aryan society in ancient history. One of the best-known books on the lance's symbolic significance is Trevor Ravenscroft's *The Spear of Destiny* (1973) which has all the hallmarks of an Indiana Jones film. Ravenscroft served with the Royal Fusiliers during the war and was captured during a raid on Rommel's HQ in Libya in November 1941. Ravenscroft's source was Walter Stein who claimed to have known Hitler when he was a struggling art student in Vienna before the First World War. The future Fuhrer, claimed Stein, 'attained higher levels of consciousness by means of drugs and made a penetrating study of medieval occultism and ritual magic'.

According to Stein/Ravenscroft, Longinus' spear, which was believed to have been acquired by the Habsburgs before the collapse of the Austro-Hungarian empire in 1918, was grabbed by Hitler after the *Anschluss* (union) with Austria in 1938. It had magical powers and whoever owned it could rule the world.

The movements of the lance in 1945 are obscure. It may have been part of the regalia discovered by historian Walter Horn, working with the Monuments, Fine Arts and Archives Program under General Patton's Third Army. The work of this dedicated little group was celebrated recently by George Clooney's movie *The Monuments Men.*

As for Himmler's links with the occult, a great deal of nonsense has been written over the last forty years. He was a 'planetary doppelganger', an 'anti-human in a human body', rather than a failed chicken farmer with murderous and anti-Semitic tendencies.

The spear itself is currently on display in the Hofburg Museum in Vienna. It was tested metallurgically in 2003 in laboratory conditions and was dated as seventh or eighth century, about the time that Charlemagne (who was once believed to have owned it) was crowned emperor of the West (AD 800). In its shape and design, the weapon bears no relation to anything carried by the Romans.

THE SPITFIRES THAT WEREN'T

The British were wrong-footed in the early stages of the war in Burma. The surrender of Singapore led to soldiers being worked to death on the notorious Burma railway. One of the major reasons for the failure of the army was a lack of weaponry and ammunitions, although it was much more complicated than that. By the end of the war, the situation had changed and it was the Japanese army that surrendered. By that time, too, so the rumour ran, the RAF had delivered – and buried – 124 Spitfires at their airborne base at Mingaladon, now Rangoon's city airport.

The RAF's records show that only thirty-seven aircraft, in three transport ships, were delivered in 1945-6 and most of them were re-exported within months. The order to bury the planes was given by Lord Mountbatten of Burma, although exactly why remains a mystery.

For seventeen years, a research team led by David Cundall, has been combing the area, talking to locals, finding eye-witnesses to events (including Stanley Coombe, ex-RAF, who saw the burials at the time). Cundall hoped to excavate the Spitfires and fly them home, expecting the find to be as important in its way as Howard Carter's discovery of the tomb of the Egyptian pharaoh Tutankhamun in 1922.

It has now been decided, inevitably, that the buried Spitfires are a myth and the search for them, officially called off in 2013, just part of World War Two foaflore (friend-of-a-friend story). Incidentally, for the older generation of archaeologists who were not brought up with such gadgetry, the Spitfire burial story is a stern warning against an over-reliance on geophysics.

STALIN THE POET

Ioseb Besarionis dze Jughashvili, later known as Stalin (Man of Steel), had a rise to power that was, in its way, as peculiar as Adolf Hitler's own. Both came from poor backgrounds, both had unhappy childhoods, both despised their fathers, had run-ins with the establishment, were no strangers to prison cells and shared unquenchable ambitions.

There is a further similarity in their creative streaks: Hitler was an artist and a poet, and Stalin himself was a poet before rising through the ranks during the Bolshevik Revolution, the events of which in 1917 turned Russia on its head and terrified the capitalists and imperialists of Western Europe.

Stalin became a fan of writers such as Goethe, Shakespeare and Walt Whitman. He wrote anonymously, using the pseudonym Soselo, and later attempts by his admirers to collate his works for publication were personally stopped.

How Stalin and Hitler could reconcile the kindness and beauty found within their prose with their actual actions cannot be easily understood. Stalin's poem *The Moon* goes;

> Sail on, as tirelessly as ever,
> Above an earth obscured by clouds,
> And with your shining glow of silver
> Dispel the fog that now abounds.
>
> With languor, bend your lovely neck,
> Lean down to earth with tender smile.
> Sing lullabies to Mount Kazbek,
> Whose glaciers reach for you on high.
>
> But know for certain, he who had
> Once been oppressed and cast below,
> Can scale the heights of Mount Mtatsminda,
> Exalted by undying hope.
>
> Shine on, up in the darkened sky,
> Frolic and play with pallid rays,
> And, as before, with even light,
> Illuminate my fatherland.
>
> I'll bare my breast to you, extend
> My arm in joyous greeting, too.
> My spirit trembling, once again
> I'll glimpse before me the bright moon.

A second darker, more ominous poem goes as follows;

> He knocked on strangers' doors,
> Going from house to house,
> With an old oaken *panduri*
> And that simple song of his.
>
> But in his song, his song
> Pure as the sun's own gleam
> Resounded a truth profound,
> Resounded a lofty dream.
>
> Hearts that had turned to stone

Were made to beat once more;
In many, he'd rouse a mind
That slumbered in deepest murk.

But instead of the laurels he'd earned,
The people of his land
Fed the outcast poison,
Placing a cup in his hand.

They told him: 'Damned one, you must
Drink it, drain the cup dry...
Your song is foreign to us,
We prefer to live in a lie!'

Like Hitler, Stalin never returned to his poetry once he assumed power.

STRENGTH THROUGH JOY

For anyone who has watched the British comedy show *Hi-de-Hi!* they may find it amusing to know that the Nazis had their own holiday camps. Strength Through Joy (*Kraft durch Freude*) was a programme dedicated to improving the leisure time of its members, having 30 million subscribers by 1936. KDF organised a wide-range of activities such as holiday camps, skiing holidays, cruises, hikes and days out to the theatre. It was the world's largest tour operator in the '30s and was presented in German newsreels as a paragon of good living. It was all part of the Labour Front which had replaced trades unions in the police state.

As well as holidays, KDF also organised evening social activities. In many ways, it can be argued that KDF was pioneering for its time; it allowed workers to experience activities that would have only been affordable to the middle class and there was nothing like it, for example, in Britain. As always, there was more to it than that – the primary role of the KDF was to keep people busy and occupied as the Nazi leadership worried that those with too much time on their hands may be prone to engage in anti-government activities. In 1939 KDF essentially ceased to exist, as all attention was now turned to the war effort. And the joy disappeared, day by day, from Germany.

SOVIET APE-MEN

The tale of Ilya Ivanovich Ivanov, a Russian biologist and his 'ape-men' is one that should be approached carefully, and without getting swept up in rumour.

Briefly, the allegations go as follows: Ivanov gave a presentation to the World Congress of Biologists where he explained to his colleagues the possibility of creating ape-human hybrids. He'd had success with other animals, so believed this was a scientific possibility.

He went on with his experiments, setting off and travelling to the far reaches of the world. In the 1920s his trials involving the use of human sperm to inseminate female chimpanzees failed to produce any results. He then tried using ape sperm with human volunteers, though this failed when his Orangutan died on the way to Russia.

In the bewildering world of Soviet intrigue, Ivanov was arrested and exiled to Alma

Ata where he would die in 1932.

In later years, tabloid newspapers got their hands on this story, where they claimed Joseph Stalin had ordered Ivanov 'the Red Frankenstein' to create a mutant army of ape-men, who would follow orders without question and conquer the world! It's unlikely Ivanov would have ever been on Stalin's radar, and there is no evidence that either of them had the slightest interest in creating ape soldiers.

Some years after the war a creature called Oliver (1957 – 2012) was believed by some to be a human-chimpanzee hybrid. Science has shown this is clearly not the case and he's an ordinary ape but once again the myth never quite died.

STRUWWELHITLER

The 'Nazi story book' by Robert and Philip Spence was an excellent piece of propaganda and a superb parody of the cautionary tales for children written by Heinrich Hoffmann in 1843. It cost 1s 6d and was sold in aid of the *Daily Sketch* War Relief Fund. With careful copies of the original illustrations, suitably adapted and brought up to date for a wartime readership, the book was hysterically funny, yet grimly prescient.

'When the children have been good,
That is, be it understood,
Good at killing, good at lying,
Good at on each other spying,
When their fourteen Pas and Mas,
Grandmamas and Grandpapas,
Great Grandparents too, are sure
That their Aryan stock is pure,
They shall have the pretty things
Krupp Von Bohlen kindly brings,
And the blessings, only listen!
Brought by Stinnes, Frick and Thyssen,
Who will welcome all your savings
While you feed on grass and shavings.
Only such as these shall look
At this pretty picture book.'

At a stroke, the Nazi obsession with race is highlighted and the greed of the German arms manufacturers against a background of economic hardship for ordinary German people. As early as 1936, Herman Goering had given the public a stark choice – guns or butter. With a bitter irony, he wrote, 'I do not want to have rearmament for military ends or to oppress others.'; that was the year that the Germans marched illegally into the Rhineland.

Struwwelhitler lampooned Hitler himself –

'Here is cruel Adolf, see!
A horrid, wicked boy was he.'

Goebbels became Gob and Ribbentrop Ribby, two of the inky boys punished by the great magician in the original (here played by 'Comrade Joseph' Stalin). Mussolini is sent up as the man who went shooting – Greeks, rather than the original goats. Goebbels the journalist/propagandist has his thumbs cut off by the long-legged scissorman –

'No more will echo roof and rafter,
To *Angriff* and to *Beobachter.*'

Hess became Flying Rudolf as a result of his mysterious flight to Scotland in May 1941 –

'Has he come to seek for solace,
On the soil of Bruce and Wallace?'

They don't write them like that any more!

SUBMARINE TANKS

By the beginning of the Second World War, the tank had come of age. From the hopeful line-drawings of Leonardo da Vinci, to the clumsy inadequate 'ironclads' of Cambrai in the First World War, tanks had made a slow and hesitant start. By 1939 however, the cavalry was born again in motorized vehicles that ran on caterpillar tracks and could cope with almost any rough terrain. Heinz Guderian's panzers crashed through the forest of the Ardennes as part of the blitzkrieg that hit the west in 1940 and Bernard Montgomery's Crusaders halted the advance of the Afrika Korps at El Alamein.

It was a different story with the Panzerkampfwagen III als Tauchpanzer which was an underwater variant designed in 1940 for the planned invasion of Britain, Operation Sea Lion. Once the Royal Air Force had been overwhelmed by the Luftwaffe (so ran the strategic theory of the German High Command), there would be a small window of opportunity for the Kriegsmarine (German navy) to launch assault troops on British soil. What could be more terrifying than tanks roaring up out of the surf and snarling up English beaches on the south coast? Prototypes were built and proved successful.

An estimated 168 Tauchpanzers were built but because of the RAF's success in the Battle of Britain, there was no opportunity to use them in the Channel. Instead, they were used in river crossings in Operation Barbarossa, the invasion of Soviet Russia in June 1941. Most of them were converted to land vehicles later in the war.

THE SUN GUN

As if straight out of a sci-fi comic, one of the most imaginative and 'out there' ideas concocted by the Reich was the 'Sun Gun'. The Nazis didn't actually pioneer it. As early as the sixteenth century, the Scottish mathematician and astronomer John Napier (he of the logarithm so dreaded by generations of schoolchildren) was thinking along similar lines. The plan was to build a giant orbital mirror in space, 20,000 miles above the Earth, which would focus the sun's rays to scorching point when aimed at a target area, like a child killing ants with a magnifying glass; except that the ants would be cities and the whole world would be at Germany's mercy. The Sun Gun was the brainchild of renowned scientist Hermann Oberth who estimated it could be constructed in fifteen years at a cost of three million marks. Fortunately, the war ended before the plans could come to fruition and the Sun Gun and its variants are now weapons of choice for Hollywood villains.

SWASTIKA NIGHT

The Second World War is *the* hotbed for alternative and speculative fiction, the likes of which the world has never seen before. No period of human history has fascinated writers and readers quite so much. And the most tantalising question is, 'What if the Nazis had won the war?' Famous examples include Robert Harris' 1992 novel *Fatherland* and the 1964 movie *It Happened Here*. This obsession continues to the modern day, with popular retellings such as the televised series *Man In The High Castle*, originally a 1962 novel by science fiction writer Philip K. Dick, and the BBC series *SS GB*, originally published in 1978 by Len Deighton.

There are so many hypothetical questions that intrigue us; what if Germany continued its relationship with China and did not ally with Japan; what if Japan attacked the Soviet Union instead of the US; what if Finland fell to the Soviet Union and the Molotov-Ribbentrop Pact was fulfilled; what if the US entered the war before Operation Barbarossa had commenced; what if Spain or Turkey joined the Axis; what if Roosevelt did not stand or win a third term as US President, the list goes on and on.

Of the countless works to have been penned regarding this most famous 'what if?', surely Katharine Burdekin's *Swastika Night* must win the prize for the most imaginative. The book is not mentioned here because it is weird, but because it was written *before* the war. The grimly prescient book was first published in 1937, two years before the outbreak of the conflict.

The story follows an alternative history, one in which Germany and Japan have conquered the world. Set 700 years in the future, the story follows the protagonist, Alfred, an Englishman, who goes on a pilgrimage of holy Nazi sites, including a Munich plane that Hitler flew to Moscow to win the war. Hitler is remembered by the world as a seven-foot, blue-eyed, blonde deity. Women are reduced to the caste of baby-makers, shaven-headed pathetic creatures hidden from the world and used solely for breeding. As the story develops, and Alfred learns the truth behind the lies and horrors of the Empire, he believes a spiritual rebellion must happen urgently, and fears any armed conflict – which the Germans would win – would reassert the world's delusional belief that violence and strength of arms is linked to righteousness and the favour of the gods. At the end, soldiers beat Alfred so viciously that he dies of his wounds. In dying, he fantasises about finishing his book and exposing Hitler to show what sort of a man he really was.

Adam Roberts says of *Swastika Night*, 'Burdekin's pre-war story reads as horribly prescient and its feminist emphasis ... provides a very valid critique of fascism.' Largely forgotten, it gained a new lease of life when it was republished in the 1980s.

THE SWORD OF ISLAM

Leptis Magna is one of the largest excavated sites of Roman civilisation in the world. Until recently, a well-informed Libyan archaeologist would show tourists around, marvelling at the architecture and the full-size chariot circus at the sea's edge. When he came to a few lumps of concrete topped by twisted metal, he was less fulsome in his praise. This, he said, was what the Italians had built in 1930, under the dictator Benito Mussolini and it was noticeable that they were in worse condition than the surrounding buildings which were two thousand years older!

Mussolini had delusions of grandeur and wanted to recreate the Roman Empire which had been the most impressive in the ancient world. It included a broad sweep of North Africa from Morocco in the west to Egypt in the east. Accordingly, Italians settled in Libya, bringing with them western culture and Christianity. By the early 30s, a third of the population of Tripoli and Benghazi was Italian. Inevitably, tensions rose and over a ten year period, an estimated 100,000 people were killed in local rebellions and harsh reprisals by Mussolin's 'new Rome'.

Il Duce was not a religious man, but he understood the need to make his African colonies work. He set up mosques and Quaranic schools and referred to Libyans as 'Italian Muslims of the fourth shore of Italy'. By championing Islam, he hoped to impress other Muslims in Algeria, and British Muslims in Egypt. It was not a success.

In 1937 Mussolini visited Libya, entering Tripoli riding on a white horse like a Roman Emperor, at the head of 2,600 cavalrymen. A huge statue of his was erected in the city, only to be hauled down by the Allies in 1943. At that triumphal entry in 1937, the Berber Chief Iusuf Kerisc presented the Italian with a curved scimitar, known as the Sword of Islan, the traditional gift for a successful (and popular) military commander. In fact, Mussolini was neither of these things and the sword was just as fake. It was not Berber, nor Libyan nor even Islamic. It was made to Mussolini's specification by an Italian art firm!

The sword was displayed in the summer residence of the dictator, Rocca delle Caminate, an iconic totem of Mussolini as some kind of descendent of the Ottoman Turks and the 'protector of Islam'. It did not make sense and did not fool anybody. When the Caminate estate was overrun by Italian partisans who had turned against their leader in 1943, the sword disappeared and has never been seen since.

TEDDYBÄR

An odd trend swept through Germany in the 1920s, and continued for another forty years – individuals and crowds posing for the camera with people dressed in polar bear costumes. The bizarre pictures may have never seen the light of day but are known to us thanks to collector Jean-Marie Donat, who collected the photographs for a limited edition book, *TeddyBär*.

Various pictures survive, those posing with the polar bears including German soldiers, a holidaying family at the Baltic Sea, a young girl who is in the League of German Maidens uniform and the after-service of a wedding. Later pictures include posing with black GIs and youngsters from what appears to be the Swinging Sixties.

What is weirdest here is that the reasons for the polar bear phenomena aren't clear. Unsatisfactory answers include: links to the soft drink Fanta as a mascot; the belief that polar bears were simply popular in the country; or the idea the costumes would encourage people to have their photograph taken with a stranger. A theory it was all to celebrate the arrival of a polar bear at Berlin Zoo doesn't stand up well to scrutiny either.

Attempting to explain this oddity Jean-Marie Donat said, 'These photographs were found during 20 years of research, all over Germany, in shops that sell old photos, or in markets dating from 1920 to 1960. All these individual moments add up to the story of Germany over 40 years.'

THAT MOUSTACHE

Much to lament of Charlie Chaplin and others, the toothbrush moustache will always belong to Hitler. So iconic was the moustache and the 'slash-over' haircut, that any cartoon with those embellishments is instantly recognizable over seventy years after the man's death.

According to those who served with him in the First World War, the young corporal Hitler originally sported a handlebar moustache. This in itself, usually stiffened with wax, was made popular by the Kaiser, Wilhelm II. In fact, a piece of Second World War British propaganda has a spoof German alphabet –

'K was the Kaiser. On both of its Fronts
His moustache was the joy of all Germany once.'

Photographs of Hitler recuperating from a gas attack at Pasewalk Hospital at the end of the First World War shows him with a much larger, 'Kaiser' version. This was ironic since, as chemical warfare developed and the use of gas masks became standard, Hitler was ordered to clip it so he could put on his respirator properly. The moustache was an accepted symbol of middle class establishment figures for men in the 1930s and '40s, but increasingly, politicians were going for the clean-shaven look.

THAT'S ALL FOLKS!

Propaganda was considered a crucial part of the war effort for all sides of the conflict. Efforts to encourage public support for a cause and demonise an enemy, have existed since the first word was written. However, what was unique about the Second World War was the sheer intensity of it. Soldiers and civilians were bombarded constantly, and unlike earlier wars, which were usually fought in a field far-away, this war was unavoidable.

Propaganda even found its way into children's cartoons. The list is far too long to detail here, but hundreds of cartoons were created throughout the six-year conflict. The use of propaganda, and the manner in which it was presented, is fascinating. It reveals that the war was never a simple case of good and evil, black and white. A close friend and ally one moment could be a bitter enemy the next, and vice versa.

Der Fuehrer's Face is a 1943 cartoon featuring Donald Duck having a bad dream - he dreams that he's a Nazi. Interestingly, this cartoon was temporarily banned as extremist material by a Russian court – in 2010! Spike Jones' song of the same name became a favourite for the soldiers.

Herr Meets Hare and *Bugs Bunny Nips the Nips* were two outings for the Warner Bros animal. The former generally sees him irritating the Nazis, particularly Goering 'the golden pheasant'; the latter sees him outsmarting the Japanese.

The more sensible and compassionate *Education for Death: The Making of the Nazi*, follows a newborn baby named Hans through his brainwashed childhood and depicts German children as victims.

Comic books heroes also joined the fight; DC and Marvel Comics stalwarts Wonder Woman, Superman, Captain America, Daredevil, Batman and Flash Gordon were constantly fighting the bad guys. Superman, the Man of Steel – the fact that he shared his name with 'Uncle Joe' Stalin is notable here – was already punching Nazis a year before America joined the war. Some cartoons of Asian people were so ridiculous they would be funny, were they not so racist.

It wasn't just the Allies who were hurling their propaganda messages at children; the Axis was doing the same. *Nimbus Libere* from 1944 is a very odd, short cartoon, made by the Germans but aimed at the French. In this Mickey Mouse, Popeye and Donald Duck are the crew of Allied bombers, promising the French salvation, but instead kill them in a bombing run.

The Italian cartoon *Il Dottor Churkill* sees Winston Churchill as a deranged Dr. Jekyll and Mr. Hyde type monster, a greedy sociopath who lives in the Bank of England and robs his friends, before being defeated by a combined Italian and German airforce.

Momotarō no Umiwashi (Momotarō's Sea Eagles) was a 1942 contribution showing the attack on the 'Devil's Island' (Pearl Harbor). Bluto, the nemesis of Popeye – now a drunk sailor - defends the US.

Perhaps the most peculiar, though, is *Omochabako series dai san wa: Ehon senkya-hyakusanja-rokunen* (Mickey Mouse invades Japan). A monstrous Mickey Mouse terrorises Japanese children before eventually being defeated by a samurai. This cartoon stands out for special attention because it was actually made by the Japanese in 1936, five years before the nations were even at war with each other.

THERESIENSTADT – THE MODEL VILLAGE

While the war continued in Germany's favour, news of the existence of concentration camps, ghettos and the brutal treatment of civilians under their control did not particularly concern the Nazis.

But as the tide of war turned and the Allies made inroads into Europe, the situation changed. It dawned on SS and Nazi leaders that perhaps they may be held accountable for their inhumanity and cruelty after all.

After the D-Day landings, their concerns increased. The international community wanted to know if so-called extermination camps existed – surely they couldn't? Surely, they were just ridiculous lies to demonise the Third Reich? The first Danish Jews had arrived in 1943, and facing increasing pressure from the Danish Red Cross, the Nazis finally allowed the charity to investigate the claims. They were to be permitted to visit Theresienstadt, a camp, they were told, which was representative of all the others dotted throughout Europe.

The Nazis went into overdrive in preparation for the visit. They deported a large number to Auschwitz to show the camps weren't overcrowded. Orphans and the sick were removed – they'd be a depressing sight. It was cleaned up, fake shops and cafes were built. Flowers were planted, benches and playgrounds were created. The residents who were to be visited had freshly painted homes, no more than three to a room.

The Red Cross visit was on 23 June 1944. Following a very specific route on their tour, they were apparently impressed by conditions in the camp, young ones sang and danced, the smell of bread wafted from the bakery, and the scent of the newly planted flowers filled the air. They even attended a children's performance of *Brundibár*. What was all the fuss about? The tales of the shocking, brutal treatment of Jews was all an absurd lie. In the First World War the Allies had accused the Germans of rendering corpses to make oils for the war effort. This was, in reality, a complete fabrication. The Danes knew that the British had lied before, why should they be trusted now? The Red Cross left contentedly, and the ruse worked

After the visit, a propaganda film was made of the seemingly lovely conditions at Theresienstadt, directed by an inmate Kurt Gerron, an experienced director and actor who had previously worked with Marlene Dietrich. Naturally, after the film was made, Gerron and the cast and crew were murdered at Auschwitz. Only 17,000 were left when the camp was finally liberated, the Red Cross briefly taking over administration on 2nd May 1945. The complete film of this disturbingly fake toy-town no longer exists, but some footage has survived.

TIME MAGAZINE

Although much has been made of Adolf Hitler being Time Magazine's 'Man of the Year' in 1938, it is important to put it into context. The award was not an endorsement or compliment, and to say someone is great does not mean they are good. Unlike more recent examples that have a 'head and shoulders' image, the cover of the magazine is not flattering and shows the tiny dictator in a cathedral playing 'a hymn of hate' on a large organ. The artwork was done by Baron Rudolph von Ripper, a Catholic who had fled Germany. The article which followed Hitler's nomination also stated he was the 'greatest threatening force that the democratic, freedom-loving world faces today' and is generally very unflattering -

'The man most responsible for this world tragedy [Munich and the invasion of Czechoslovakia] is a moody, brooding, unprepossessing 49-year-old Austrian-born ascetic with a Charlie Chaplin moustache.'

Hitler was in fact out done by the equally cruel Josef Stalin who was 'Man of the Year' twice in 1939 and 1942.

TIMUR'S CURSE

Timur, or Tamerlane (Timur the Lame), was a 14th century Turco-Mongol ruler. The Great Khan of 1369 is remembered as the last of the great nomadic conquerors. An estimated 17 million people were killed under his brutal reign. On his death during a campaign to China, he was entombed in the Gur-e-Amir mausoleum in Samarkand,

Uzbekistan.

But what does any of this have to do with World War Two?

A legend says that Timur's tomb bore two inscriptions. The first read, 'When I rise from the dead, the world shall tremble,' while the second, on his casket, read, 'Whosoever disturbs my tomb will unleash an invader more terrible than I.'

On 19 June 1941, Soviet anthropologists opened the tomb to examine his remains. Operation Barborossa, the largest military assault in history, was unleashed against the Soviet Union three days later.

Timur was reburied and put to rest in November 1942, soon after the Soviets were victorious and turned the tide of the war after the pivotal Battle of Stalingrad.

This legend does run in a similar manner to that of the curse of the Egyptian pharaoh Tutankhamun, which did in fact throw up some very odd coincidences. Even the most skeptical among us must admit that it's a great story at least. Gur-e-Amir has since been renovated and remains a popular tourist attraction.

THE TITANIC

Joseph Goebbels was the head of Nazi propaganda, minister for the majestically named *Reichsministerium für Volksaufklärung und Propaganda* (Reich Ministry of Public Enlightenment and Propaganda). Goebbels' style was haphazard and often disastrous. His Degenerate Art Exhibition, mocking modern art, was ironically a raging success. He used a Jazz band to broadcast Nazi songs, to the amusement of Churchill and others, and many of his works were counter-productive – and harmful to Hitler's message.

The sinking of the RMS *Titanic*, which resulted in the death of 1,500 people on 15 April 1912, became a worldwide tragedy. The sinking of the 'ship that couldn't be sunk' sent shockwaves around the world and is perhaps, to this day, the best known seaborne disaster to many.

Ignoring the fact there already was a 1929 German filmed 'Atlantik' telling the story of the ill-fated ship, Goebbels decided he wanted it filmed again. In 1943, 'Titanic' was released. This version added an entirely fictitious German hero, First Officer Peterson, and blamed the sinking on Western capitalism. The film's director, Helbert Selpin, who was frustrated with the drunken actions of the extras on set, was arrested for his off-colour remarks and detained. Later that same day he was found hanged in his prison cell, whether this was murder or suicide isn't entirely clear though murder seems much more likely.

Oddly, this movie, having cost 4 million Reichmarks to make, was then suppressed by Goebbels, who realised that showing more tragedy, despair and panicked people desperately looking for their families could be detrimental to the spirits of the German audience. Particularly as they were suffering air raids themselves.

Ironically, the ship used for the film was the SS *Cap Arcona*, which would suffer a tragedy even greater than the real life Titanic disaster.

Cap Arcona, known as 'the floating palace', would later be used in 1945 as part of

Operation Hannibal to evacuate soldiers and civilians from East Prussia to West Germany and away from the advancing Red Army. The journeys across the Baltic Sea would have been terrifying, with the ships constantly being hunted by Soviet submarines and the perennial threat of mines. The greatest maritime disaster in history, the sinking of the *Wilhelm Gustloff* and costing 10,000 lives, took place during these evacuations.

So nerve-wracking must these journeys have been that in February 1945 the ship's captain, Johannes Gertz, shot himself in his cabin rather than endure another trip across the Baltic when he was ordered to go back East.

And, of course, a ship linked to the cursed RMS *Titanic*, was never going to escape the war unscathed.

It was 3rd May 1945. Hitler was dead and the remnants of the Nazi leadership were in flight. Intelligence had reached the British that the Nazi and SS leaders were gathered at Flensburg in Germany, preparing to sail to Norway aboard the SS *Cap Arcona* and a few other ships. They hoped to escape by disappearing into society where they could live unpunished and return to a normal existence. To aid their getaway, they 'unburdened' themselves of the concentration camp prisoners that were with them. The emaciated corpses of their victims – men, women, children – soon littered the foreshore. Heinrich Himmler was there, and his intentions were clear. A signed note from 14 April 1945 read, 'no prisoner must be allowed to fall into the hands of the enemy alive.'

This was it, the day of wrath and justice. The sadistic Nazis who had orchestrated a six-year war leaving tens of millions dead, were gathered in one place at the same time. This would be like shooting fish in a barrel, it was too good to be true.

Squadrons of RAF Hawker Typhoons attacked *Cap Arcona* and the flotilla at Lubeck Bay, dropping their bombs and strafing the survivors in the water without mercy. *Cap Arcona* caught on fire and capsized.

The tragedy is, the RAF didn't know the full story. These ships actually *were* laden with concentration camp survivors. Crucial information from the Red Cross that a mass of survivors were present on the ships had not reached the RAF pilots. The poor souls had survived years of anguish, only to be drowned or shot by their liberators. 7,400 prisoners were killed. Of the 5,000 aboard the *Cap Arcona*, only 350 were saved. It was the stuff of nightmares – the survivors ran the gauntlet of drowning or being shot at by the SS and the mistaken RAF at the same time.

This depressingly tragic event is even harder to bear when you realise that the war in Europe ended only a few days later, on 8th May 1945. For the prisoners this must have been an unbearably horrific finale to the Second World War. Theories survive that the British kept this incident secret from both the pilots and the public, and it should have been sealed for 100 years, not being released to the population until 2045, but it was de-classified early for unknown reasons. What is more likely is that the details of the incident were released in 1972 after the Public Records Act 1967 reduced the amount of time similar state records were to be kept classified. The remains of victims of this tragedy continued to wash up on land as late as 1971.

Having said all that, there is one aspect that should not be forgotten. Despite obvious denials from the Nazi survivors, who sought to mitigate their actions and plans, there was clear and corroborated testimony during the subsequent war trials that, had the Nazis actually completed their journey across the North Sea, they had a plan to ensure their security. This was simply to blow up the three vessels while all the prisoners remained on board. It's unlikely the ships were even seaworthy. It would appear that the only reason why they were loaded aboard in the first place was not in order to sustain their lives, but so the Allies could not interrogate them and hear their damning personal accounts. The three vessels would have sunk with the 10,000 prisoners sealed within, dying from the explosions, from drowning, or asphyxiation. This final crime would have been covered up - presented as an unfortunate accident or a regrettable incident of friendly fire, assuming the Allies had not got to them first.

TO HELL AND BACK

What do you have to do to get your name in a book? *Chambers Biographical Dictionary* (1990 edition) has four Murphies. One was a nineteenth century Irish playwright; another is an Australian dancer; a third was an American doctor and the fourth is Eddie, the black American 'comic performer'. But, bizarrely, the most famous Murphy of them all is not included. He was a genuine hero of the Second World War and arguably accomplished more in his brief military career than all of *Chamber's* other Murphies put together.

Audie Murphy was born in a Texas farming community, one of twelve children. The family was broken up when Audie's father abandoned them and his mother died when the boy was sixteen. With his fresh, freckled face and clear blue eyes, he went to join the US Marines in 1942 but at 5ft 5in he was too short. He must have 'walked tall' (as he did in innumerable Fifties Westerns later) as the army *did* take him. He claimed to be eighteen, which he was not, and saw action in North Africa, Italy (the battle of Anzio and the liberation of Rome) and the south of France.

His greatest moment came on 26 July 1945 near Holtwihr in eastern France. His unit was attacked by six panzers and a force of 250 men. The Americans fell back, but not Murphy. He clambered into a blazing tank and blasted away with a machine gun, killing fifty of the enemy in a hail of bullets. When his unit had time to reform, Murphy, bleeding from wounds in both legs and out of ammunition, attacked with them.

By the end of the war, Murphy was only 21 years old, but he had won every single medal awarded to American soldiers, including the coveted purple heart, the highest accolade for a wounded man's gallantry in the field. Hollywood could not leave this man alone. Like James Stewart, Errol Flynn and Glenn Ford who also saw active service, Murphy was the stuff of legend before he ever put on a ten-gallon hat! He starred in over forty feature films, mostly Westerns, in a simplistic era when the good guy in the white hat always got the girl and beat the baddie.

In reality, the heart-throb who looked like the boy next door suffered from post traumatic stress disorder as a result of his wartime experiences. Few people recognized the condition, believing it to be shell-shock only experienced in the trenches of the First World War. Murphy highlighted the problem and brought it to the public's attention for perhaps the first time. In his darkest moments, which no one outside a chosen few ever knew about, he suffered from insomnia and nightmares and slept with a loaded pistol under his pillow.

Audie Murphy was killed in a plane crash in Virginia in 1971 and was buried with full military honours in Arlington National Cemetery. It is one of the most commonly visited war graves.

In 1955, Hollywood made a movie called *To Hell and Back* based on the man's 1949 autobiography. Who played him? Audie Murphy.

TRUST NO FOX

'Trau keinem Fuchs auf grüner Heid und keinem Jud auf seinem Eid' or 'Trust No Fox in the Green Meadow and No Jew on His Oath', was a children's book written by 18-year-old kindergarten teacher Elvira Bauer and illustrated by Philipp Rupprecht.

It was published in 1936 by Sturmer-Verlag, run by chief Nazi propagandist Julius Streicher. It saw seven editions and 100,000 copies produced and was distributed to schools throughout Germany, aimed primarily at children around six-years-old.

The content of the book is, frankly, appalling, and the fact it was read in schools to impressionable youngsters makes it all the more grim. The title itself comes from a quotation of Martin Luther's, the leader of the Protestant reformation in 1543.

The colourful and bright book glosses over the usual Nazi diatribe we have come to recognise. A poem accompanies each page and image, riddled with the usual racist nonsense. According to this title, Jews are the children of the devil (Jews in fact don't believe in the devil in the Christian sense, believing humans are capable of making enough evil on their own), and they murdered Jesus. An explanation of Jewish naming customs is looked at to allow children to 'catch out' Jews. A baptised and assimilated Jew is still an insidious double agent. They are naturally greedy, filthy, lecherous. Worse, they are, paradoxically, lazy and parasitic –yet also wealthy and cruelly industrious. Jewish doctors delay the death of their patients for as long as they can, knowing each Jew is bound straight for hell.

Before Jews were completely segregated from 'Aryan' schools in 1938, the children suffered what surely must be every parent's worst nightmare. Innocent Jewish children would be forced to stand at the front of the class to be humiliated: discussed and jeered at by their teachers. The children would naturally find themselves the victims of bullying and beatings by other students as a result. This happened more than perhaps we'd like to admit, because by 1937, 97% of teachers were members of the National Socialist Teachers League. The 1938 segregation didn't give the Jewish children any reprieve either, the more fanatical youngsters of the Hitler Youth would wait outside these schools to beat up the children.

'Trust No Fox', together with two other equally disgusting and disturbing books, would be used as evidence at the Nuremberg trials. Julius Streicher was hanged in 1946, as for Elvira Bauer, well, we may assume she skulked back into normal life unpunished, if she survived the war.

U-1206

U-Boats, the predatory submarines of the Reich, were the terror of all sailors during the war. It was particularly the case for the Merchant Navy, whose mariners made their nerve-wracking journeys across the Atlantic, bringing food and supplies from the US to keep Britain fed, supplied and equipped. The U-Boats could strike unseen and without warning, their victims who survived the initial blast would, if there was no help in sight, very likely freeze to death in the icy waters. Churchill himself is quoted as saying 'The only thing that ever really frightened me during the war was the U-boat peril.'

As the war progressed, the Allies became increasingly more efficient at deterring, detecting and fighting back against this menace. Though there was one U-Boat, U-1206, which the Allies would themselves never have to face.

6 April 1945 saw U-1206 set off on patrol from occupied Norway. Its mission was to hunt and destroy Allied shipping. For U-Boat crews themselves, life was dangerous and thoroughly unpleasant. Living for days in cramped and squalid conditions, even tasks such as using the toilet needed to be carefully thought out in order to avoid causing danger. In emergencies, the crew had to use buckets, which couldn't be emptied until the submarine next surfaced. The smell of urine, faeces, human body odor and diesel must have been overwhelming.

The U-1206 had a new and improved plumbing system, but it was complex, and the flushing of the toilets could only be performed by specialists. While hunting shipping off the coast of Scotland, Captain Karl Adolf Schlitt had to go and relieve himself. Rather than call on one of his specialists, he attempted to operate the toilet. Failing, he eventually called for a specialist to flush it after him, but at this point his embarrassment appears to have turned into a disaster. The wrong valve was opened, and water poured into the submarine. At risk of flooding and sinking, the submariners were horrified when inrushing seawater overwhelmed the battery bank. Soon noxious fumes of chlorine gas from the batteries filled the hull. As the air became unbreathable, the Captain had to order the vessel to surface. But here, it was a sitting duck. Allied forces soon discovered her and attacked. Four crewmen died before Captain Schlitt gave the order to abandon ship. He and the remaining forty-six crew were captured and taken prisoner.

It could be argued that the malfunctioning toilet (or operator) saved the lives of the majority of Schlitt's crew, because living onboard an U-boat was perilous: only 25% of U-Boat sailors survived the war.

Never, in the field of human conflict, was so much owed, by one flush, to one loo.

UNCLE ADOLF

Hitler, they say, loved children and dogs. Several of the children of his closest advisers, such as Josef Goebbels and, in the early days, Putzi Hanfstaengel, called him 'Uncle Adolf' and found him great fun. But one of the many myths about the Fuhrer is that he really did have a nephew, William Patrick Hitler and there is a connection with Liverpool.

The story has been accepted by some historians that between November 1912 and April 1913, Hitler lived with relatives in the city. The tale belongs, in a way, to various countries centuries ago hijacking Jesus Christ. His mother Mary went to live in Gaul (France) after the crucifixion. His disciple, James, sailed to Spain in a stone boat. Jesus himself visited England (then on the edge of the Roman province of Britannia) in the company of his uncle, Joseph of Arimathea. Even by these standards, however, Hitler the Scouser takes some beating!

The tale probably originated in a typescript written in 1940 by Brigid Dowling-Hitler, the wife of Adolf's half brother Alois. The couple's son, William Patrick, according to *My Brother-in-Law Adolf*, was taken to Germany to be brought up as a good Nazi before Brigid, having chatted to such luminaries as Hess and Himmler, got him out. Robert Payne, in *The Life and Death of Adolf Hitler*, accepts the Dowling-Hitler memoir and claims that this explains Hitler's delay at Dunkirk, giving the BEF time to evacuate and his various attempts at peace with Britain.

In fact, Hitler was living in Vienna in 1912-13 and never visited Britain at all.

Nevertheless, stories still survive of William Patrick trying to blackmail the Fuhrer with 'evidence' of his Jewish ancestry within the family. There are other rumours that various off-shoots of the Hitlers have made a pact not to reproduce, so that the bloodline dies out. Contrary to the myth of the blue-eyed children of *The Boys from Brazil*, however, there is no evidence that anti-Semitic megalomania is either genetic or hereditary!

UNIT 731

Officially it was the Epidemic Prevention and Water Purification Department of the Kwantung Army (actually run by the *kempeitai*, Japan's military police) and it became an experimentation centre on thousands of people, mostly Chinese, Koreans and Mongolians. As the war continued, Allied prisoners were added to the list of victims, up to 250,000 of whom died before 1945. In the grim codename humour of the time, the victims were known as 'logs'.

Many of the inmates of Unit 731 were vivisected and deliberately infected with disease. Limbs were amputated to assess blood loss; other body parts were removed to see whether a human being could survive without them. Germ warfare resulted in huge numbers of deaths and pathogens used included anthrax, bubonic plague and cholera.

That anyone survived the horrors of this supposedly scientific programme is astonishing, but one who did was Robert Peatley, a major in the Royal Army Ordnance Corps. He kept a diary of his time with 731 and this is available from the Public Record Office at Kew, London. His taped reminiscences are available at the Imperial War Museum, also in London.

In a 2003 statement, the Japanese government claimed to have no record of Unit 731.

THE UNLIKELY AGENT

A blind soldier lies in the psychiatric ward of Pasewalk hospital, Bavaria. It is mid-November 1918 and the bloodiest war in history has just finished. Millions are dead and Germany is in ruins. The blind soldier is a decorated hero, with the Iron Cross and the Black Wound Badge to his credit. Captain Karl Mayr, head of the army Information department says of him, 'He would have worked for a Jewish or a French employer just as readily as for an Aryan. When I first met him, he was like a tired stray dog looking for a master.' His name is Adolf Hitler.

We all have an image of the Fuhrer born of the propaganda, pro- and anti- Nazi which grew up in the 1920s and continued to 1945 and beyond. We know the broad events of those years because they are so astonishing and terrifying. It is when we dissect a monster's life that we find evidence that is not just weird, but almost defies belief.

During the First World War, Hitler had, like thousands of other young men, joined up to do his bit. As a despatch runner dodging shells and bullets in the trenches, he did more than many and deserved his decorations. Even so, there was something odd about Hitler. He never got drunk, never visited a prostitute. He always had his head in a book. He disliked Communists and he disliked Jews, but that was by no means unusual in wartime Germany. And as for his blindness, caused, he said, by a gas attack, that was psychosomatic – he was not blind at all.

The Jewish officer, Lieutenant Hugo Gutmann, had put Hitler forward for the Iron Cross and he was not the only superior who believed the corporal could be useful. Germany was falling apart at the end of 1918, not least Munich, where Hitler's regiment was based. It was taken over by the Communists under the journalist Kurt Eisner and soldiers like Hitler, bitter and disillusioned at being let down by their government in what was being referred to as 'the stab in the back' were bewildered and confused. Against the new Communist regime were a number of right-wing groups, collectively called the *Freikorps*. One of these was the SDAP, the not yet National Socialist Workers' Party. The very name 'Socialist' implied a confusion which also gave the group a wide appeal. At first there were several Communists among its members.

And one of the new faces that turned up at meetings in the Munich bierkellers was Adolf Hitler. There is little doubt that he was working for Mayr or someone else in the army's Intelligence unit. In other words, he was a spy. For the sake of verisimilitude, he had to join the NSDAP, which he did as party member 555. In later years, he would claim that his number was 7 – in other words, he had been a founder member – one of the many pieces of misinformation that the Nazis cultivated in the years ahead.

It was in those chaotic months of 1919-20 that Hitler discovered his skill for oration. Kurt Ludecke, who heard him, wrote, 'I forgot everything but the man. Clanking around, I saw that his magnetism was holding these thousands as one.'

Under the tutelage of Dietrich Eckart, poet and journalist who invented the much-hear battle-cry of these years – *'Deutschland Erwache!'* (Germany, awake!) – Hitler became the mob orator par excellence and slowly by surely replaced the railway worker Anton Drexler as head of the party. He embraced the Thule Society which promulgated Aryan racial supremacy. He designed the *hakencreuz*, the broken cross or swastika that had become the party's emblem. By July 1921, the Nazis had become national and if there was ever anything socialistic about their policies, that was phased out.

Eckhart died two years later, by which time Hitler was launching his abortive coup in Munich and writing *Mein Kampf,* the bible of the Nazi party. His last words were – 'Follow Hitler. He will dance, but it is I who have written the music ...'

From undercover agent to Fuhrer; it only took thirteen years. From Fuhrer to a petrol-soaked corpse in a bombed garden in Berlin; that took thirteen years too.

UNROTATED PROJECTILE

The Second World War saw conflict of a scale never seen before, for this was not a war of land or sea. For the first time the air became a hotly contested battle zone. As well as the dreaded U-boats, the Royal Navy understood perfectly the terrible threat posed by the Luftwaffe and the Japanese air force.

Normal air defences included batteries of 4" and 40mm guns. As always with technology, the next advancement was sought. The enigmatically named 'unrotated projectile' was the cover name for a new concept: twenty smoothbore tubes which would fire spin-stabilised rockets. Thus they were 'unrotated' unlike most other rockets.

This weapon deserves a mention as the rockets weren't aimed at aircraft, but some distance in front of them. The rockets would launch, and at a preset height detonate a small charge. This would release an 8.4 ounce mine which was itself attached to three parachutes on a 400ft wire. The concept was that, as a plane snagged the wires, it would become tangled, or, better, draw the explosives into contact with the aircraft's fuselage or wings.

The idea of an aerial minefield is sound, but the unrotated projectile didn't impress the Royal Navy. If the enemy dodged the wires, the minefield was useless. During a demonstration of the weapon at Scapa Flow, a change of wind meant that some of the mines flew back towards the vessel, becoming entangled in its rigging. Fortunately these were dummy rounds and there were no casualties.

The most famous ship to have the weapon was HMS *Hood*, which was sunk by the pride of the *Kriegsmarine*, the seemingly indestructible Bismarck. Anti-aircraft weapons advanced at an astonishing rate, but the unrotated projectile was scrapped.

UNSINKABLE SAM

Although this tale has been written off as a sailors' yarn, it is still an intriguing one. Unsinkable Sam served in both the *Kriegsmarine* and the Royal Navy (prompting the obvious question – whose side was he on?), and he was a black and white cat. Sam first saw service on board the legendary battleship *Bismarck* as the pet of one of the sailors. In its day, the *Bismarck* was the most powerful warship afloat, but it was sunk on 18 May 1941 and only 118 of the crew of over 2,000 survived. Hours after this, the British destroyer HMS *Cossack* came across him floating on a board in the sea, where he was collected. The crew named him Oscar.

Five months later, HMS *Cossack* itself was torpedoed by a U-Boat (U-563) off the Bay of Biscay, killing 159 crewmen; Oscar was among the survivors. Now nicknamed 'Unsinkable Sam' he was transferred to the aircraft-carrier HMS *Ark Royal*, which ironically had been involved in the search for the *Bismarck*. *Ark Royal* met a similar fate and was attacked by U-81 in November 1941 near Gibraltar. All but one of the crew were saved from this attack, including Oscar who was clinging to flotsam and was described as 'angry but unharmed.'

This was Oscar's last active service and he spent the remainder of his career working with the governor of Gibraltar before retiring with a sailor in Britain. The truth of this is somewhat doubtful and relying on the word of sailors isn't recommended. Besides, as a mascot he didn't appear to be a particularly lucky one!

V FOR VICTORY

Winston Churchill's famous V fingered sign was in fact the brain child of Belgian minister Victor de Laveleye in 1941. Belgium speaks two languages and the V stood for victory in French (*victoire*) and freedom (*vrijheid*) in Dutch. The idea was to demoralize the Nazi occupiers with the constant display on this sign in graffiti and banners to show that the people were not with them. By July, the symbol was being used throughout occupied Europe and Winston Churchill approved its use in a speech, often using it himself. The V finger sign was intended with the palm facing the recipient but Churchill's erroneous use with the palm towards him gave the symbol an added meaning!

The use of two fingers as a term of contempt is much older and goes back to the Hundred Years War (1340-1453). The war-winning weapon then was the English longbow, which fired at six times the speed of the French crossbow. French troops would cut off the bow string fingers of English prisoners to make sure they never fired a bow again. The archers who waved their fingers at the French across the field of, say, Agincourt, were making a statement.

In 1942, the British occultist Aleister Crowley claimed he invented this gesture. This was never corroborated; 'the great beast' made a fool of himself by applying to British Intelligence to aid the war effort – he was turned down. In any case, the symbol infuriated the Nazis, who simply decided that they in fact invented it, adding their own V's to walls and vehicles and even plastering a giant V across the Eiffel Tower.

THE VALKYRIE GIRLS

The Mitford sisters came from a fascinating upper class British family, and though there was also a brother (Thomas), it was the six daughters who caught the imagination of the public. They were the socialite children of Lord and Lady Redesdale, called by the children 'Farve' and 'Muv' and soon became celebrities and favourites of the newspapers.

Diana married Oswald Mosley, the leader of the British Union of Fascists after a scandalous divorce from Bryan Guinness, of beer fame, in 1929. When the war broke out, she was interned, along with her new husband, under Defence Regulation 18B and spent several weeks in Holloway. Her devotion to Fascism never wavered.

Unity went one better; she was a huge admirer of Adolf Hitler and eventually got to meet him in Berlin. They became close, which sparked rumours of a relationship. Known as 'Bobo' to her siblings, her middle name was Valkyrie and with all the associations with Nazi/German legend, she became a pin-up girl for Josef Goebbels' propaganda machine. Days after war was declared, she shot herself in the head and was invalided home.

Jessica ('Decca') at the other extreme, became a communist fighting in the Spanish Civil War, before moving to America and becoming a civil rights campaigner and author.

Nancy was a socialist and moved to Paris to become a writer. Deborah had no interest in politics, and was content to live a quiet country life as the wife of the Duke of Devonshire at Chatsworth House. Pamela, known as 'Woman' in the family, married a scientist and became an adventurer, driving around Europe and flying across the Atlantic. As for Thomas, he was killed in action in Burma in 1945, one more victim of the war. A convinced Fascist, he refused to fight Germany but had no issues confronting the Japanese.

VANISHING CELEBRITIES

What do the Duke of Kent, Joseph Kennedy Junior, Wladyslaw Sikorski, Leslie Howard and Glenn Miller have in common? They all died in mysterious plane crashes, some vanishing without trace.

The first to go was Howard, known on both sides of the Atlantic as the quintessential English gentleman actor. Slim and dapper, he didn't look the hero but his roles were certainly heroic. He was Ashley Wilkes in the epic tearjerker *Gone With*

The Wind released in the year that the war began. More pertinent perhaps to his disappearance were the British roles he took. He was the Spitfire engineer R.T. Mitchell in *The First of the Few* and a British agent operating in Nazi Germany in *Pimpernel Smith.* As a propaganda icon he was irreplaceable.

In June 1943, Howard and his agent Alfred Chenhalls were flying to London from neutral Lisbon in a Douglas DC3, a civilian aircraft clearly marked and in broad daylight. There were thirteen passengers and four aircrew. Somewhere over Biscay, a squadron of Junkers 88 from KG40 shot the plane down. Not only was Howard an obvious loss, the shooting down of a civilian aircraft was contrary to the Geneva Convention which Germany had signed years before. Questions were raised in the Commons and one of the fingers of suspicion pointed to the Prime Minister. Churchill travelled frequently by air, visiting Allied leaders and theatres of war and the description of a thickset man smoking a cigar boarding the plane at Lisbon may have been enough for Nazi agents to make the assumption that it was the Prime Minister and to tip off the Luftwaffe accordingly. The man was probably Alfred Chenhalls. Other theories followed. Was the real target Wilfred Israel, founder of the Jewish Refugee Mission in London? Or were there top secret papers on board the DC3 which the Abwehr wanted destroyed?

Less than a month later, General Wladyslaw Sikorski joined the list of the missing. Sikorski was the unpopular leader of the Polish government in exile based in London and he too went down over Biscay when his RAF Liberator took off from Gibraltar. Astonishingly, there was a survivor, Edward Prchal, the Czech pilot, who made it clear that there were no German aircraft involved. If there was a bomb on board, the target had to be Sikorski, but who wanted him dead?

Most obviously the Germans, but there was a problem. In April, a mass grave containing the bodies of 10,000 Polish officers was found by the Germans in Katyn Forest near Smolensk. Long before this, Sikorski had been deeply suspicious of Stalin and the Red Army. He was strongly anti-Communist and until Operation Barbarossa, the Russians had been Germany's allies and happily partitioned Poland. The Katyn Massacre was clearly attributable to Stalin and this is now accepted fact. It was awkward to both the British and the Americans that the Polish government broke off diplomatic relations with the Soviets. To that end, Goebbels' propaganda machine broadcast from Berlin that the British had engineered Sikorski's death, calling him the last victim of Katyn.

On 7 July 1943, the RAF had a court of inquiry in Gibraltar. Prchal was an experienced pilot and said the controls seized up. This was not due to an error by his co-pilot Squadron Leader W.S. Herring; neither was it because the Liberator was overladen. As the only survivor, Prchal naturally came under suspicion and was officially cleared by a second inquiry launched by Churchill himself. Yet the rumours have never quite gone away.

By August 1944, the Allies were pushing eastwards across France. That was the month that Lieutenant Joseph P. Kennedy died. He was the oldest son of the ex-American ambassador to Britain whose pro-Nazi views before the war made him deeply unpopular. Joseph Jnr was a pilot with the US Naval Reserve and on 12 August he flew out of Fersfield airbase in Suffolk in a B24 Liberator bound for a V3 rocket launch base near Calais. At 6.20pm, the Liberator suddenly blew up in mid-air. Since the plane was a stripped down version filled with twelve tons of explosives, the catastrophe was hardly surprising, but Kennedy and his co-pilot, Wilford Willy, were supposed to bail out and the aircraft would carry on to its destination as a flying bomb controlled by radio. All this could be dismissed as what it was, a tragic accident engendered by the use of volatile technology, were it not for the weird testimony of Karl-Heinz Wehn.

Wehn wrote in 1986 that he had interrogated an American airman captured from a plane crash in the sea off Normandy. This was on 14 July and the American gave his name as Joseph Kennedy from Hyannisport near Boston. His father had been an ambassador and owned a Boston shipping line. *This* Joe Kennedy was shot while trying to escape and was buried in the churchyard of St André sur Orme. Was someone else impersonating Kennedy in order to get preferential treatment from his captors? Or did Karl Heinz Wehn get his facts and dates wrong? In the event, of course, Joseph Kennedy Jnr became, with hindsight, the first casualty in the family curse that saw the murders of both his brothers, John and Robert, in the 1960s.

Three days before Hitler launched the counter-attack in the Ardennes known as the battle of the Bulge, Glenn Miller disappeared. It was 15 December 1944 and Miller's band flew to Orly in France to begin a six-week tour of US bases and field hospitals. Bad fog was disrupting flights over the Channel and Miller persuaded Flight Officer John Morgan to take him in a Noorduyn Norseman from an airstrip near Bedford. The plane never arrived and no wreckage was ever found. Officially, Miller, his pilot Morgan and friend Lt Colonel Norman Bressel were declared dead by the US government a year later.

Large sections of the public found it very hard to accept the sudden loss of their hero. Miller's big band sound was part of the mythology of wartime, especially for the Americans and rumours about his actual fate proliferated. Some said that he had cracked up mentally or become a cocaine addict and had been quietly removed to a sanatorium. Perhaps he had been murdered by the SS, anxious to destroy the Allies' musical world's best known protagonist. Then again, he could have been a Nazi spy, flitting under the showbiz cover between Britain and France, conveying all kinds of secret information to the enemy. Most lurid of all were the claims that he had been seen in a Paris brothel and had been knifed in a fight over a girl.

The theory which is given considerable credence today is that the Norseman was hit by 'friendly fire' when 149 Squadron's Lancasters, returning from a raid in Seign, Germany, jettisoned their remaining bombs in what was standard practice and may have hit Miller's plane by accident.

THE VICTORY PARADE

The London Victory Celebrations of 1946 was a time of joy and jubilation; six long and hard years of war were finally over. The Allies had defeated Nazi Germany, Imperial Japan, Italy and all of the minor Axis powers. Britain, the United States, France, China and countless other nations joined in the merriment, but there was a darker side to the parade.

The Soviet Union had an ambiguous position within the Allied nations and the other countries were rather ambivalent in their feelings towards the Russian Bear.

Originally friendly to Germany, the Soviets secretly carved up eastern Europe with the Nazis in the Molotov-Ribbentrop pact, and only joined the Allies out of necessity after the shock of the German onslaught of Operation Barbarossa in June 1941.

The elephant in the room was Poland. The attack on the nation by the Nazis sparked the Second World War in September 1939, but the Soviets themselves attacked from the east a few weeks later, eventually meeting the Germans at Brest-Litovsk. It was to become the German/Soviet border. The Polish put up a brave defence, but ultimately their position was untenable and their armed forces crumbled in the face of being attacked on both fronts. The Polish government-in-exile continued to function from London, with over 200,000 Poles fighting for the British throughout the course of the war. As the war was ending, it was clear that the nations between Germany and Russia would not see a return of democracy, but would fall, as Churchill prophesied, under an 'iron curtain' of puppet Soviet governments.

By 1946 tensions between East and West were already growing, and the first icy snowflakes of the impending Cold War could be felt. Political pragmatism forced the British to recognize the new communist government of Poland and the Soviets refused to allow the Poles to attend the victory celebrations. The Soviets themselves declined the invitation.

Britain and France had gone to war in 1939 to protect their ally, Poland, and her sovereignty. But after six years of war, the world had changed. Imperialist Europe was no longer top dog, having been replaced by the superpowers of the United States and the Soviet Union, and Poland would remain behind the iron curtain until 1989.

THE VON TRAPP FAMILY

All of us who have seen and heard *The Sound of Music* will be familiar with the Von Trapp family. The charming 1965 movie received criticism for its historical inaccuracies, but considering it was a Hollywood musical adaptation of a Broadway musical adaptation of a German film adaptation of Maria Von Trapp's book, that is hardly surprising!

Maria Kutschera was born in Vienna, Austria in 1905. In 1925, she became a nun at Nonnberg abbey in Salzburg. By 1926, sister Maria became a tutor to one of the children of Georg Von Trapp, a widowed former U-boat captain. She excelled at her work and eventually took on the other six children.

Georg became enamored of Maria and asked for her hand in marriage. Just one minor problem – she was a nun! Maria panicked and returned to her mother abbess for advice. The mother abbess reassured her she should follow her heart and that it was God's will. She left the sisterhood, accepted the marriage proposal, and moved in with the family in their home at Villa Trapp. Georg and Maria had three children of their own, bringing the number of their brood up to ten.

However not everything was rosy, the family were in dire straits financially. They had to dismiss their servants and rent out various rooms in their home to make ends meet. Then along came Father Franz Wasner to act as their chaplain. He heard the Von Trapps singing and encouraged them to pursue a professional singing career. They took his advice, and the 'Trapp Family Choir' was formed. They sang at concerts and festivals, and even on the radio.

The family's budding musical career began to develop against the backdrop of growing anti-Semitism following Hitler's 1938 *Anschluss*, the annexation of the country. Hitler, of course, was himself Austrian, not German, and had long wished to see Austria formally attached to 'Greater' Germany. Georg was now in a difficult position. He was inducted into the *Kriegsmarine,* but he despised the Nazis and what they stood for. Torn, he refused his commission, but he knew that both he and his family would be at risk of arrest and persecution. So in 1938 he and the rest of the family fled – first to Italy, then England, and finally settling in America at Vermont, New England. Their successful musical career continued for decades.

As for their old home, Trapp Villa ended up in Heinrich Himmler's hands. The picturesque building was covered in barbed wire, draped in swastikas and filled with SS guards. It was to become Himmler's summer vacation home.

In modern times, Trapp Villa has since been restored to its former glory and is now one of the most popular tourist attractions in Austria. The Von Trapp family's story and *The Sound of Music,* continue to charm the world.

VOLKSSTURM

Of all of the desperate, unnecessary and futile sacrifices of the war, the creation of the *Volkssturm* (People's Storm) is one of the most tragic. As the Nazis were in retreat by October 1944, it was a last desperate roll of the dice. All German males between 16 and 60 were ordered to join the units and fight tooth and nail to the death for the glory of the Reich. Millions of young boys joined and so did old men who had probably already suffered the nightmare of the First World War.

The *Volkssturm* were poorly equipped, received next to no training and were not given official uniforms, many using their old First World War uniforms or uniforms from their jobs such as postmen. Many of the conscripts were not even armed, and had to share weapons within their units.

Goebbels, with his usual style of propaganda, made out the People's Storm was a heroic response from the people of Germany itself, rallying to the cause – but most were exhausted and saw through the lies. The sight of old men and boys without uniforms or weapons made many realise how desperate the situation had become.

Unsurprisingly, the militia, often unsupervised and without direction, would surrender to the enemy when the chance came, particularly in the West, where the Allies were generally more merciful. In the East however, many units fought bravely and fought hard against the might of the Red Army. Many more units would simply go into hiding and wait for the war to be over. In the ruins of Berlin, many of the militia fought to the death against the Red Army simply through the fear of being captured. It is estimated that in the last four months of the war, over half a million men and boys of the *Volkssturm* died.

THE VOYAGE OF THE DAMNED

Anti-Semitism in Germany became more structured from 1935 onwards. The Nuremberg Laws deprived Jews of their citizenship and the 1938 *Kristallnacht* on 9 November was the signal for systematic attacks on Jewish businesses, synagogues, schools and people. Many Jews who could afford it applied for foreign visas, but due to the immigration quotas of various countries and the time it took to process, many of them came too late.

On Saturday 13 May 1939, one such group of 937 people were able to escape when they boarded the SS *St. Louis* bound for Cuba. The Captain, Gustav Schröder, ordered his staff to treat the Jewish passengers as they would treat everyone else. Leaving their homes and loved ones behind, the passengers enjoyed the luxuries of life on the cruise ship, eating well, making friends and relaxing. When the ship finally got to Cuba, things did not go to plan; due to technicalities and recent changes in the law, those on board could neither be classified as tourists nor refugees, despite paying for visas and permits, which had been retroactively made worthless.

The ship stayed at anchor for six anxious days and only 29 of the passengers were allowed to disembark as they were US, Spanish and Cuban citizens. In despair Captain Shröder took the ship to Florida, where the Americans too refused to allow them to make port. In the end, there was no choice but to return to Europe. Britain agreed to take 288 passengers; France took 244; Belgium 214 and the Netherlands 181. Those who went to Britain survived the war, but for those who ended up back in Europe, it is estimated that only 365 of the 620 lived, the rest being murdered once these countries came under Nazi control from 1940 onwards.

For his valiant efforts, Captain Shröder was honoured by Germany after the war and was named as 'righteous among the nations' by Israel. Stuart Rosenburg's 1976 film *The Voyage of the Damned* dramatizes the fateful voyage of SS. *St Louis*.

WAR AGAINST THE POTATO BEETLE

Autumn 1940: things were going well for the Axis. France had fallen, and only Britain – hiding beyond the English Channel – stood in opposition to them. However, they were confident the Luftwaffe's attacks would soon bring the British to submission. In the meantime, there was another enemy on the horizon which would either have to fall in line or be crushed, the potato beetle.

The Colorado bug first appears to have had a run in with potato plants around 1859, sweeping east and destroying American crops. The Americans warned Europe about the bug, and imports were stopped, but it was too little, too late and by 1877 the bug was firmly established in Europe. The devastation was so great that in the First World War the French looked into weaponising the insect against the Germans. In the Second World War, the Germans tried doing the same to the French. Allegedly, the Nazis researched the bug in controlled facilities, and tested it on themselves near Frankfurt in 1943. It has been claimed that the British ordered 12,000 from the Americans. Whatever the truth of that, the bug ate both nation's crops – neither nation deployed it as a weapon, and it wasn't taking sides.

After the war, East Germany, now under communist rule, became infested – possibly as a result of the Frankfurt test. The pro-Stalin nation called the bug 'Amikfaer', the American beetle, as the cold war was crystalizing. The Soviet agents of propaganda got their hands on this one, American capitalist planes were secretly dropping the bug on farms to starve out the inhabitants. The beetle was even compared to the atomic bomb, America's nightmarish weapon of mass destruction. Though the bugs were smaller, it was a weapon of 'US imperialists' – no doubt the work of the CIA. Farmers had to spend countless hours picking the eggs and bugs by hand, community bug killing days were launched – and the Young Pioneers youth movement did their bit too.

The Colorado bug still occupies America and Europe and has been the bane of gardeners ever since. Though have they now switched allegiance from the CIA to the KGB? In the troubles in Ukraine from 2014 onwards, the term *kolorady*, referring to the beetle, is used disparagingly to refer to pro-Russian separatists.

THE WAR OF THE WORLDS

'Who would have believed that on 30 October 1938, millions of Americans were duped into believing that the Martians had landed and that New Yorkers were vapourised by ray guns.'

This is a paraphrase (sort of!) of the start of H.G. Wells' brilliant science fiction story which was dramatized by the actor Orson Welles on CBS radio on the date above.

The foaflore existed for years that American listeners really believed

Wells'/Welles' fiction, assuming that it was a live-coverage broadcast. On 8 November 1938, Hitler referred to the panic that ensued as a classic example of the 'corrupt condition and decadent state of affairs in democracy'.

In 1930s America, as elsewhere, radio was a new kid on the block in terms of attention-grabbing media (rather as television is battling against YouTube, Tik Tok, Twitter and the rest today). Newspapers like the *New York Times*, anxious not to lose advertising revenue to radio claimed that 'terror by radio' was an example of the immorality and irresponsibility of the new outlet. Among the fake news stories that the papers ran were colossal traffic-jams bringing American cities to a standstill, mobs rioting in the streets and suicides happening all over the place. Bearing in mind the genuine hysteria from time to time in the United States, usually to do with race, nothing surprised the world any more; over 10,000 newspaper articles ran in the weeks after the show was aired. Such was the pull of all this that thousands who had not heard the play claimed that they had and remembered the ensuing panic too. CBS researchers phoned 5,000 households – only 2 per cent had actually heard it!

The play made Orson Welles' reputation and it did no harm to the bank balance of H.G. either. In fact, America need not have worried at all. The Welles' version is set in Princeton, but the 'real' Martian landing, as envisaged by Wells, happened in Woking, England. And to prove it, a statue of an alien 'grey' stands on the site today!

WELCOME TO BRITAIN

America's entry into the Second World War undoubtedly turned the tide in favour of the Allies, but logistics dictated that the US army had to be based in Britain as a springboard for the invasions of North Africa, Italy and France. Although the presence of the GIs was generally accepted by the British – and actively welcomed by some – there were problems. They were 'over-paid, over-sexed and over here' and that in itself led to confrontation. 'Have you heard about the new Utility knickers?' one joke ran. 'One Yank and they're off!' The satirical magazine *Punch* summed up the situation brilliantly in 1942 –

> 'Dear old England's not the same,
> The dread invasion, well, it came.
> But no, it's not the beastly Hun,
> The god-damn Yankee army's come!'

A Welcome to Britain was a 1943 movie, produced by the Ministry of Information to advise American servicemen entering the country how to, and how not to behave. Starring Burgess Meredith (the Penguin from the TV series of *Batman*) as a young GI, we follow him exploring an English pub, a school-room, a station and other places. The movie is surprisingly funny and endearing, and scenes where Meredith tries to work out what '3 and 9' is (about 50 cents at the time), talking to a retired teacher and trying to pronounce Worcestershire are still hilarious. The final scenes where he hasn't finished exploring Britain and is still trying to finish his film before being sent off to fight is a sad foreshadowing of what so many brave soldiers, who were the film's intended audience, would sacrifice at Bloody Omaha and beyond.

WENT THE DAY WELL?

Most of the war movies relating to 1939-45 were made in the 1950s and early '60s, starring the lantern-jawed British and American heart-throbs of the day. John Wayne often featured, even though he never saw an actual day's action in his life. Jack Hawkins, Anthony Steele, Richard Attenborough and John Mills provided the British muscle with a number of cheeky chappies like Harry Fowler and Victor Maddern to provide the light relief.

Went the Day Well? is different from all these, if only because it was made in 1942, when the war was at its height. From a short story by Graham Greene, directed by Alberto Cavalcanti, the film was produced at the Ealing Studios by Michael Balcon, perhaps Britain's most famous producer at the time. In a plotline often copied since, the fictional village of Bramley End (actually Turville in Buckinghamshire) is overrun by Wehrmacht troops in disguise. This is the start of a German invasion which was very much on the cards when Greene wrote the original story and it highlights the fear surrounding the existence of a fifth column spy network in the country. The actor Leslie Banks played the local squire in league with the Nazis and David Farrar was the handsome lead. The ever-reliable Mervyn Johns was the narrator, looking back on the events at Bramley End from the perspective of a war that was won (even though at the time, no one could have known the outcome). It was Thora Hird's first film and yes, of course Harry Fowler was in it!

The film's title comes from a poem written towards the end of the First World War by John Maxwell Edmonds –

Went the day well?
We died and never knew,
But, well or ill,
Freedom, we died for you.

Despite the fact that there is very little violence in it, it was included in *100 Greatest War Films* in 2005. Its black and white quirky nostalgia sets it apart from the more obvious gung-ho heroics of later movies and sums up superbly the hopes and sang-froid of a generation.

THE WEREWOLVES

The Werewolves first saw the light of day in 1944 as the Allies pushed east after D-Day. Partisans and resistance fighters, they were units of commandos working within the Allied areas, operating in secret and carrying out sabotage and reprisals behind enemy lines. The name probably comes, not from the shape-shifting lycanthropes of occult lore (although Germany was the focus of this in the traditional 'horror' genre) but from a novel by Hermann Lons, written in 1910 but set at the time of the Thirty Years War (1618-48).

5,000 Werewolves were trained, but their effectiveness was doubted by military commanders who needed all the regular soldiers they could get. Due to the clandestine nature of the group, it's unclear what activities were committed by them and not by regular soldiers. Whether myth or reality, the fear and paranoia this group caused the Allies and Soviets led to many harsh reprisals and thousands of German civilians being arrested. The American Armed Forces Radio station broadcast –

'Every friendly German civilian is a disguised soldier of hate ... A smile is their weapon by which to disarm you ... In heart, body and spirit, every German is Hitler.'

In March 1945, Goebbels gave the *Werwolf* speech in which he ordered every German to fight to the death leading to many stories and rumours throughout Europe. Some historians believe that their attacks were still taking place five years after the war ended.

WEWELSBURG CASTLE

Heinrich Himmler saw his SS as the modern equivalent of the Teutonic Order, a band of chivalrous knights serving the Fatherland, protected by runic symbols and ancient artefacts. For an ex-chicken farmer who also ran the death camps to have this romantic notion seems bizarre, but the facts speak for themselves.

Wewelsburg Castle was a seventeenth century three-walled fortress which Himmler used as the SS headquarters. In 1933, he signed a 100-year lease for its use. He planned to make the castle into the spiritual home of the SS but the claims that he believed himself to be a reincarnated Arthur and that he wanted to dress up his 'knights' in armour in a Nazi Camelot are baseless. The idea of clandestine Nazi rituals involving magical items, held under the cover of darkness by torch-light certainly capture the imagination, but it is next to impossible to separate the truth from the myth.

As with most Nazi grand plans, the war ended before it could be completed. As with Hitler's architectural dream of Germania, a new city to replace Berlin, Himmler's architectural ambitions for Wewelsburg never materialized. To what degree Himmler's men believed in the 'New Order' or whether they simply went along with it is a matter of opinion. Hitler didn't visit the castle himself and seemed quite unimpressed by 'Himmler's nonsense', but allowed him to get on with it. Today Wewelsburg Castle is a museum, youth-hostel, one of the largest in Germany, and is a popular tourist attraction.

THE WHITE DEATH

The Soviet invasion of Finland was supposed to be a walk in the park. It wasn't. The Finns were outnumbered, outgunned and technologically inferior to the Red Army but they put up an incredibly brave resistance. The 'Winter War' as it was known was a three-month conflict that began in 1939. The Soviet invasion was declared illegal by the international community and they were dismissed from the increasingly ineffectual League of Nations as a result.

The Finns were experts in winter combat, wearing white camouflage and engaging in daring hit and run tactics before escaping, often on skis. The most famous of these guerillas was Simo Hayha, who killed 505 Russians during the war and remains to this day the sniper with the highest body count in the Second World War.

After realizing this was the work of one man, the Red Army named Hayha, 'The White Death' and were desperate to stop him. He was eventually shot in the jaw by an enemy sniper. His injuries were horrific but Hayha didn't die; he remained comatose for four days before finally regaining consciousness on 13 March, the day the Winter War ended. He became a Finnish hero and lived peacefully until he died at the age of 96 in 2002. The image of outnumbered ski-troops fighting an overwhelming mechanized enemy, as far north as Lapland, became one of the period's most romantic.

When asked, in 1998, why he was such a good shot, his answer was simply, 'Practice.'

WHITE ROSE

The White Rose was a German resistance group made up of academics who opposed Nazi rule by non-violent means, using graffiti and the written word to spread their message.

Their first known actions were in 1942 in Munich, when they distributed around 15,000 pamphlets warning people of the atrocities and crimes being committed by the government.

They produced seven leaflets in total, with poignant messages such as:

'Why do you allow these men who are in power to rob you, step by step, openly and in secret, of one domain of your rights after another, until one day nothing, nothing at all will be left but a mechanised state system presided over by criminals and drunks? Is your spirit already so crushed by abuse that you forget it is your right – or rather, your moral duty – to eliminate this system?'

Though brave and commendable, it was only a matter of time before the police and the Gestapo caught up with them. Those found to be members of the White Rose could expect brutal treatment: punishment and the farcical show trials of the 'People's Court'. Of those caught, many were executed, some of their number beheaded by guillotine, including the heroic siblings Hans and Sophie Scholl.

Despite the end they suffered, their message was not forgotten. The final leaflet produced by the small but dedicated team of the White Rose made it into the hands of the Allies. In July 1943 they dropped millions of copies from planes, scattering them and their message over Germany and the dwindling Reich.

Sophie Scholl is a hero in Germany to this day. Lillian Garrett-Groag, a playwright, summarized her thoughts of the White Rose on 22 February 1993:

'It is possibly the most spectacular moment of resistance that I can think of in the twentieth century. The fact that five little kids, in the mouth of the wolf, where it really counted, had the tremendous courage to do what they did, is spectacular to me. I know that the world is better for them having been there, but I don't know why.'

THE WHITE ROSE OF STALINGRAD

The war in the east would be over quickly. Von Runstadt unleashed his blitzkrieg (lightning war) on the west with the overthrow of four countries in three month, Hitler could now turn his attention to his real goal – the subjugation of the Soviet Union. The Russians were genetically inferior *untermenschen* (sub-human), he believed and against the combined might of the Wehrmacht and the Luftwaffe, stood no chance. Operation Barbarossa, named after a Medieval emperor who had led the third crusade, was launched on 22 June 1941. Perhaps it was an unlucky code-name; Barbarossa never reached the Holy Land but drowned in a swollen river on his way to war.

Initially all went as planned. Stalin seems to have been blindsided by his former ally and was caught napping. In clash after clash, the massive Red Army fell back, exactly as earlier Russian armies had done in the First World War and against Napoleon in 1812. The problem was that the German fighting machine relied on speed and success – it was not equipped for a long, drawn-out struggle in which the Russian weather took its toll and petrol froze in fuel tanks. At Leningrad, Moscow and Stalingrad, the Red Army held on with a tenacity that was unexpected by anyone.

Women had fought in the Revolution of 1917, both for the Reds and the Whites, and by 1941 there were perhaps 800,000 of them serving in the army and 200,000 in air defence (see 'The Night Witches'). The Germans had their own Teutonic legends of the Valkyrie, terrible female spirits who swooped down onto battlefields to take the souls of the dead to a warrior-heaven called Valhalla. But they had never seen anyone like Lilya Litoyak. She signed up as a pilot although she had very little flying experience, refused to crop her hair as other Russian women did. She was punished for snazzing up her uniform with a fur collar but most party commissars, paid snoopers who insisted on slavish devotion to the party line, turned a blind eye.

Lilya's first known victory was over Erwin Meier, a Luftwaffe fighter pilot shot down by her over Stalingrad. He survived and was taken prisoner, but never believed that the petite blonde he had been introduced to, had actually brought him down. She was the first woman in history to kill in aerial warfare, and her plane, painted with a lily on the fuselage and with a cockpit full of flowers, assumed the same kind of totemic power of Manfred von Richthofen's red tin-plane in the First World War.

Her reputation grew as kill after kill was credited to her. In the British and American press, the lily morphed into a rose, hence the nickname and title of this section. By the age of 21 she was a squadron leader.

Lily flew her last mission on 1 August 1943. Her plane was shot down, but whether she died in the burning cockpit or was taken prisoner was unknown.

'WHO DO YOU THINK YOU ARE KIDDING, MR. HITLER?'

The Second World War was marked, among other things, by some spectacular photographs. Before it began, we have the British Prime Minister Neville Chamberlain holding up the worthless 'scrap of paper' on which Adolf Hitler promised peace in Europe. We have the dome of St Pauls Cathedral in London, still standing as the Blitz of 1940 rages all around it. We have British Tommies wading out to the 'little boats' that would rescue them at Dunkirk. We have the young men of the RAF's fighter command – Churchill's few – 'scrambling' to their Hurricanes as the air raid siren sounds. We have the American ships at Pearl Harbor, blazing and belching black smoke. We have terrified British and American troops about to leap out of their landing craft onto the Normandy beaches on D-Day. We have hundreds of parachutes floating like mushrooms over Holland in Operation Market Garden. We have the Stars and Stripes being lifted by battle-weary GIs on Iwo Jima. We have three utterly destroyed cities – Berlin, Hiroshima and Nagasaki.

Each photograph tells a poignant story of the bloodiest war in history. But there are some photographs that tell a vastly different tale. Expert Martin Dammann has collected hundreds of war photographs and has published them in a 2018 book, *Soldier Studies: Cross Dressing in Der Wehrmacht.* For years there were black propaganda stories of Nazis wearing women's clothing which were designed to blacken their reputations still further. Homosexuality was illegal across Europe in the 1940s and was a particular anathema to the Nazis who put people in concentration camps for it.

The truth was that pre-war Berlin was highly cosmopolitan, with a transexual elite personified by the characters in the musical *Cabaret*. The Nazi regime contrasted sharply with the decadence of Weimar and yet Damman's photographs are living proof that homosexuality, even sometimes in jest, was rife in the German armed forces.

WHO, ME?

A top-secret, war-winning weapon was being developed by the British SOE (Special Operations Executive.)   Correspondence from August 4, 1943 between British Intelligence Officer TR Bird and his American counterpart Stanley Lovell from the OSS (Office of Strategic Services) discusses the development of 'S Liquid', the S standing for stench!

The plan was for the S Liquid to be given to resistance agents in occupied Europe, who would then secretly pour it onto the clothing of Axis forces. The humiliated victims would then smell so bad they would be scorned and mocked by their comrades.

TR Bird said of the weapon, 'Since the air in any ordinary public meeting room is generally free from smell, almost any strange smell which cannot readily be accounted for would arouse suspicion which might easily culminate in fear or even panic.'

The Americans were impressed, and planned their own variant known as Who, Me? or Why Me? spending two years working on a weapon with 'the revolting odour of a very loose bowel movement'.

The weapon didn't quite go to plan; the S Liquid was highly volatile and unpredictable. The attacker would often end up smelling as bad as, or worse than, their victim. It was abandoned two weeks later.

WHOSE SIDE ARE YOU ON?

While most of us in the west have a clear idea of the broad brush-strokes of the Second World War, there are always little hidden corners which history has overlooked. One of those was the war in Finland.

From the Russian point of view, the Second World War was an opportunity to spread the word of Communism beyond the boundaries of the Soviet Union, and Finland, geographically so near, was an obvious example. One young man affected by this was Lauri Törni who despised communism and joined the Finish army to fight it. A determined and physically impressive soldier, he came to his superiors' attention at the bloody clashes at Lake Ladoga in the south of the country. The Red Army was vast and powerful but it had little experience of guerrilla warfare in heavy snow and across frozen lakes. The Finns fought them to a standstill, but inevitably had to agree an armistice when no help was forthcoming (despite being promised) from France or Britain. Soviet losses in this war were appalling.

By June 1941 Törni was wearing a different uniform. At the height of the Russo-Finnish war, operating deep behind enemy lines and causing havoc, there was a bounty of three million Finnish markka on his head. Now, he had joined the Waffen SS. Three years later, Finland and the Soviet Union had come to an agreement that any German forces still in the country must be demobilised and expelled.

By January 1945, Törni was in Germany being trained as a saboteur and found himself fighting against the Red Army near Schwerin. Here he surrendered to British troops and was marched to a POW camp at Lubeck a month after the war ended. Back in Finland, Törni tried to rejoin the family he had not seen for over two years but he was arrested in Helsinki and tried for treason for joining the German army. He was sentenced to six years in prison.

Having already escaped from the camp at Lubeck, Törni had something of a taste for it and he got out again before another re-arrest. In December 1948 he was pardoned by President Juho Paasikivi.

There can have been fewer spirits more restless than Lauri Törni. He went to Sweden and, under the alias of a Swedish seaman, took a ship bound for Venezuela. When the craft docked in the United States, Törni jumped it and became a political refugee in 'Finntown', New York's Finnish-American community in Brooklyn.

By 1954, Lauri Törni had become Larry Thorne of the United States Army, joining the Special Forces and becoming a captain by 1960. Three years later, he was fighting the communists again, this time in the form of the Vietcong in the grim jungles of Vietnam. He won a Bronze Star and no less than five Purple Hearts.

In 1965 Törni's luck ran out. The man who had fought in three armies, but all of them against the left, was in a CH-34 helicopter when the craft disappeared in smoke over Laos. It was not until 1999 that the wreckage was found and what was left of Törni's body was brought back to be buried with full military honours at Arlington National Cemetery. His arch-enemy, Russia's Soviet Union, had been buried twelve years earlier.

THE WIGWAM MURDER

Criminologists call it 'the last of the classic cases' but if it remains relatively unknown today, it is because it was a crime that happened in wartime. As Graham Greene wrote in *The Ministry of Fear* in 1942, 'Nobody troubled about single deaths ... in the middle of a massacre'.

The single death came to light on 7 October of that year, when a couple of marines on a routine march in woodland in Hankley Common on the Surrey-Sussex border stumbled on the decomposing body of a girl. Detailed forensic work and the discovery of personal items scattered nearby confirmed that her name was Joan Pearl Wolfe and she was a sixteen year old runaway.

The problem for the Surrey CID was that, not only was there a war on, with all police forces stretched to breaking point, but the murder scene was surrounded by army camps. Thousands of British and Canadians were in the area and any one of them – or more of them – could have killed Joan Wolfe.

As was customary in those days, the local police called in the homicide experience of Scotland Yard, in particular the lantern-jawed Chief Inspector Ted Greeno, who led the inquiry. House-to-house investigations and the full support of the military led to Joan's identity. She was what was still referred to in 1942 as a 'camp follower', a teenager tempted by the lure of young men in uniform. There had been several in Joan's young life, but the current 'squeeze' was August Sangret of the Regina Rifles of Saskatchewan.

Sangret was a Meti, a half-blood Cree native Canadian and French trapper from early colonial days. Strikingly good-looking and taciturn in the extreme, Sangret was grilled by Greeno for five days and produced the longest statement in British criminal history up to that point. He admitted that he knew Joan and they he risked punishment by nipping out from the camp to be with her in the 'wigwam' he built for them both in Hounsdown Wood, near a tank-training ground. Newspapers at the time and a number of ill-informed commentators since, have pictured the scene out of one of Edward Curtis's photographs of the 1880s – a plains 'Indian' in full war bonnet living in a buffalo-skin tepee. In fact, the Cree built their lodges of bent branches and leaves and August Sangret never wore anything except his Canadian khaki.

Sangret's story was that Joan had told him she was pregnant and they had fallen out about it, after which she disappeared and he spent some time trying to find her. The forensics of the case were carried out by Keith Simpson, the Home Office pathologist who concluded that the girl was first stabbed in the forehead with a pen-knife with a broken blade – 'like a parrot's beak'. She was then bludgeoned from behind with a birch branch which shattered her skull.

Sangret was arrested and put on trial at the Old Bailey in March 1943. The jury and the crowd gasped when Simpson produced Joan's skull to prove his point; it was the first time that such an exhibit was shown in court. Joan was Sangret's girl. She was pregnant which may have displeased him. They lived together on and off. The penknife with the peculiar blade was Sangret's. The jury found him guilty and he was sentenced to death by Mr Justice Macnaghten.

It all might have ended there, but today we would not be as certain as the jurors of 1943 over Sangret's guilt. It was Sangret's knife, but did he use it? The weapon passed through any number of hands while the case was being investigated. There were traces of blood on a blanket that Sangret owned, but it could not be tied to Joan Wolfe. She was not pregnant as she had claimed, so a potential motive disappeared. There were a number of other men in Joan's life who were not questioned once Sangret slotted into the frame.

He was hanged by Albert Pierrepoint who would go on to execute a number of Nazi leaders at Nuremberg three years later, at Wandsworth Prison. 'He lay there,' Molly LeFebure, Simpson's secretary remembered, 'muscular, well-built ... his handsome bronzed skin marked only by the imprint of the hangman's noose around his neck ...'

The judge had said during his summing up – 'there is no evidence that there ever was blood on this man'. The jury disagreed. Despite the dishonour surrounding his death, the Overseas Canada's Roll of Honour of 3 May 1943 includes his name – 'Royal Canadian Service Corps – Sangret, August, Pte. L27572'. As far as most of the world knows today, he died a soldier's death.

WILLIAM LONKOWSKI

Unravelling the facts and fiction from the murky world of espionage is often a near-impossible and ultimately futile task. Truths, half-truths, confusion, deliberate lies, rumours and omissions are hopelessly intertwined. Despite this, many espionage stories are known to us.

One such case was that of William Lonkowski, a German *Abwehr* agent, operating in the United States. Lonkowski found work in Long Island, New York at the Ireland Aircraft Corporation. He began feeding back vital plans and information to his handlers, and soon befriended two German-Americans, Otto Voss and Werner Gudenberg, who joined his spy ring. His next cover was taking on a job with *Luftreise*, a German aviation magazine.

Lonkowski almost slipped up on 25 September 1935. He was stopped by a customs official as he was boarding the ocean liner *Europa*. Within Lonkowski's violin case, a favourite of fictional spies ever since, were aircraft drawings. He was interviewed by military authorities and explained he needed the pictures for his magazine article. He was told to return three days later. He didn't bother. Instead he went to Canada and headed home on a German freighter. He received a hero's welcome.

Is any of this true? What really happened? Welcome to the shadowy world of espionage. *Confessions of a Nazi Spy,* (1939) Hollywood's first anti-Nazi film was inspired, in part along with the Rumrich spy case, by Lonkowski.

WINDKANONE

As the war progressed, Hitler became increasingly obsessed with his *wunderwaffe*; his wonder weapons, which he believed, would miraculously turn the course of the war back in his favour. Many prototypes and ideas were floated: most were either unworkable, dismal failures or simply an unacceptable diversion of men and resources that could be better placed elsewhere.

One of the most odd weapons of the wunderwaffe arsenal, but one which was actually made, was the *Windkanone* (Wind Cannon). It was an anti-aircraft weapon developed in Stuttgart that fired a jet of compressed air and water vapour, similar to the effects of turbulence, designed to assault enemy planes. The idea behind this was that the weapon could knock down low-flying aircraft, without needing ammunition. A wind cannon was installed on a bridge over the River Elbe in 1945, but we have no evidence of its effectiveness.

The weapon was scientifically impressive in a sense, but the war ended before the windkanone was capable of doing much more than smashing 25mm thick wooden planks from a distance of 200m – itself hardly enough to turn the tide.

WINKIE THE PIGEON

23 February 1942 saw a Bristol Beaufort bomber, having sustained severe damage, crash into the merciless North Sea. The crew were stranded 100 miles from home, their odds of survival were next to nothing – with no points of reference, and struggling in the freezing waters, the men could not radio their position.

But the four men still had one hope – a pigeon named Winkie. The blue chequered hen bird was set loose, in the faint hope it could make it back to its home in Broughty Ferry, Scotland.

Against all the odds, Winkie did make it home, after flying 120 miles, exhausted and covered in oil – but Winkie wasn't carrying a message. Remarkably, the RAF calculated the time difference between the bomber crashing and the pigeon arriving, allowing for wind direction and the bird being covered in oil, and were able to pinpoint where the Bristol Beaufort crashed.

A rescue mission was launched and the crew, resigned to their fates, were saved within fifteen minutes, in what must have been a time of elation. Back at base, a dinner was held in her honour. She received the Dickin Medal on 2 December 1943 for 'delivering a message under exceptional difficulties'.

WINTON'S CHILDREN

He was an unlikely hero, a stock broker from London: Nicholas Wertheimer. He had been born in 1909 to German Jew parents, but in an effort to integrate with their new society, they anglicized their surname to Winton and converted to Christianity.

When Hitler's grip began to tighten over Germany, life became increasingly unbearable for Jews. It was never going to be as simple as 'just leaving'; they had families, friends, homes, careers. Emigrating was expensive, so most couldn't afford it. Besides, other countries had strict immigration quotas – British Mandate Palestine was political dynamite, so they couldn't go there either. As one survivor would later state, the world was divided into countries where they couldn't stay and countries they couldn't go.

It was December 1938 and time for the stockbroker to take a well-deserved holiday, the skiing in Switzerland was excellent and would make a perfect getaway. But before he left, he received a chance letter in the post., It was from an old friend Martin Blake, who was in Prague. 'I have a most interesting assignment and I need your help. Don't bother bringing your skis.' He accepted Blake's invitation and headed to Prague.

Prague shocked Winton, the appalling conditions not just of the Jews, but of all the refugees who were fleeing in the face of Nazi Germany's annexation of the Sudetenland. Winton set up an organisation, linked to the *kindertransport* program, to help Jewish children at risk of the growing anti-Semitism. Thanks to the pressure of humanitarian groups and the Quakers, Britain agreed to take them in temporarily until the crisis was over, provided a home could be found for them.

We can only imagine the real desperation and despair of the parents, to allow their children to go off unaccompanied to the other side of Europe, through the heartland of the Reich, and into the arms of strangers. Innocently naïve children would occasionally give them Hitler salute as they left.

There were still hurdles, the Netherlands had closed its borders to Jewish refugees and the police would send back any refugees they discovered. Eventually the Netherlands got on board and allowed the safe passage of the children through their country to reach Britain.

The effort was overwhelming, but Winton and his friends worked tirelessly to advertise the plight of the children and find caring homes for them. His own mother helped out. Time was ticking, Winton sent a plea for help out to the world, and to Roosevelt's United States in particular, but it fell on deaf ears. Only Sweden agreed to join Britain and assist.

Winton's work in Prague came to an end on 1 September with the outbreak of the war. Tragically, the last trainload of 250 children which was due to set off was unable to depart due to wartime restrictions. Of these 250 children, only two survived the war. However some 10,000 children escaped the clutches of the Nazis through the *kindertransport* program, and Winton himself personally saved 669 of them.

With the war beginning in 1939, Winton first joined up as a conscientious objector with the Red Cross. He had a change of heart in 1940, when he discovered he had the strength within him to fight.

Winton's story is remarkable enough. He was one of the untold humble heroes of the war. But there was a surprise in store for him.

It was 1988, four decades since the war had ended, and Winton's wife Grete was having a rummage in their attic. While doing so, she came across a peculiar scrapbook, inside which were the names and addresses of all the kind souls who had agreed to take Winton's children in. It also contained the names and addresses of the children's parents. Winton didn't remember this scrapbook. 'Isn't that odd,' they must have thought, to have forgotten that they had it.

He was knighted in 2003. 2008 saw him receive the Pride of Britain award. Two years later he was named as a British Hero of the Holocaust. A statue of the altruistic hero with a couple of his children still stands at Prague railway station, mingled in with the hustle and bustle of the modern world.

It is believed that 370 of Winton's children have never been traced, and probably remain oblivious of their own past.

Winton died peacefully in his sleep at the age of 106 in 2015, 76 years to the day that 241 of his children, because of his kindness and hard work, left certain death behind them at the platform.

He was featured on the children's program *Blue Peter*. Wojtek's popularity never diminished, and countless statues and tributes have been paid to him, the most recent being a 2015 statue in Princes Street Gardens in Edinburgh.

WOJTEK THE BEAR

Operation Barbarossa, the surprise Axis invasion of the Soviet Union changed everything. For the Allies, the Soviet Union turned from an enemy to a friend.

The Soviet Union had joined the Nazis in carving up Eastern Europe in 1939, and many Polish soldiers and deported civilians found themselves in brutal gulags as a result. With the Reich closing in on the Soviet Union in 1941, they released the Polish prisoners, who set off for Iran, nominally independent but in reality ruled by the British.

On their journey, the Poles came across a young Iranian boy near the town of Hamadan, the boy had a bear cub with him, after hunters had shot its mother. Lt. Anatol Tarnowiecki was taken in by the bear. The bear spent three months with the group at the Polish refugee camp near Tehran.

In August 1942 the bear was donated to the 22nd Artillery Company and given the name Wojtek (Happy Warrior). Wojtek fitted in well with his comrades, he was rather fond of food and enjoyed marmalade, honey and syrup and even shared cigarettes, though he sometimes preferred to eat them rather than smoke them. He liked play fighting and was taught to salute and joined the soldiers' journey, without complaint, through Syria, Palestine and Egypt.

When the Polish were to join the British in the Italian campaign, Wojtek was officially enlisted with the rank of private, to ensure his place on a transport ship. He received a pay book and rations, although any pay was substituted with double rations.

During the battle of Monte Cassino, Wojtek did his part by carrying 100 pound crates of shells to the gun crews. In fact the image of Wojtek carrying a shell became the official symbol of 22 Company.

After the war Wojtek retired to Britain. He lived at Edinburgh Zoo, where old Polish comrades would continue to sneak him cigarettes, but he didn't have matches or a lighter so he would have to eat them.

WOLFSKINDER

War is not neat, it doesn't 'end' on an arbitrary date. The tremors continue. Post-war Europe and Asia were chaotic, and soldiers didn't go home for years as they were sent to occupy conquered countries and uphold the law. Millions of homeless refugees streamed to and fro, while civilians wandered desperately, trying to discover news of family and friends. Some scars, physical and emotional, would last for decades; some would never heal at all, and followed the victims to their graves.

Among the dead were countless German parents. Many orphans, who may once have been in children's homes or other institutions, now found themselves without any care at all. Thousands of these children were slaughtered by bombs and reprisals, so for some the best bet was to take their chances in the wild by foraging, begging and stealing. Others had sick or dying parents, and it was up to the children to care for them.

These groups of wandering semi-feral children became known as *wolfskinder* (wolf children). As the children were German, the Soviets would punish harshly any adults found to be caring for them. Children who were caught were often deported East, many of whom would not survive the journey. Despite this, many adults took a risk and did help, particularly in rural farms. Lithuania alone took in around 45,000 wolf children.

It was only in 1991, after the fall of the Soviet Union, that the wolfskinder and their carers were free to reveal the children's identities without reprisals. However, 45 years had passed, and the children were now adults themselves. In later years, some would look in vain for any information about their old lives and family, while many more were oblivious to their past.

XX COMMITTEE

The XX double-cross system was a top secret part of the British Security Service. Despite the hysteria generated by the British propaganda machine, Nazi spies in Britain weren't particularly effective and all of them were captured or surrendered themselves by the war's end, except one possible case of suicide.

Captured spies would be taken to Camp 020, hence XX as its code, which was Latchmere House, in a quiet cul-de-sac in Richmond. Here, they would be interrogated, either being imprisoned or executed or given a chance to become double-agents. The brains behind this system were those of John Masterman, who wrote a book on the subject years later, outlining as much of the story as the still-paranoid censors would allow. Those spies deemed useful would then be used by the British to provide misinformation to their handlers in Germany, confusing and distracting the German war effort. The XX Committee had many successes including classic deception on the landing sites of V1 and V2 rockets being fired at London and confusing the Nazis as to the location of the inevitable D-Day Landings.

The code names of XX's agents still survive and even today some of them remain unknown. Taken at random from the list: Artist was Johnny Jebson; Beetle was Petur Thomsen, based in Iceland; Carrot was a Pole, but his name is lost; Charlie was Kiener, a British-born German; Moonbeam was based in Canada; Mutt and Jeff were Norwegians; Snow was a Welshman, Arthur Owens. Women were among them – Bronx was Elvira Chaudoir; Le Chat was Mathilde Carré. Perhaps the best known today is the black marketeer, Eddie Chapman – Zigzag.

And in case you think all this espionage was kept under wraps, when MI5 moved its location to the obscurity of a London prison, bus conductors on the route would call out, 'All change for the Scrubs and MI5!'

YANG KYOUNGJONG

Yang Kyoungjong was, allegedly, a Korean who had the dubious honor of being forced to fight for the Imperial Japanese Army, the Red Army and the Wehrmacht.

The story goes that Yang Kyoungjong was conscripted by the Japanese into the Kwangtung Army, at this time Korea was under the rule of Japan. He was sent to fight the Red Army during the border skirmishes of Khalkin Gol. Captured, he was sent to a gulag before being forcibly enlisted into the Soviet army in 1942. He was next sent to fight the Germans on the Eastern front. Again, after the battle of Kharkov, he was captured and joined the 'Eastern Battalions'. His final posting was as a guard in northern France along the Atlantic Wall. After the D-Day landings of June 1944, Yang Kyoungjong was captured one last time by the Allies.

It is claimed that after the war, he became a US citizen, living the rest of his life in Illinois before dying in 1992.

ZIGZAG

Whose side was he on? Spy fiction is full of examples of double, triple, quadruple agents, but Eddie Chapman was real. The best *actual* agents are unobtrusive, anonymous, careful (think George Smiley in the John le Carre novels). The least successful are the flash attention-seekers, the 007 wannabees who substitute violence, fast cars and beautiful girls for clever espionage.

What raises alarm bells about Chapman is that he was a career criminal and did nothing without serious payment. His handler in wartime Britain was John Masterman of the XX Committee, itself known as Double Cross, not just because of the Roman numerals but because it was specifically the Committee's job to 'turn' agents from their original masters. Masterman wrote in his memoirs that Chapman arrived from Jersey in December 1942, where he had been imprisoned for safe-blowing. Jersey of course had been occupied by the Wehrmacht and Chapman had offered his services to them in exchange for freedom. He was dropped by parachute near Ely, one of the very few enemy agents who was not interrogated and hanged as common criminals.

Chapman was charming and debonair, the arch conman, with a fund of useful information about enemy radio transmissions and military operations in the Nantes area of France. His task for the Germans was to sabotage the de Haviland works at Hatfield in Hertfordshire where they made Mosquito aircraft. He carried £1,000 in cash and explosives and had been promised £15,000 (a vast sum) to pull the bombing off.

Masterman took a chance. He 'turned' Chapman (although the jury is still out as to how much of that was required), gave him the codename Zigzag and faked a successful attack on the Hatfield factory. The Germans bought it, gleefully viewing the photos of 'bomb damage' on 29 January 1943 and taking press reports as genuine.

With British SIS connivance, Chapman got a job as steward on the merchantman *City of Lancaster* and when it reached Lisbon in neutral Portugal, he contacted the Germans and was secretly hailed as a hero. He had ambitious plans, which he outlined to Masterman, to set up a Fifth Column in France and even assassinate Hitler as a one-man killing machine. The idea was taken up by Geoffrey Household in this short story *Rogue Male*, later televised and starring Peter O'Toole. In the event, Masterman turned him down.

Little was heard of Zigzag until 1944 when news reached Masterman of someone in neutral Oslo speaking bad German in a loud voice. He had two gold teeth, awful clothes and lived on a private yacht. He also had, although few people knew it, an Iron cross given to him by a grateful nation! In June of that year, he parachuted near Cambridge with two wireless sets and £6,000 spending money. He had been fully accepted by the Nazi authorities in Nantes and his task this time was to report on the damage caused by V1 and V2 missiles and the organization and whereabouts of US airbases. He reported that Berlin looked like the 'ruins of Pompeii' and that morale in the Germany Kreigsmarine (Navy) was particularly low.

The problem was that by now, Chapman had let his successful double life go to his head. He began to talk about his cases and that, to Masterman at least, was the kiss of death. He was dropped from all future operations.

After the war, it could all come out – or at least, Chapman's version of it. In 1954, he wrote an autobiography, *The Eddie Chapman Story*, but whether he was actually Zigzag, as the British knew him, or Fritzchen, his German codename, will probably never be known.

Other titles by BLKDOG Publishing for your consideration:

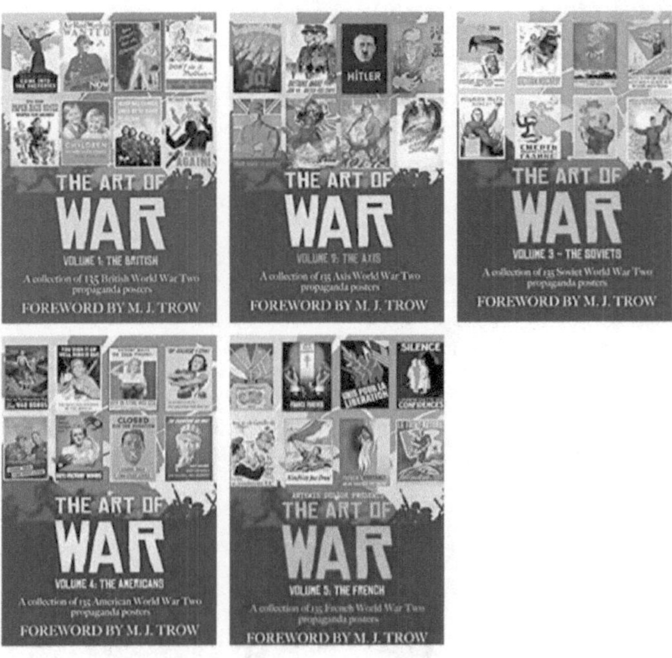

The Art of War series by Artemis Design. Each book contains 135 historical propaganda posters and a foreword by M. J. Trow.

The *Citizen Survivor* series. A collection of dystopian tales set in an alternate history where Britain has been knocked out of the Second World War.

BLKDOG

www.blkdogpublishing.com